An Analytical Guide to Television's
Battlestar Galactica

An Analytical Guide to Television's *Battlestar Galactica*

by
JOHN KENNETH MUIR

McFarland & Company, Inc., Publishers
Jefferson, North Carolina, and London

Frontispiece: The Cylons and humans fight it out in outer space.
(Illustration by Mindy Easler.)

> The present work is a reprint of the library bound edition of
> An Analytical Guide to Television's *Battlestar Galactica*,
> first published in 1999 by McFarland.

LIBRARY OF CONGRESS CATALOGUING-IN-PUBLICATION DATA

Muir, John Kenneth, 1969–
    An analytical guide to television's *Battlestar Galactica* / by John
Kenneth Muir.
        p.   cm.
    Includes bibliographical references and index.

    ISBN 0-7864-2455-9 (softcover : 50# alkaline paper) ∞

    1. Battlestar Galactica (Television program)   I. Title.
PN1992.77.B353M85   2005
791.45'72 — dc21   98-38737

British Library cataloguing data are available

Manufactured in the United States of America

McFarland & Company, Inc., Publishers
Box 611, Jefferson, North Carolina 28640
www.mcfarlandpub.com

For John, Jacob, and Mindy,
architects of dreams
and teammates through life

Acknowledgments

The author gratefully acknowledges the support, assistance and guidance of Kevin McCorry, John and Mindy Easler, Ken, Loretta and Kathryn Muir, Professor Stuart Wheeler and the entire Classics Department at the University of Richmond in Virginia. Special thanks also to the creators and maintainers of the Richard Hatch Home Page, and to the myriad *Battlestar Galactica* fans across the Internet who answered questions, proposed new ideas and shared their passion with this author. Thanks, too, to Glen Larson and Universal/MCA for creating a series worthy of scholarly examination.

Contents

Acknowledgments vii
Introduction 1

Part I. The History 9

Part II. *Battlestar Galactica* 37
Critical Reception 37
Series Overview 40
Cast and Credits 52
Episode Guide 54

1. "Saga of a Star World" 54
2. "Lost Planet of the Gods" 61
3. "The Lost Warrior" 64
4. "The Long Patrol" 68
5. "Gun on Ice Planet Zero" 71
6. "The Magnificent Warriors" 75
7. "The Young Lords" 78
8. "The Living Legend" 81
9. "Fire in Space" 84
10. "War of the Gods" 89
11. "The Man with Nine Lives" 94
12. "Murder on the *Rising Star*" 98
13. "Greetings from Earth" 101
14. "Baltar's Escape" 105
15. "Experiment in Terra" 107
16. "Take the *Celestra*" 110
17. "The Hand of God" 114

Part III. *Galactica: 1980* 119
Critical Reception 119
Series Overview 120
Cast and Credits 126
Episode Guide 127

1. "*Galactica* Discovers Earth" 127
2. "The Super Scouts" 135
3. "Spaceball" 138
4. "The Night the Cylons Landed" 140
5. "The Space Croppers" 144
6. "The Return of Starbuck" 146

Contents

Part IV. Morality and Mythology 151

**Part V. The *Galactica* Universe Today:
Converts, Computers, and Collectibles** 175

Part VI. Epilogue: A Shining Quest 205

Appendices 209
A. Planets Visited by the *Galactica* 209
B. *Battlestar Galactica* in *Buck Rogers in the 25th Century* 211
C. A Catalogue of Science Fiction Television Clichés
in *Battlestar Galactica* 213
D. Ten Recommendations for Improving *Battlestar Galactica*
Should It Be Revived 215

Notes 217
Bibliography 221
Index 223

Introduction

In the grand Valhalla of science fiction television drama, there are multiple levels of honor and dishonor. Most honored are the productions of virtually unchallenged merit. These classic, even worshipped, shows are the modern American myths, the standard-bearers for all future genre efforts. In this esteemed category, the memorable visions of the sixties reign supreme. Dwelling in this realm of distinction are Rod Serling's *The Twilight Zone* (1959–64), Leslie Stevens' and Joseph Stefano's *The Outer Limits* (1963–64), Gene Roddenberry's original *Star Trek* (1966–69) and Patrick McGoohan's nightmarish exploration of personal freedom lost, *The Prisoner* (1966).

Further down in the pantheon, many other high-quality TV programs are precariously perched. These are the efforts which have large, dedicated fandoms, but about which critical and fan opinion is polarized. Ironically, these are frequently the most daring of science fiction TV odysseys — creative, innovative, stylish and determinedly different from *Star Trek*. At this level, one might find video visions as varied as J. Michael Straczyinski's complex and ever-growing *Babylon 5* (1993–98), Terry Nation's subversive *Blake's 7* (1978–81) and Gerry and Sylvia Anderson's maligned but brilliant exploration of gothic space horror, *Space: 1999* (1975–77). Others vying for a spot in this position include Rick Berman and Michael Piller's *Deep Space Nine* (1993–), perhaps the best of all *Star Trek* spin-offs; Dan Curtis' tongue-in-cheek *Kolchak: The Night Stalker* (1974), surely an inspiration for the 1990s hit *The X-Files*; *Planet of the Apes* (1974), an exploration of race integration; and *U.F.O.* (1970), the jingoistic but fascinating Anderson series. All of these TV epics have their detractors — sometimes quite prominent ones — but all nonetheless express philosophical underpinnings as powerful, if not as popular, as those of *The Prisoner, Star Trek, The Outer Limits* or *The Twilight Zone*.

Below that level, matters in the science fiction TV roster deteriorate rapidly, and turn ugly. There exist several TV series whose appeal is somewhat difficult to comprehend objectively. Derided by most viewers and ravaged by scornful critics, but nonetheless popular to a core group of diehard aficionados, these are the misconceived blunders that are failures from virtually every critical perspective imaginable: production values, originality, plotting, dialogue, acting, writing, special effects, philosophy and story resolution. Irwin Allen's campy *Voyage to the Bottom of the Sea* (1964–68), the short-lived *Logan's Run* (1977), Harlan Ellison's Canadian misfire *The Starlost* (1973), *Manimal* (1983), Steven Spielberg's *Amazing Stories* (1985–87), *Automan* (1983), *SeaQuest DSV* (1994–96) and *Misfits of Science* (1984) all unhappily reside at this level of shame.

Apart from the top-to-bottom roster, there is one other notable position, existing outside the critical parameters detailed above. This strange corner in the pantheon is reserved for what might be called the "guilty pleasure." A guilty pleasure is best defined as a science fiction production that suffers from typical television problems such as indecisive writing, a derivative central premise and blatant scientific ignorance, yet still manages, seemingly by magic or chemistry, to weave a distinctly pleasurable spell for the audience. There is something inherently and almost indefinably enjoyable about this category of programming. Rarely can the spell be explained in logical, critical or objective terms; yet one cannot deny its reality or power. It is in the unique category of the guilty pleasure that many genre viewers place the single-season 1978 outer space adventure *Battlestar Galactica*.

This series was troubled from the start. It premiered the year after George Lucas' blockbuster film *Star Wars* (1977) and was derided far and wide in major periodicals such as *Time* as an out-and-out *Star Wars* rip-off. *Battlestar Galactica* compounded the problem by relying on genre and TV clichés once it began its regular run on the ABC network. Several episodes were unimaginative rehashes of Western films and genre standbys such as *The Magnificent Seven* (1960) and *High Noon* (1952).

As if the Wild West clichés were not troubling enough for discriminating science fiction lovers, *Battlestar Galactica* frequently made basic errors about the realm of outer space as well. Galaxies and solar systems were continually confused ("The Long Patrol," "The Hand of God"); in one episode ("Fire in Space"), flames burned out of control in the vacuum of space — and were put out by propelled streams of water shot from zooming starfighters. Although *Battlestar Galactica*'s youngest followers may not have been at all troubled by these errors, prominent genre figures such as Isaac Asimov, as well as *Star Trek* aficionados and other groups, were all too aware of the show's failings.

Significantly, *Battlestar Galactica* was also the most fascistic American science fiction program of all time, rigorously and mindlessly espousing complete faith in the military "hawk" point-of-view, treating all peace attempts by a civilian government as misguided and stupid at best, and evil at worst.

Despite these scientific and philosophical shortcomings, *Battlestar Galactica* did boast some rather remarkable and memorable strengths. After just a few short weeks, the series regulars were firmly entrenched as interesting, surprisingly believable people whom audiences found they truly cared for. Like *Little House on the Prairie* (1974–83) or even *Lassie* (1954–71), *Battlestar Galactica* featured a tragedy each and every week: an emotional, family-oriented tearjerker. Central characters were killed off or marooned, heroes lost loved ones, and mankind faced an endless quest in the solitude of outer space. Series regulars Richard Hatch, Dirk Benedict and Lorne Greene, unfairly derided by many as bland clones of *Star Wars* prototypes, succeeded admirably in creating unique, memorable personalities — people arguably more interesting and believable than the comic book cut-outs who populated *Star Wars* and its sequels.

Battlestar Galactica may have been a hokey space opera, but it was nonetheless sincere and heartfelt TV. For all of its many weaknesses, it struck a chord as solid TV drama, and resonated with many viewers in a powerful and unexpected way. Today it is almost universally remembered with nostalgic fondness by viewers not interested in the carping and infighting of genre critics.

This 20-year-old adventure TV series was based on a simple premise: In a distant galaxy, 12 colonies of mankind (named after the 12 signs of the Zodiac) flourish. The Colonies have been locked in deadly war with a race of mechanical devils called Cylons for nearly ten centuries. Following the total destruction of all the Colonies in a Pearl Harbor–like surprise attack, Commander Adama (Lorne Greene) of the spacecraft carrier *Galactica* and ace warriors Cpt. Apollo (Richard Hatch) and Lt. Starbuck (Dirk Benedict) flee to the deepest regions of space, leading a ragtag, fugitive fleet of human survivors in search of a mythical thirteenth colony. This legendary world is known only in ancient texts as "Earth." The Cylon Empire, intent on the final extermination of man, is always in hot pursuit of the *Galactica* and her fleet, forcing the *Galactica* ever further into the depths of uncharted territory. The Cylons are led by the villainous

Baltar (John Colicos), a human turncoat responsible for the destruction of the human civilization.

The brainchild of veteran television producer Glen A. Larson, creator of *McCloud* (1970–77), *Knight Rider* (1982–85), *Alias Smith and Jones* (1971–73) and another thoroughly enjoyable guilty pleasure, *Buck Rogers in the 25th Century* (1979–81), *Battlestar Galactica* premiered in the autumn of 1978 boasting the largest budget in TV history, reportedly $1 million per episode. At that exorbitant rate, *Battlestar Galactica* cost roughly three times per episode what Gerry and Sylvia Anderson's impressive British import *Space: 1999* had cost only two years earlier! Easily the publicity bonanza of the fall season, *Battlestar Galactica* was even afforded a terrific prime-time slot: Sunday nights at 8:00 P.M. What's more, it was very successful in the all-important ratings game. It finished its year ranked as number 24 in the critical Nielsen sweepstakes, the best showing ever for a network sci-fi program until the heyday of *The X-Files*. Even the "popular" *Star Trek*'s highest finish for the NBC network had been a lowly 52 in these weekly contests.

Strangely, placing 24 for the year was not deemed sufficient cause for renewal when *Battlestar Galactica*'s astronomical cost was factored in by anxious ABC bean counters. Most industry pundits had predicted *Battlestar Galactica* would be the top-ranked show of the season; Larson's epic fell far short of that lofty mark. For the record, the number one show of 1978 was *Laverne and Shirley* (1976–83), a spin-off from the popular sitcom *Happy Days* (1974–84). Although rival networks CBS and NBC briefly considered picking up *Battlestar Galactica* as early as a mid-season replacement in 1979, negotiations failed for undisclosed reasons, and the expensive space program ceased production after just 17 stories.

Six months after *Battlestar Galactica* was canceled, ABC brought it back in a cheaper and thoroughly embarrassing format called *Galactica: 1980*. Many critics suggested that this sequel series was purely an attempt to continue the popular *Battlestar Galactica* toy merchandise line sponsored by Mattel and make further use of the expensive special effects seen in the original series. *Galactica: 1980* was so bad, so thoroughly juvenile, that even creator Larson has now reportedly disowned it, referring to it in 1997 as "Lt. Starbuck's nightmare." The new series featured an entirely new cast save for Herb Jefferson, Jr. (Boomer), and Lorne Greene (Adama). Audiences despised the sequel series, and it was canceled after only six episodes.

Still, in its original format *Battlestar Galactica* brought a whole new world of outer space special effects to network TV. John Dykstra, the brilliant artist responsible for the fantastic miniatures, optical effects and explosions of *Star Wars*, worked laboriously for many months to insure that the world of *Battlestar Galactica* would be spectacular and unforgettable, and he certainly succeeded. The amazing spaceships moved faster and more believably than ever before on TV, and the laser blasts were more frequent and zippier. Beyond its visual accomplishments, *Battlestar Galactica* is worth remembering today for some very interesting character arcs — a literary device heralded as revolutionary in *Babylon 5* — as well as two other important details.

The first of these details was the way the universe of *Battlestar Galactica* exploited the rich human history of mythology. Savvy series writers made use of many legends and names from various cultures to remind audiences that Earth and these far-off galactic colonies had originated from the same ancient source, a mother world called Kobol. Characters such as Lucifer, Apollo, Athena, Adama, Cassiopeia and Cain shared characteristics with their mythological counterparts, and these significant names added a layer of depth to the weekly events. The references to the Bible, ancient history and Greek mythology supported *Battlestar Galactica*'s Erich Von Däniken–style universe, and successfully afforded the show a larger context and a distinct lexicon. Consequently, the series was not merely space adventure. It was the epic story of mankind's heritage, forever interconnected with our myths, legends and history.

The entire background of *Battlestar Galactica* was steeped in this unusual mythological context. As it represented one oppressed race's great exodus to a new home, *Battlestar Galactica* was essentially the story of Moses and the Israelites transplanted to the realm of outer space. In the first episode of the series, Commander Adama led the *Galactica* and the civilian fleet through a red-hued space minefield. He did so by clearing a path through the deadly explosive objects. It was not precisely the Red Sea that Commander Adama parted, but it was close enough for viewers to make the connection. Even though *Battlestar Galactica*'s ongoing attempt to revise, revamp and reinterpret Earth mythology was sometimes unsuccessful, it gave the series a consistent motif, an admirable facet missing from contemporary competition such as *Buck Rogers in the 25th Century*, *Salvage One* (1979), *Logan's Run* (1977) or *The Fantastic Journey* (1977). Such an accomplishment should not be forgotten.

The second memorable detail was a certain race of alien beings — aliens who were surely the prototype for the "revisionist" and modified

Klingons explored so thoroughly in *Star Trek: The Next Generation* (1987–94) and *Star Trek: Deep Space Nine* (1993). Since the Klingons are probably *Star Trek*'s most popular race to date, *Battlestar Galactica* deserves some recognition for creating the Borellian Nomen. Members of this warrior race, introduced in the episode "The Man with Nine Lives," were obsessed with honor, and they prided themselves on skillful combat and physical prowess. If by that description they do not seem to resemble the aggressive Klingons of the modern *Star Trek* spin-offs, it may help to remember that the Borellian Nomen of *Battlestar Galactica* sported bumpy, bulbous foreheads, an extraterrestrial affectation Klingons never sported in the universe of *Star Trek* until *Star Trek: The Motion Picture* in 1979 — almost a full year after the Nomen had appeared on *Battlestar Galactica*.

Before *Battlestar Galactica*, Klingons in *Star Trek* were bearded, swarthy space pirates with absolutely no concept of honor. They were human in appearance through-and-through. After *Battlestar Galactica* introduced the bumpy-headed, honor-bound Borellian Nomen, Klingons also become bumpy-headed, honor-bound warriors. To this author's knowledge, that fact has never been acknowledged in *Star Trek* fandom, or by critics and genre historians. It could easily be an example of spontaneous creation, but *Galactica* hit the concept first.

In the final analysis, *Battlestar Galactica* may be no more than a prominent example of the guilty pleasure, but it was nonetheless a memorable attempt to make science fiction accessible to the mainstream TV viewing audience; and it is historically important for all the reasons noted above. For both its mistakes and its successes, *Battlestar Galactica* is well worth a second analytical look two decades after its initial network run, especially in an era when *Star Trek* clones and sequels continue to dominate the cathode ray galaxy.

For those who still believe that "life here began out there" and that "God is an astronaut," this analysis and critical commentary should bring back good memories of an exciting and unusual space adventure. For those who believe that *Battlestar Galactica* and *Galactica: 1980* did not influence the science fiction initiatives of the '80s and '90s such as *Star Trek: The Next Generation* (1987–94), *Star Trek IV: The Voyage Home* (1986), *Independence Day* (1996) and the Fox series *Space: Above and Beyond* (1995–96), this book may provoke a reconsideration, and may even permit one to see the Glen Larson series in a more positive light.

A *Battlestar Galactica* revival movement has been gaining steam since early 1995. At this writing, it seems possible that a new *Battlestar Galactica* series will be produced in syndication around the year 2000. Before a new and (let's hope) improved *Battlestar Galactica* can appear on our television sets, it is vitally important to review the past, and remember what both the genre and this series looked like in the bygone days of 1978.

PART I

The History

The State of the Genre in the Mid-'70s

Although the spectacular events of *Battlestar Galactica* occurred in a vacuum, it is important to remember that the TV series was not created in one. On the contrary, the origins and convoluted 20-year post-broadcast journey of *Battlestar Galactica* are understood best when the series is viewed within its historical context. Although to this day many critics and fans prefer to dismiss the ABC series as an out-and-out clone of *Star Wars*, as well as a cynical attempt to cash in on Lucas' unexpected success, there is much more to *Battlestar Galactica*'s genesis and history than that flawed and rather biased perception. Like all productions, *Battlestar Galactica*'s origins do flow directly from a specific time and place, but popular opinion to the contrary, its primary antecedents are not necessarily *Star Wars*. To appropriately set the stage for *Battlestar Galactica*, one must remember the multitude of productions and events that preceded its parturition.

In many important ways, the early to mid-'70s represented a good time for science fiction TV. It was a period of growing pains, of adolescence, to be sure, but growth nonetheless. For the first time in history, science fiction seemed to be entering the American mainstream. Although new TV shows such as *The Starlost* (1973), *Planet of the Apes* (1974) and *The Fantastic Journey* (1977) had been devoured in the Nielsen contests, *The Six Million Dollar Man* (1974-78) starring Lee Majors achieved bionic ratings on the tube, and the MGM film *Logan's Run* (1976) starring Michael York was nothing short of a box office phenomenon. *Logan's Run* was so successful that it spawned a series of *Logan's Run* novels, a comic book series from Marvel Comics and a short-lived CBS-TV series starring Gregory Harrison, Heather Menzies and Donald Moffatt.

Perhaps more importantly, *Star Trek* was alive and prospering. It was more popular than ever thanks to ongoing reruns. Mego's line of *Star Trek* toy merchandise, which included action figures, playsets, utility belts and the like, actually sold best between 1975 and 1977, nearly eight years after the series' untimely cancellation by the short-sighted NBC network. The continuing popularity of *Star Trek* in syndication, coupled with the runaway success of Mego's toy line, proved that science fiction TV could generate sustained enthusiasm among viewers, as well as represent a bonanza for related merchandise.

In 1975, Sylvia and Gerry Anderson's outer space odyssey *Space: 1999* premiered in syndication, and was an immediate ratings hit. Like the *Battlestar Galactica* toys, *Space: 1999* merchandise reached the American market before the first show even aired. By the time of the premiere episode, "Breakaway," in September 1975, hordes of six-year-old American boys wanted a model of the trademark Eagle spaceship. Although *Space: 1999* soon met with fierce resistance from many *Star Trek* fans, including those writing for genre magazines, it undeniably featured the next generation of convincing visual special effects. Spaceships were more detailed and convincing than in *Star Trek*, *Lost in Space* or *The Starlost*, and they streaked across screens in a very believable fashion. *Space: 1999* also featured incredible pyrotechnics and explosions in space, the mainstay of later efforts like *Star Wars*, *Battlestar Galactica* and *Buck Rogers in the 25th Century*. Though this British-made series folded after two seasons and 48 episodes, it still was one of the longest-running "outer space" shows of the decade. Significantly, *Space: 1999*–related merchandise sold well in America into 1979, two years after its cancellation.[1]*

The successes and inroads created by *Star Trek*, *The Six Million Dollar Man*, *Logan's Run* and *Space: 1999* established several important facts about science fiction productions, and the entertainment industry took note. The twin ratings successes of *Star Trek* in syndication and *The Six Million Dollar Man* on network television established that genre TV had a huge fan following — what network executives lovingly refer to as a "built-in" audience. Secondly, the show-related merchandise sales proved there was much money to be mined from ancillary tie-ins like model kits, action figures and utility belts. Thirdly, and perhaps most significantly, the new special effects era ushered in by *Space: 1999* demonstrated that outer space adventure could at last be produced believably. Sparklers and visible wires were out. Convincing, mind-blowing forays to alien landscapes were in.

See Notes section beginning on page 217.

Considering this historical background, it is perhaps difficult to understand why so many members of the genre press and the critical mainstream were blind-sided by *Star Wars* in the summer of 1977. They reacted as if *Star Wars* was no less than the "second coming." Except for a few curmudgeonly hold-outs such as Harlan Ellison and David Denby, most critics and journalists seemed to believe the film had emerged from the head of George Lucas as a full-blown act of genius, without any historical precedent or context. On the contrary, Lucas proved above all else with *Star Wars* that he was a savvy businessman with an uncanny knack for timing. His film came out at precisely the right time to capitalize on the three prong successes (ratings, merchandise and special effects) generated by *Star Trek*, *Space: 1999* and *Logan's Run*.

Because of *Star Trek*'s widespread success and permeating influence in American living rooms, Lucas was in 1977 able to create a bold space drama accessible to the masses. *Star Wars* was littered with references to things like "tractor beams," "proton torpedoes" (a close relative to *Star Trek*'s photon torpedoes, no doubt), holographic projections, weapons set on "stun" and the like. These futuristic terms were not originated by Roddenberry's series, but they were undeniably popularized by the ubiquitous *Star Trek*. This jargon would not have been familiar, let alone comprehensible, to the average moviegoer watching *Star Wars* for the first time in '77 had *Star Trek* not been rerun *ad infinitum* by then. Even the noteworthy Cantina scene in *Star Wars* had its antecedents in the multi-racial alien banquet scene in the second season *Star Trek* episode "Journey to Babel" by D. C. Fontana. Significantly, at the ten-year anniversary of *Star Wars*, Lucas confided to *Trek* creator Gene Roddenberry that he had watched *Star Trek* reruns while writing the screenplay to *Star Wars*.[2] It certainly shows. Although *Star Wars* was determinedly different from *Star Trek* in many important ways, it spoke very much the same language. It was able to tell its mythic story so effectively only because *Star Trek* had already indoctrinated or "primed" millions of viewers into the "vocabulary" of outer space adventure. Would fans have responded so enthusiastically to the beauty of the Force and the myth of the Jedi had they been focusing instead on comprehending hyperspace, tractor beams, scanners, sensors and the like? *Star Trek* had made outer space jargon as familiar to red-blooded Americans as Archie Bunker's living room or Hawkeye's tent in *M*A*S*H*.

While putting together his special effects team for *Star Wars*, Lucas first attempted to enlist Brian Johnson, the technical wizard responsible for the special effects magic of *Space: 1999*. Since Johnson had a commitment to that ongoing series, he was unable to join Lucas. However, the special effects of *Star Wars* (heralded far and wide as technological "breakthroughs") were actually the logical extensions of the fabulous work pioneered in Johnson's two years on *Space: 1999*. Joe Viskocil, who designed the impressive space explosions for *Star Wars* and later for *Battlestar Galactica*, once stated, "Gerry Anderson's shows were very influential. No one else was doing full time explosions."[3] He added, "Anderson usually had very well-choreographed explosions — they looked like they took the time to break down the sets and place explosions where there should be explosions."[4] Already it is clear that, visually at least, *Star Wars* capitalized on the TV work pioneered by Gene Roddenberry and Gerry and Sylvia Anderson.

Considering that *Star Wars* followed a three- to four-year period of intense genre growth and acceptance, it would actually have been a surprise had the movie failed at the box office in 1977. It had the advantage of *Star Trek*'s built-in audience, an audience starving for new space adventures, plus a then-whopping budget of $10 million — more than the cost of an entire season (24 episodes) of *Space: 1999* in 1976. It is no wonder that *Star Wars* looked so very good on the big screen, and made such an impact. Yet neither the Andersons nor Roddenberry ever sued Lucas for copyright infringement, as Lucas later sued the makers of *Battlestar Galactica* in 1978.

Why is any of this back history relevant to the creation and lifespan of *Battlestar Galactica*? Because for 20 years *Battlestar Galactica* has been accused of ripping-off *Star Wars* because of a misperceived similarity in special effects and story concept, as well as its timing. In point of fact, *Battlestar Galactica* no more copies the details of *Star Wars* than *Star Wars* copies the details of *Star Trek*, *Logan's Run* or *Space: 1999*. When planning his new science fiction series, Glen Larson did precisely what Lucas had done before him. In essence, he "leap-frogged" off the successes of the genre (this time *Star Wars* as well as *Star Trek* and *Space: 1999*) and took those successes to the next logical plateau. If it was valid for Lucas to create *Star Wars* capitalizing on the technological skill of *Space: 1999* and the mainstream popularity of *Star Trek* and *Logan's Run*, then certainly it was equally valid for Larson to create *Battlestar Galactica* following the box office success of *Star Wars*. Larson was just unlucky enough to be the *first* producer to follow *Star Wars* with a major outer space effort. Even so, with its "lost in space"-style premise and tragic happenstance each week, *Battlestar Galactica* had more in common thematically with the serious-minded *Space: 1999* than the upbeat *Star Wars*. And the bantering, enjoyable characters of *Battlestar Galactica* were as reminiscent of *Star*

Trek as they were of *Star Wars*. Seen in its historical context, *Battlestar Galactica* was clearly the next logical genre step to follow *Star Trek*, *Space: 1999*, *Logan's Run* and, yes, even *Star Wars*. It was not "solely" reminiscent of Lucas' film any more than Lucas' film was solely reminiscent of *Space: 1999* or *Star Trek*. Each program and film owed a debt to the productions and history that preceded it.

But alas, perception is slow to change, and *Battlestar Galactica did* follow closely on the heels of *Star Wars*. For many skeptics, the chronological placement is enough evidence to condemn the Larson series as a pale copy of a perceived masterpiece. After all, *Star Wars* was not just a success, it was the biggest box office hit of all time — at least until *Titanic* (1997). It became so popular so quickly that it literally consumed the minds of the nation. With *Star Wars* shower curtains, *Star Wars* breakfast cereals and *Star Wars* toys everywhere, it became virtually impossible to think of outer space without thinking of R2-D2, Darth Vader, Luke Skywalker, Chewbacca and the rest — despite the seldom-reported fact that Lucas had been influenced by *The Seven Samurai* and other films by Japanese director Akira Kurosawa (*The Hidden Fortress, Rashomon*) when creating his masterpiece.[5] Today, critics and fans downplay the fact that much of *Star Wars* took place on a desert planet, and that the golden droid C-3PO (himself reminiscent of the robot in *Metropolis* [1926]) even mentioned "spice mining": two very important elements in Frank Herbert's classic novel *Dune*.

Nevertheless, *Battlestar Galactica*, a show described frankly and openly by Glen Larson as an outer space *Wagon Train*, was instead mislabeled in 1978 as a *Star Wars* "rip-off." In 20 years, it has never escaped that damning label. And, importantly, that label has never been applied to *Star Wars*. Not once.

Glen Larson: Imperious Leader

Battlestar Galactica's lingering status as a *Star Wars* "rip-off" was caused not just by timing but, ironically, by the successful TV career of its creator, producer and frequent teleplay writer Glen A. Larson. A once-member of the Mormon Church and former singer in The Four Preps, Larson is no ordinary TV personality. In fact, he is a man who has often been perceived by industry skeptics to have built his TV reputation and empire by targeting a successful trend in movies, and then adapting it immediately to the venue of television. In his 1996 book *City on the Edge of Forever*, acclaimed writer Harlan Ellison coined Larson "Glen Larceny" for this practice of stealing movie concepts and translating them to the big screen with only a few minute changes in detail.

It would be wonderful to report that Ellison's assertion of intellectual piracy has no basis in fact. However, there is a noticeable pattern that lends credence (if not actually support) to the allegation. Larson created the western *Alias Smith and Jones* in 1971, one season after *Butch Cassidy and the Sundance Kid* (1969) cleaned up at the box office. He produced *McCloud* (1970) shortly after *Coogan's Bluff* (1968) proved popular. He also created *B. J. and the Bear* (1979), a TV show about a trucker and his chimpanzee, right after a Clint Eastwood movie about a trucker and his orangutan (1978's *Every Which Way but Loose*) made a bundle of money on the big screen. Following this pattern to its logical conclusion, many people assert that Larson watched *Star Wars* in 1977 and responded with *Battlestar Galactica* in 1978. Whether this so-called pattern is a coincidence or something less honorable is perhaps impossible to prove or disprove, but the "Larceny" reputation must be a continual source of frustration for Larson.

On the other hand, in TV the bottom line is success, and Larson has proven himself successful with a surprising number of TV series. Other than the efforts listed above, he is responsible also for *Quincy* (1976–83) starring Jack Klugman, *The Hardy Boys/Nancy Drew Mysteries* (1977–79) with Shaun Cassidy, Parker Stevenson and Pamela Sue Martin, *Sword of Justice* (1978) and *Knight Rider* (1982–85) starring future *Baywatch* icon David Hasselhoff.

Larson is undeniably a controversial figure in TV history because of his reputation for producing video facsimiles of popular films, but scholars, fans and critics should also consider that "similarity" is the name of the game in the fast world of TV productions. Shows are frequently purchased, produced and promoted by networks *not* for their differences from popular productions, but because of their similarities. It may not be right, artistically satisfying or very noble, but it is true. *Kolchak: The Night Stalker* begat *The X-Files* begat *Dark Skies* (1996), *Profiler* (1996) and the like. *Raiders of the Lost Ark* (1981) begat the Bruce Boxleitner series *Bring 'em Back Alive* (1982) and the Stephen Collins series *Tales of the Gold Monkey* (1982). *American Graffiti* (1974) begat *Happy Days* begat *Laverne and Shirley*. *Star Trek: The Next Generation* begat *Deep Space Nine* begat *Babylon 5*. *Seinfeld* begat *Ellen* begat *Friends*. Perhaps the trick to creating a new TV series is to walk a thin line. One's creation must be similar enough to a hit show to appeal to the hit show's audience, yet simultaneously offer some unique qualities to avoid charges of plagiarism or intellectual property theft. One can argue that Larson rather successfully walked this particular line to get his personal visions on the air. However, it is not the main concern of this text to defend Larson, or argue for the validity of his life's work, but only to discuss and analyze the creation and life of *Battlestar Galactica*.

At least in the case of *Battlestar Galactica*, it does seem fair to assert that Larson did not "suddenly" develop an affinity for science fiction after the premiere of *Star Wars*. On the contrary, he has stated repeatedly that his interest in science fiction began during his youth while listening to radio programs such as *Superman* and *Dimension X*. Once he entered the cutthroat world of Hollywood, Larson became story editor for the series *It Takes A Thief* (1968–70); his mentor on the series was none other than *Star Trek* producer Gene Coon. It was during this time, the late 1960s and early '70s, that Larson first began serious contemplation on what would one day become *Battlestar Galactica*. He told *Starlog* reporter Karen E. Willson about his notion in 1980:

> It was a show called *Adam's Ark*, and it was kind of the reverse of *Galactica*. All the great people from this planet were leaving Earth and going some place else because of an imminent disaster. They were tricked into going....[6]

Adam's Ark never saw the light of day because of *Star Trek*'s failure to capture a sizable audience during its original three-year run on network TV. By the time he was ready to produce *Battlestar Galactica* in 1978, Larson had absorbed almost a decade's worth of new science fiction influences, undoubtedly up to and including the popular *Star Wars*. All of these "new" visions had to be carefully considered when producing his *magnum opus*. One such influence was the literary speculation of Swiss author Erich Von Däniken (1935–) in a work called *Chariots of the Gods* (1968). This text suggested that ancient astronauts may have visited the Earth in the distant past and been responsible for such miracles of architecture as the Great Pyramids. Von Däniken's speculations, though routinely dismissed by scientists, proved immensely popular to a wide readership in the '70s, and he followed his first success with no less than six sequel texts: *Gods from Outer Space* (1971), *Gold of the Gods* (1973), *Miracles of the*

Gods (1975), *In Search of Ancient Gods* (1976), *Signs of the Gods* (1980) and *Pathways to the Gods* (1980).

For Larson, Von Däniken's in-vogue contemplations were to be the primary source for his *Battlestar Galactica* imaginings. He revealed his inspiration to James Delson of the periodical *Fantastic Films* shortly before *Battlestar Galactica*'s 1978 premiere:

> The characters could be people like us, or the people before us. Maybe the ones who built the pyramids.... Think in terms of the archaeological discoveries off Bimini — those giant stones and highways. How the heck did they build those things? ... The reason I like Von Däniken so much is that he doesn't say, "This is what happened," but "This *might* have happened." That's what makes science fiction truly fascinating.[7]

That the heroes of Larson's new TV series should be brothers of man out in distant space, brothers who may have been ancient astronauts, gave *Battlestar Galactica* a different feel than space series like *Space: 1999* or *Star Trek*. Both of those series had been rooted firmly in a near-future or far-future Earth: they were Earth-centric. By peppering his new drama with Biblical and other mythological names, Larson also imbued *Galactica* with a distinctly different feel from the universe of *Star Wars*. *Star Wars* introduced the Jedi, a Samurai-like order of warriors, and their Zen philosophy of life involving "the Force." There was no connection tying the heroes or villains of *Star Wars* to life on Earth. The adventure all took place "a long time ago, in a galaxy far, far away."

Conversely, Earth was to be the object of the grand quest in *Battlestar Galactica*. It was the destination of a cosmic, homeless fleet looking for their long-last ancestors/brothers. Viewers would tune in each week to see exactly how the "trek" of our space brothers related to our life on this planet. Did they colonize Earth thousands of years ago, and then depart for some mysterious reason? Are the Colonials the source of all our myths and our historical mysteries? Or will these space brothers arrive in the present, or in the future, just to find we only half-remember our relationship with them?

These are the tantalizing questions raised by Larson's vision, the questions of mankind's very heritage. Who are we? Where do we come from? *Star Wars* never concerned itself with such contemplations. *Battlestar Galactica* did.

The Series Launches at Light Speed

ABC-TV was quick to support Larson's and Universal Studio's initiative to bring outer space science fiction drama to television with a bang. *Battlestar Galactica*, known alternately as *Star World, Battle Star Galactica, Galactica: Star Worlds* and *The Saga of the Battlestar Galactica*, was first given the network green light as a seven-hour miniseries to air in the fall of 1978. It was only when impressed network executives saw the quality of the production that they realized they wanted *Battlestar Galactica* on their 1978 fall schedule as a weekly series.

To bring his opus to life in prime condition, Larson surrounded himself with the best talents available. Ralph McQuarrie, who had done the pre-production art for *Star Wars* and *Close Encounters of the Third Kind* and an aborted version of *Star Trek: The Motion Picture*, expertly performed the same task for *Battlestar Galactica*. John Dykstra, *Star Wars'* special effects expert, was hired not only as *Battlestar Galactica's* effects supervisor but as a series producer as well (a title given him to validate the salary he was drawing for his special effects expertise). Series costumes were designed by Jean Pierre Dorleac with an eye towards various unique cultural mixes. From Dorleac, Joe Johnson and Andy Probert came the Cylons, robotic soldiers who wore chrome armor reminiscent of Japan's samurai, and the Colonial Warriors, men and women garbed in Egyptian-style space helmets. Also on board with Dorleac, Dykstra, Larson and the rest were skilled art director John Chilberg and music composer Stu Phillips.

In the casting department, Lorne Greene of *Bonanza* was hired to lead the series as the Colonial patriarch, Commander Adama. After 14 years as the head of the Ponderosa, Greene was perfectly suited to lead another noble family through a dangerous frontier, this time the wilderness of space. Greene would be ably assisted in this new effort by two young Colonial warriors played with aplomb by actors Richard Hatch of *The Streets of San Francisco* (1976-77) and *All My Children*, and Dirk Benedict of Aaron Spelling's short-lived helicopter drama *Chopper One* (1974) and the sci-fi snake movie *SSSSSSS* (1973).

Another member of the *Battlestar Galactica* cast was Maren Jensen as Adama's daughter Athena. Although Jensen, a lovely cover girl model, had no prior acting experience except for one guest-shot on Larson's *The Hardy Boys*, she proved almost instantly on the set that she had dynamic screen presence. Rounding out the cast were Herb Jefferson, Jr., a veteran black performer who, after graduating from the American Academy of Dramatic Arts in New York City, appeared in guest starring roles on diverse TV series such as *Columbo*; *Rich Man, Poor Man*; and *McCloud*; as well as in a Los Angeles stage production of *Streamers*. Also aboard were actress Laurette Spang as the cosmic call girl Cassiopeia and young Noah Hathaway as Cpt. Apollo's adopted son, Boxey. Playing the evil Baltar was John Colicos, the talented thespian who had once played Hamlet opposite Lorne Greene's Claudius on stage, and who had menaced William Shatner's Cpt. Kirk in the *Star Trek* first season episode "Errand of Mercy" (1967). Another genre vet was Jonathan Harris, who was employed on *Battlestar Galactica* to give voice to the Cylon robot Lucifer. Harris, of course, had made waves in science fiction circles as the villainous and cowardly Dr. Smith in *Lost in Space* and the gentle Commander Gampu in *Space Academy* (1976).

No expense was spared to bring *Battlestar Galactica* to TV viewers across the world. The original Imperious Leader costume design and headpiece cost $50,000, and then was kept hidden entirely in shadows when Larson declared he did not like the final results.[8] The massive *Galactica* bridge set was lined with real, functioning computers designed by Tektronix Corporation to mimic spaceship functions such as life support, engineering and ship propulsion. Tektronix experts, who had also put their advanced computer equipment aboard many NASA spacecraft, estimated that the massive bridge set alone cost the *Battlestar Galactica* production over $850,000, with $23,000 of that sum going for the purchase of TV monitors alone.

The bridge was not the only spectacular setting. The John Dykstrabuilt, so-called "miniature" of the *Battlestar Galactica* was a whopping 72 inches long, and it weighed over 60 pounds. The incredible, crocodile-shaped warship represented an apex in television special effects design. It was believable, highly detailed and suitably futuristic. Interestingly, *Star Trek: Voyager* has introduced a ship not unlike the *Galactica* in design. The *Voyager* boasts a long, elliptical alligator-style nose, just like the battlestar. This shape is different from the saucer configuration of most Federation standard starships. Also, *Voyager*'s nacelles extend outward horizontally from the main hull, just like the Galactica's twin docking bays — again a departure from typical Starfleet engineering. Most *Star Trek* crafts are equipped with nacelles that extend upward from the main hull, not parallel to that hull.

Thiokol, another outside vendor, provided the *Battlestar Galactica* production company with the Colonial terrestrial vehicle called a "land ram." This huge, fully built replica of a futuristic tank was used extensively in "Saga of a Star World" during the Carillon sequences, and then redressed to double as a "snow ram" in "Gun on Ice Planet Zero." Like the *Galactica*, it was utilitarian in design, and indicative of a believable, futuristic military.

Considering all of these items, it is not surprising that costs spiraled early on in *Battlestar Galactica*'s tumultuous history. Surprisingly, there has never been "one" official figure that has been proven conclusively to be correct, but various reliable sources have suggested different price tags for *Battlestar Galactica*. When the film version of Larson's epic opened in Canada, it was reported that "Saga of a Star World" alone cost Universal Television somewhere in the neighborhood of $14 million. That is not too bad, one supposes, considering that *ER* today costs $13 million per episode; and it has no special effects, other than George Clooney.

Future magazine #6 ran a 1978 cover story about *Battlestar Galactica* by David Houston called "ABC's Multi-Million Dollar SF-Gamble." It reported that the first three-hour installment of the series ("Saga of a Star World") cost $9 million to assemble. A third figure came from *Newsweek*. It also ran a cover story on *Galactica* in September 1978, and it declared that the first seven hours of the series (the length of the original miniseries) cost $7 million![9] The accepted story in *Battlestar Galactica* fan circles is that each episode of the 1978–79 series cost approximately $1 million.

Money was not the only problem to plague the early days of *Battlestar Galactica*. Since ABC changed its corporate mind in midstream and demanded that *Battlestar Galactica* become a weekly series rather than a special event miniseries, the story had to be adjusted accordingly. Actress Jane Seymour, originally playing a character named "Lyra," was to have died of a weird space cancer at the conclusion of the miniseries, leaving Apollo to raise the orphan Boxey. That entire subplot was excised from "Saga of a Star World" and Jane Seymour, now "Serina," returned for two more hours of *Battlestar Galactica* in the second episode "Lost Planet of the Gods."

Another change involved the character of Baltar. In the miniseries, he was shown being executed by Cylon Centurions before the throne of the Imperious Leader. Although that scene appeared in the theatrical version of *Battlestar Galactica*, it was removed from the television print so that John Colicos (Baltar) could return as a continuing villain.

Extensive reshoots were also required for several "adult" scenes in

"Saga of a Star World." In particular, there was one short scene in which Starbuck and Cassiopeia made love in the *Galactica* launch tube. Dirk Benedict's bare, writhing back was visible for several seconds, while Spang's hands clutched passionately at it. The inference was clear. Ultimately, this provocative moment was deemed "too adult" when the series was scheduled to air during the family hour, at 8:00 P.M. on Sundays — the most watched night of the week. In the reshot version, Starbuck is fully clothed, and he and Cassiopeia are kissing, not making love.

The resultant shooting schedule of the original miniseries-cum-series pilot became so fevered that veteran director Richard Colla was let go during mid-shoot for falling behind. He was replaced by an uncredited Alan J. Levi. Although the *Battlestar Galactica* schedule only specified one month of shooting, in the end "Saga of a Star World" took two long months, eight-to-nine weeks, to shoot.

Legal Light Sabres Are Levelled

With internal problems, budget and schedule overruns, crew firings, deleted subplots and abrupt script rewrites, the last thing *Battlestar Galactica* needed during its protean phase of existence was an external crisis. Unfortunately, the fledgling series had to deal with that eventuality as well. At the express direction of *Star Wars* director George Lucas, 20th Century–Fox sued Universal Television and *Battlestar Galactica* for infringing on *Star Wars* copyrights and representing unfair competition to Lucas' *Star Wars* movie series.[10] In its September 18, 1978, issue, *Time* reported Fox Vice-President Joseph Gallagher's assertion that Universal did not have the right to produce *Battlestar Galactica*. Furthermore, Lucas revealed to *Variety* that he felt *Battlestar Galactica* infringed on the prerogatives of *Star Wars*[11], even though he himself admitted to having been "influenced" in the creation of *Star Wars* by Alex Raymond's *Flash Gordon*, Frank Herbert's novel *Dune* and the *John Carter of Mars* book series.[12]

Importantly, Lucas revamped the central plot of *Star Wars* from another source: Akira Kurosawa's *The Hidden Fortress* (1958), a film seldom seen in America, but which Lucas had viewed in film school. In the 1993 edition of his *Video Home Companion*, Roger Ebert, the respected film critic and sparring partner to Gene Siskel, noted the startling similarities between *Star Wars* and the work of Japan's foremost filmmaker:

The debt of the *Star Wars* pictures to Kurosawa is obvious almost from the opening shots, when two hapless Army underlings, one short, one tall, stagger through an empty landscape bemoaning their fates. Then the other story elements fall into place: a brave, outcast warrior general; a proud and fierce princess who is forced to disguise herself as a commoner; a feared military leader who first opposes the princess's cause ... a mysterious hidden fortress....[13]

In the same review, Ebert notes that Lucas himself gives full credit to Kurosawa for these character and plot inspirations, just as he openly mentioned *Star Trek* to Gene Roddenberry at a convention in 1987, as well as *Dune*, and *Flash Gordon* in other venues, particularly the book *Skywalking*. Considering the eclectic filmic and literary sources which Lucas pooled to create an acknowledged modern masterpiece, how could he perceive *Battlestar Galactica* as a rip-off of his brilliant, if admittedly derivative, work? If *Battlestar Galactica* was in truth a rip-off of *Star Wars*, then *Star Wars* was surely a rip-off of all those sources to which Lucas so kindly paid "homage."

Actor Gil Gerard, who played *Buck Rogers* on TV in 1979, summarized the situation in a *Starlog* interview (February 1979):

All that desert stuff was taken out of *Dune*. That's what gets me. After lifting all of that, *Star Wars* now has the audacity to sue *Galactica* for stealing *Star Wars*. Fox acts like it did the ultimate science fiction movie and no one has the right do another one. Three hundred million dollars isn't enough.[14]

The 20th Century–Fox suit against Universal also sought to prevent the sale of *Battlestar Galactica*–related merchandise, because such a sale supposedly represented an attempt to make money on what Fox asserted was "stolen property." In response, Universal immediately countersued Fox, claiming that R2-D2 in *Star Wars* was also "stolen property," a rip-off of the small ambulatory robots (Huey, Dewey and Luey) seen opposite Bruce Dern in the Universal space film *Silent Running* (1972). Universal was also reported to have filed a second countersuit against Fox, which claimed that *Star Wars* infringed on the copyrights of the 1939 *Buck Rogers* serial starring Buster Crabbe.[15]

This unfortunate, ill-timed lawsuit cast a pall over the production of *Battlestar Galactica*. Now virtually every periodical and newspaper that covered the TV show noted *Battlestar Galactica*'s resemblance to *Star Wars*, although those same periodicals had been conspicuously silent about *Star Wars'* similarity to earlier outer space fare. Glen Larson, John Dykstra, Richard Hatch and others defended their adolescent series on the basis that *Battlestar Galactica* capitalized on the special effects breakthroughs of *Star Wars* while simultaneously telling an original story. In *Starlog #196* (1993), Richard Hatch reiterated his stance to interviewer Kyle Counts:

> *Star Wars* ripped off ideas, too. You take old books and ancient stories and you evolve them. Whatever part of *Battlestar Galactica* was triggered by *Star Wars* was evolved in new directions.[16]

Indeed, *Star Wars* had capitalized on the new public acceptance of science fiction brought about by *Star Trek's* success in syndication, as well as by the special effects work of *Space: 1999's* Brian Johnson. Nevertheless, no one sued Lucas or Fox for having peddled "stolen property." In fact, the suit against *Battlestar Galactica* seemed to many the worst kind of legal mudslinging and greedy nonsense. Was Fox actually asserting that *any* outer space movie which followed *Star Wars* somehow owed a debt to the Lucas film? That kind of thinking certainly flies in the face of logic and history, because outer space adventure movies had been a staple in Hollywood long before the production of *Star Wars*. Earlier space adventures included *Buck Rogers* in 1939, *This Island Earth* in 1955, *2001: A Space Odyssey* in 1968 and *Silent Running* in 1972, to name but a few. On TV, outer space epics had also been a regular presence, from *Space Patrol* in 1951 to *Lost in Space* in 1965, up to *Star Trek* in 1966, *U.F.O.* in 1970 and *Space: 1999* in 1975. Seen in its historical context, *Battlestar Galactica* and *Star Wars both* followed in a long line of space movies and TV shows. Sadly, *Battlestar Galactica* had the misfortune of arriving immediately after *Star Wars*, a production that millions around the world had seen (unlike *The Hidden Fortress*). As a result of the timing, the makers of *Battlestar Galactica* have for many years been accused of being money-grubbing connivers who only cared about making bucks and ripping-off a hot property. But by suing Universal for financial remuneration after *Star Wars* had already broken box office records around the world, Fox and Lucas demonstrated conclusively that Larson and Universal were not the only people in the business of making money. If so inclined, one can deem it spectacularly hypocritical that one artist can make a space adventure based on the breakthroughs of other talents (including Herbert, Burroughs, Kurosawa, Roddenberry and the Andersons) and call his work a "homage," yet a second artist can do the same thing and be accused of "ripping-off" the work of the artist perpetrating said "homage"!

Greed was the real issue behind the lawsuit against *Battlestar Galactica*. In 1976, Universal and Dino DeLaurentiis had fought it out via threatened lawsuits about which entity had the right to make a new *King Kong* film. Universal had been preparing *The Legend of King Kong* to star Barbra Streisand in the Fay Wray role, and DeLaurentiis had planned an updating of the pop culture icon to be set in the 1970s. The issue was settled when DeLaurentiis agreed to give Universal a percentage of the profits from his version. In other words, the threat of legal action gave Universal the right to Dino's hard-earned *King Kong* profits, and thus Universal did not need to spend any money producing their own version! As John Dykstra explained to *Fantastic Films* in 1978:

> Universal got ten percent of *King Kong* just for saying "we won't prosecute." Well, Fox has got the same position now, so they get a piece of the action of *Galactica*.[17]

Dykstra's remark suggests that 20th Century–Fox was perhaps motivated not only by a true concern that their product (*Star Wars*) had been "ripped-off," but also by a desire for the same kind of "sweetheart" money deal that Universal had pressured out of DeLaurentiis. Maybe the Fox executives believed they could bully Universal into giving them a piece of *Battlestar Galactica*'s profit, and thus further line their own already overflowing pockets. For whatever the reason, the lawsuit is an ugly incident in *Battlestar Galactica*'s history. It would be two long years before the issue was finally settled.

The Saga Continues

Despite the lawsuit, *Battlestar Galactica* flew onward. The *Battlestar Galactica* pilot, whittled down to two hours and marketed as a movie, premiered first in Canada to recoup Universal's production costs. This was the film seen by author Isaac Asimov for review purposes. Not surprisingly, *Battlestar Galactica*, which had been hyped in print and on TV, proceeded to make big money in Canada. In the United States, Mattel and Monogram released their *Galactica* toys and model kit lines before the first children had ever seen the series. The week of its premiere, *Battlestar Galactica* was featured on the cover of *TV Guide* with a colorful illustration of Lorne Greene, and a drawing of what appeared to be a modified version of the Discovery from *2001: A Space Odyssey* (1968). *Newsweek* also did a cover story on the series, but with a more accurate illustration of the Galactica over a planet.

The mainstream press was not alone in the coverage of the new series. *Famous Monsters* #150 called *Battlestar Galactica* "a series designed for a second season. Another *Star Trek* phenomenon."[18] *Starlog* #17 also reviewed the new series in detail, and featured a photograph from it on its cover. The era of *Battlestar Galactica* had begun.

The series finally premiered on ABC on September 17, 1978. That Sunday, at 8:00 P.M., American audiences were able to see what all the hype and fuss was about. For the most part, people were not disappointed. "Saga of a Star World" was an involving drama, even though the episode was interrupted for half an hour by news coverage of the Camp David Summit between Israel and Egypt overseen by President Jimmy Carter. Even that lengthy interruption was not enough to keep *Battlestar Galactica* down. It premiered in the top ten shows for the week of September 17. It was a bonafide hit.

Unfortunately, *Battlestar Galactica* was not an easy series to shoot. John Dykstra left after producing only five hours of the series. He expressed his unhappiness with the quality of the show, and felt that the TV pace was just too fast. He felt it was impossible to do things right, the way they should be done. He was also less than thrilled that the special effects he had planned for TV had been shown on the big screen in Canada and other places. He felt that such a venue was not the best showcase for his work, work designed specifically within the limitations of television.[19] Dykstra's departure was a major blow to *Battlestar Galactica*. One of the series' most-talked-about selling points was the fact that Dykstra, *Star Wars*' guru, was handling the special effects. After Dykstra left the series, Universal Hartland facilities took over the management of *Battlestar Galactica*'s complicated effects work.

Soon after *Galactica* was on the air, the science fiction media reviews began to filter into print, and they were almost universally bad news. *Starlog*'s editor Howard Zimmerman enraged series viewers by writing a caustic review of *Battlestar Galactica* in his editorial forum, "Lastword," in issue #19. Ironically, it seemed as if Zimmerman had not paid close attention to the details of the premiere, because he asserted early in his piece that Apollo and Starbuck had discovered the Cylon fleet in "Saga of a Star

World." Of course, it was an important plot point that Apollo and *Zac*, a raw cadet, had faced that attack. Zimmerman wondered how "two battle-hardened warriors" could react so illogically in combat the way that Starbuck [sic] and Apollo did in that circumstance, when in fact Apollo was the *only* pilot with battle experience in the scenario. His isolation out in space was an important character moment. Apollo had to choose between protecting his inexperienced brother from the Cylons, or warning the fleet of the impending attack. That Zimmerman could have made so basic a factual error in his review did not lend credence to his arguments.

Zimmerman also did not win any points with *Galactica* fans by commenting that the Colonial helmets were "stupid-looking,"[20] an unnecessarily subjective assessment of Dorleac's interesting work. Zimmerman did not attempt to understand or make allowances for the fact that the "Egyptian" helmets were part of *Galactica*'s Von Däniken motif—a crucial piece of fabric in the *Battlestar Galactica* tapestry.

Zimmerman was in good company, however. Isaac Asimov also railed against the show, as he had done against *Space: 1999* in *The New York Times* in 1975. Encouraged by the big-name support, other prominent science fiction voices such as David Gerrold (who labeled the show "cowardly") were quick to jump into the *Galactica* fray. Of course, many people felt that Glen Larson had virtually "asked" for this backlash by some of the outrageous comments he made during key interviews preceding the series. In an interview with James Delson in *Fantastic Films* #6, Larson stated flat out that *Battlestar Galactica* was better than *Star Trek* or *Space: 1999*, an amazing, egotistical boast that many *Galactica* viewers soon found completely unsupported by the uninspired science fiction unfolding on their TV sets.[21]

In the weeks following the premiere of *Battlestar Galactica*, the ratings stayed high, but then began to drop slowly but surely. This dip may have been a result of the weak, "space Western" stories such as "The Lost Warrior" and "The Magnificent Warriors," both of which occurred on frontier-type planets and featured saloons, cowboy hats and Old West clichés aplenty. The series fell unexpectedly out of the prized top ten ratings bracket and landed squarely in the top fifteen—still a respectable position for a brand new program.

In response to this little sag, Larson soon announced a series revamp, and began to reduce the importance of the Cylons. Accordingly, the robotic villains disappeared from the show after episode ten ("War of the Gods") and did not reappear until the final episode of the season, "The Hand of

God." The new thrust of *Battlestar Galactica*'s first season was to be a concentration on "the people."

Tragedy Strikes

While *Battlestar Galactica*'s Nielsen ratings continued to slide, the series was hit with its first major controversy since the lawsuit initiated by George Lucas and 20th Century–Fox. On January 11, 1979, the UPI reported that a four-year-old boy from Lilburn, Georgia, had died on December 31, 1978, three months after the premiere of *Battlestar Galactica*, when he swallowed a red missile from the Colonial Viper toy released by Mattel. The same piece reported that there had been ten other injuries resulting from the same Viper missile. On January 15, 1978, a massive toy recall was ordered, even though several noted safety inspectors defended Mattel, declaring it was not so much a case of dangerous toys as it was of children using the toys in an unsafe manner.

After the recall, Mattel immediately set about re-releasing the popular *Battlestar Galactica* toy line with missiles that were now glued firmly in their launchers, impossible to eject. Other toy companies, wary of similar lawsuits, quickly followed suit. The popular Shogun Warriors, with their flying fists and helmets, and Mego's interchangeable Micronauts line were quickly adjusted, no longer shooting missile-like projectiles. Even the special "advance" action figure from *The Empire Strikes Back*, Boba Fett, was remodeled rapidly so as not to shoot a small red rocket from his backpack. Despite all these toy-line changes, the Associated Press reported on March 23, 1979, that the family of the deceased Georgia boy was seeking $14 million in damages from Mattel for marketing what they considered a dangerous item. *Battlestar Galactica* was in legal trouble all over again, although at least this time the lawsuit was not directed at the production company itself. This would not be the last tragedy, nor the last young death, to be associated with the short-lived *Battlestar Galactica* series.

Back on the set, *Battlestar Galactica* continued to be plagued with problems. Although the writing had improved since the disappearance of the Cylons, there were other problems to consider. The last several episodes of *Battlestar Galactica*'s maiden season ("The Man with Nine Lives" through "Take the *Celestra*") did not finish principal shooting any earlier than ten days prior to their announced air-time. Even worse, post-production editing and dubbing was being completed as late as the Saturday morning before the Sunday airtime, according to Tom Shales in "Rattle-trap *Galactica*," a *Washington Post* article that ran April 8, 1979.

Still, all was not gloom and doom. After a lull in the publicity machine, *Battlestar Galactica* was finally awarded with some positive attention. *Donny and Marie*, an ABC comrade that aired Friday nights, ran a humorous skit in honor of *Battlestar Galactica* called "Cattlestar *Galactica*." In a brief special effects shot, the *Donny and Marie* satire featured the nose-cone of a *Space: 1999* Eagle spaceship pulling a wagon train through the stars. Although the *Donny and Marie* appearance was a fun bit of free publicity, what was more rewarding to Glen Larson and his cohorts was that the movie version of *Battlestar Galactica* had immediately broken the record box office grosses of the John Travolta/Olivia Newton-John film, *Grease* (1978), in Great Britain. Word from around the globe was the same. *Battlestar Galactica*, the movie, had more than recouped its cost by finding huge financial success in Japan and Canada, where it blew away not only *Grease*, but *Jaws II* (1979) as well. The theatrical *Galactica* succeeded just as well in other countries, to the surprise of many pundits and critics.

Cancellation

No network science fiction TV show had ever garnered the impressive ratings *Battlestar Galactica* did in 1978-79. Yet, amazingly, the series was cancelled in late April 1979, just before the airing of "The Hand of God" on April 29, 1979. Although there was much buzz about a second season, and even a persistent rumor that Isaac Asimov (formerly a series detractor) had been hired to lead the series through a second season as new story editor, the official word came down from ABC. The supreme space epic of the fall season was finished. This decision was especially astounding since *Battlestar Galactica* had been the twenty-fourth highest rated show of the year and the sixth highest rated new series.[22] Even more impressively, it had registered a rating of 20.4 in the Nielsens, when most successful new series needed only an 18 share to be brought back for a second season. What made the difference, and what killed *Battlestar Galactica*, was that it was so expensive. At $1 million an episode, even a spectacular rating in the top 25 shows was not enough to justify the huge cost layout. Fans around the United States were shocked at the news, but it somehow seemed appropriate. *Star Trek* had never been treated well in prime time, and it looked like *Battlestar Galactica* would not be either.

Starlog reported in October 1979 that NBC and CBS were interested in buying the series, and that CBS at one point considered adding *Galactica* to its prime time lineup as a midseason replacement.[23] Unfortunately, nothing came of that possibility, and after only 24 hours of episodes, just 17 individual stories, *Battlestar Galactica* ended its first-run in ignominy. Teleplays such as "I Have Seen Earth" by Steve Kreinberg and Andy Guerdat, "Showdown" by future *Star Trek: The Next Generation* contributor Frank Abatemarco and "The Mutiny" by Guy Magar all went unproduced. Perhaps the worst news for fans was that there would not even be enough hours of the *Battlestar Galactica* series available to make it an attractive property for syndication and local stations. Generally, shows need to air a minimum of two to three years (50–80 episodes) so they can be "stripped" and run in a daily time slot. With only one season under its belt, *Battlestar Galactica* looked poised to disappear from television forever, an expensive fiasco. Not surprisingly, many in the sci-fi media responded to *Galactica*'s cancellation with a kind of "I told you so" attitude. The implication was that the special effects had been used to sell the series, but that even special effects grow tiring to audiences. That explanation made no sense, however, considering the fact that viewers had not really abandoned *Galactica* at all. Americans had not grown tired of the series in any way, shape or form: it was still a popular show (the twenty-fourth most popular out of more than 80!). On the contrary, ABC abandoned *Battlestar Galactica* because it was too expensive to produce.

Rebirth?

Amazingly, not even a month after ABC's official cancellation, *Battlestar Galactica* had risen from the ashes. It was reported on May 18, 1979, that Glen Larson had been asked by ABC for a two-hour movie sequel to *Battlestar Galactica*. The story was widely reported to concern the *Galactica*'s arrival on Earth. Once again it was said that Isaac Asimov, a revered figure in science fiction circles, would be penning a brand new *Galactica* adventure. Although *Battlestar Galactica* was gone, faithful viewers at least had cause to hope. Their favorite show would be back for at least two additional hours.

Another tidbit of good news heralded the United States theatrical release of the *Battlestar Galactica* film. *Buck Rogers*, another Glen Larson TV production, had seen its pilot film transferred to the big screen. In no time, *Buck Rogers,* starring Gil Gerard and Erin Gray, raked in an astounding $20 million, receiving mostly positive notices from mainstream critics despite its genesis as a TV production! Glen Larson immediately saw the potential in a *Battlestar Galactica* feature film. After being modified with a technology called Sensurround, which actually "shook" people in the audience during appropriate moments of high action, the *Battlestar Galactica* movie ("Saga of a Star World") was released to theaters across the United States to decent grosses. It raked in more than $10 million, an unprecedented feat considering that the production was essentially an abbreviated rerun of a story already broadcast more than once on television! To Universal Studios, this was an act of pure genius. It had paid almost nothing to modify *Battlestar Galactica* into a movie ("Saga of a Star World" had already played as a movie in Canada and elsewhere), so every dollar it made was pure profit.

This bit of good news immediately gave Larson and the owners of *Battlestar Galactica* a morale boost, and a bold new marketing idea. They would package *Battlestar Galactica* series episodes in re-edited two-hour bundles and market them in the United States and overseas as "telefilms" or theatrical releases. In Japan and Great Britain, "The Living Legend" became a movie titled *Mission Galactica: The Cylon Attack.* Since there were not enough episodes to make an attractive one-hour-a-day syndication package, Larson assembled his 17 episodes in unique new combinations and marketed them as telemovies. There was *Battlestar Galactica* ("Saga of a Star World"), *Lost Planet of the Gods, Gun on Ice Planet Zero, The Phantom in Space* (a compilation of "The Lost Warrior" and "The Hand of God"), *Space Prison* (a combination of "The Man with Nine Lives" and "Baltar's Escape"), *Space Casanova* ("Take the *Celestra*" and "The Long Patrol"), *Curse of the Cylons* ("The Magnificent Warriors" and "Fire in Space"), *The Living Legend, War of the Gods, Greetings from Earth, Murder in Space* (a compilation of "Murder on the *Rising Star*" and "The Young Lords") and *Experiment in Terra.*[24] Later, *Conquest of Earth,* a compilation of the *Galactica: 1980* episodes "*Galactica* Discovers Earth" and "The Night the Cylons Landed," was added as the thirteenth *Battlestar Galactica* "movie." The *Battlestar Galactica* telemovies were sold to many local stations, including Atlanta, Denver, Indianapolis, Kansas City, Los Angeles, Memphis, Milwaukee, Nashville, New York City, Philadelphia, Sacramento, Salt Lake City, Tampa and Washington.[25]

The surprising success of post–ABC *Battlestar Galactica* in worldwide theaters also led Universal to create a new attraction to their popular studio tour. On June 9, 1979, "The Battle of Galactica" at Universal Studios began sending red- and white-striped trams full of camera-snapping tourists into the malevolent hands of the mechanical Cylons and their Imperious Leader.[26] The *Battlestar Galactica* tour lasted only 2 minutes and 45 seconds because it had to accommodate the park's daily visiting population of 24,000 people, but it nonetheless featured an impressive laser battle between a costumed Colonial Warrior and the chrome Cylon Centurions. Good showmanship was the order of the day, and the Cylon robots were specially modified to split right down the middle when struck by the blasters of the Colonial warrior. At the finale of the show, after a brief appearance by the carnivorous Ovions, the tram full of studio visitors rocketed through a hole that was "blown out" of the Cylon baseship, where they escaped to safety (and further attractions). It was a hi-tech concept: Sensurround, operational five-watt lasers, smoke effects and sophisticated robots were all employed in the brief but fast-paced show designed by Robert Zraick.[27] So successful was "The Battle of *Galactica*" that it lasted throughout the 1980s, long after *Battlestar Galactica* was gone from first run television and movie theaters. The Cylons and the tour also appeared in the *Get Smart* (1965–70) revival film *The Nude Bomb* (1980).

Tragedy Strikes Again

The last rerun of *Battlestar Galactica* aired on August 8, 1979. Two weeks later, on August 25, a terrible story was reported by the Associated Press. In St. Paul, Minnesota, a 15-year-old *Battlestar Galactica* fan named Eddie Seidel, Jr., jumped to his death from a 200-foot bridge over the Mississippi River. He committed suicide because he was despondent about ABC's cancellation of the space series. A solid "B" student and part-time supermarket stockboy, Seidel posthumously captured the attention of a shocked nation, and poor *Battlestar Galactica* was again at the center of a very negative story. People wondered how a TV show, especially one as decidedly "mediocre" as *Battlestar Galactica*, could have been so important to even the most impressionable youngster. It was reported that the Seidels briefly considered suing ABC for their son's death, but no such lawsuit emerged. Still, in the brief 11 months it had been on the air, *Battlestar Galactica* had been associated with the deaths of two youngsters. It was, of course, a coincidence, but it was undeniably strange and disturbing. There had always been the threat of lawsuits over *Battlestar Galactica*, but for the specter of death to haunt the series was perhaps the final blow. From conception to lawsuit, from re-writes to sagging ratings, from toy-related deaths to a suicide in St. Paul, *Battlestar Galactica* had lived a seemingly cursed existence.

Vindication

Battlestar Galactica hooked many fans during its short life on ABC television. What it had *not* done was win many critical kudos from contemporary critics. Therefore, *Battlestar Galactica*'s "clean sweep" at the Academy of Science Fiction, Fantasy and Horror Awards in October of 1979 was all the more sweet. Larson's outer space creation won the award not only for the Best Dramatic TV Series of 1978, but star Dirk Benedict (Starbuck) won the award for Best TV Actor. Laurette Spang (Cassiopeia) was similarly honored, taking home the award for Best TV Actress.[28] These victories were a respite from the lawsuits, tragic deaths, critical brickbats and short-sighted network bent on cancellation.

Galactica: 1980

Less than six months after *Battlestar Galactica*'s last rerun, *Galactica: 1980* was on the air. This fact was perhaps the ultimate victory for Larson and devoted *Battlestar Galactica* fans. No matter how much network executives tried to candy-coat the sudden appearance of the revival, the facts of the matter were plain: *Galactica: 1980* was an acknowledgment that *Battlestar Galactica* should never have been cancelled. It was an acknowledgment by the network bean counters that they had killed a series which had performed better on Sunday night than any show in recent memory. Also, ABC had watched with envy as Larson's *Buck Rogers* made its NBC premiere in the fall of 1979 and made good, if not spectacular, ratings. The show finished in the top 35, even though it was pitted against top-rated *Laverne and Shirley* and *Mork and Mindy* (1978–82) for a time. Nevertheless, *Buck Rogers* survived to a second season, forcing ABC executives to realize that they had prematurely killed another outer space show, one not unlike *Buck Rogers* in expense, but one with far better ratings! For once, it seemed as if the networks had truly learned a lesson. *Battlestar Galactica* was to be given a second chance. The rapid-fire revival was an unusual, unprecedented move that gave many observers of the genre cause to hope. Rumors had already floated around the entertainment industry for some time that Isaac Asimov would be involved with the new series. This was excellent news, considering Asimov's extraordinary storytelling ability. When the word came down that *Galactica: 1980* would land on Sunday nights, the same night as its predecessor, fans were even more enthusiastic. It looked like the universe of *Battlestar Galactica* was to be allowed a second chance, and the ill-considered cancellation was but a brief interruption, a hiccup in the grand saga.

Such was not the case. Scarcely a year after *Battlestar Galactica*'s original cancellation by ABC, *Galactica: 1980* was off the airwaves forever. This fact was perhaps the ultimate defeat for Larson and devoted *Battlestar Galactica* fans. The *Galactica* cosmos had returned for only ten weeks (six episodes) worth of stories, and had failed to recapture the magic of the original series. The central situation of the new show was that the *Galactica* had reached Earth, but discovered once it got there that it was hardly worth the trip. The Earth people were primitive, warring and destructive. Thus it was up to the stalwart Colonials to save Earthlings from themselves, and bring their technology up to a level where Earth could defend itself from Cylon aggression. This unique premise went mostly unexplored; *Galactica: 1980* instead spotlighted silly technology (invisibility devices, flying motorcycles) and even sillier "fish-out-of-water" humor. Series leads Kent McCord and Barry Van Dyke did their best with the leaden material, but their characters were underdeveloped, personality-deficient variations of Apollo and Starbuck.

Galactica: 1980 was and is a hated creation, hated all the more because so much hope had been attached to the project. How, fans asked, could Larson have foisted this nonsense upon them? He had taken a serious, sentimental space program filled with interesting characters and spectacular special effects, and turned it into an Earthbound sitcom complete with car chases and superhero gimmicks such as children with "super powers"!

Dirk Benedict and Richard Hatch wisely turned down the offer to reappear in *Galactica: 1980* as regulars, although Lorne Greene and Herb Jefferson, Jr., both returned in their respective roles of Adama and Boomer. Benedict and Hatch have gone on record as saying that they considered *Galactica: 1980* an effort to cheaply capitalize on the ongoing popularity of the *Battlestar Galactica* series they struggled so long and hard on. They often worked 18–20 hours a day on the set of *Battlestar Galactica* in an attempt to make it a worthwhile venture. Hatch told interviewer David

Bassom in *TV Zone* Special #17 his reasons for not reprising the role of Cpt. Apollo in *Galactica: 1980*:

> I felt that they were going to just cut the show down and really cheapen it. They weren't going to put the same amount of energy and commitment that they did in the first show.[29]

Larson apparently felt differently at the time. He believed that *Galactica: 1980* could be the ultimate expression of his *Battlestar Galactica* ideals. He felt that the Earthbound format actually offered the series more possibilities than limitations. Outer space adventure was still an option, and "*Galactica* Discovers Earth" added time travel to the *Galactica* universe. Yet these interesting options were never explored in the short run of the series. Instead, *Galactica: 1980* was mainly an outlet to reuse Dykstra-generated stock footage that had already been overused in the original series, as well as tell juvenile "message" stories about the dangers of pollution, racism and nuclear power.

Galactica: 1980, like *Battlestar Galactica* before it, started strong in the ratings. Curiosity viewing accounted for the blockbuster ratings of "*Galactica* Discovers Earth," but audience interest rapidly faded after ridiculous stories such as "The Super Scouts" and "Spaceball." By May 1980, the series was out of first-run. It was considered such an embarrassment that it was not rerun in syndication until its acquisition by the Sci-Fi Channel in 1996. ABC had learned its lesson well: science fiction just did not play on TV. Of course, what ABC did not realize was that in the circumstances of both *Battlestar Galactica* and its unfortunate sequel, the network had not permitted adequate development time. After the making of "*Galactica* Discovers Earth," Larson had literally only weeks in which to prepare for *Galactica: 1980*'s regular run, a fact which many pundits insist accounts for the low quality of the sequel series.

After *Battlestar Galactica* and *Galactica: 1980* were gone from television, the lawsuit brought against *Battlestar Galactica* and Universal by George Lucas and 20th Century–Fox was finally resolved. Irving Hill, a Los Angeles Federal Court judge, announced on August 22, 1980, his decision that Larson's *Battlestar Galactica* did not infringe on the copyright of Lucas' *Star Wars*. By the time of that announcement, Universal's *Silent Running* countersuit against 20th Century–Fox had already been resolved. It was found that, likewise, *Star Wars* did not infringe on the copyright held by the Douglas Trumbull space film. Hill's decision was recounted in *Starlog #41* (December 1980):

Judge Hill stated that the two films were very different when viewed as a whole. *Star Wars* features a group of rebels attempting to usurp the tyrannical hold of the Empire on the galaxy ... while *Battlestar Galactica* centers on the last survivors of the human race vigorously trying to escape from a robot race bent on exterminating them.[30]

It had been nearly two years in the coming, but the beleaguered *Battlestar Galactica* was finally vindicated. No less than the law of the United States had declared that the science fiction series was *not* a rip-off of *Star Wars*. Ironically, *Battlestar Galactica* was already off the air, revived, off the air again, and out of the public eye by the time this ruling was handed down. It had lived under the cloud of the 20th Century–Fox lawsuit its entire video life.

Lost in the Void: A Decade *without* Battlestar Galactica

After *Galactica: 1980* folded, *Battlestar Galactica* was essentially a dead property. The toys and models disappeared from stores, and the Marvel comic book series ended in 1981 after only 23 issues. The actors, crew members and creators who had made *Battlestar Galactica* a special program went on to other projects and did not look back. Richard Hatch starred in less-than-stellar movies such as *Prisoners of the Lost Universe* (1983) with Kay Lenz and *Charlie Chan and the Curse of the Dragon Queen* (1981) with Michelle Pfeiffer, while Dirk Benedict hit it big as "Face" in the long-running hit *The A-Team*. In one especially funny moment on that action series, Face found himself on the Universal Studios back lot, and Dirk Benedict performed a delightful double-take as a Cylon Centurion strolled by him. It was a nice in-joke recalling the heyday of *Galactica*. Laurette Spang appeared in a recurring role on *B.J. and the Bear*, and the rest of the *Battlestar Galactica* cast found themselves starring in genre films of varying quality. Maren Jensen was the lead of the 1981 Wes Craven flick *Deadly Blessing* opposite Sharon Stone, Doug Barr, Michael Berryman and Ernest Borgnine. Anne Lockhart guest-starred in *Buck Rogers in the 25th Century* ("A Dream of Jennifer") and played a wood nymph in the motion picture *Troll* (1986). As a teenager, Noah "Boxey" Hathaway returned to the world of acting to star in Wolfgang Peterson's rousing version of the fairy tale *The Neverending Story* (1984). John Colicos fared best of all *Battlestar Galactica* alumni, and played major roles in high-profile productions such as *The Postman Always Rings Twice* (1981) with Jessica Lange and Jack Nicholson and *The Changeling* (1981) with George C. Scott. In recent years, Colicos has also been a recurring guest star on *Star Trek: Deep Space Nine* as the Klingon warrior "Kor."

Even Ed Begley, Jr., who played the warrior Greenbean, also became a major star. He appeared on *St. Elsewhere* for many years and had a starring role in the film *She-Devil* (1989) with Roseanne Barr and Meryl Streep. More recently, he appeared as a guest star in the two-part *Star Trek: Voyager* episode "Future's End." Lorne Greene was the only *Battlestar Galactica* actor who immediately landed in two other series, first *Galactica: 1980* and then *Code Red*, another one-season wonder which aired on Sunday nights during the family hour. *Galactica* producers and writers Glen Larson and Donald Bellisario continued to be major players in the production of new TV series, and both had hits such as *Knight Rider* and *Magnum, P.I.* to their names.

To the delight of many fans, *Battlestar Galactica* did not disappear entirely in the 1980s. The series was picked up briefly in syndication in its regular series format by some stations such as WWOR-TV in New York City. The show aired once a week on Saturday evenings instead of nightly, but the appearance was enough to sate the appetites of series devotees. In the mid–1980s, Universal/MCA obligingly released several episodes of *Battlestar Galactica* on videotape, although the selections were not necessarily favorite episodes of fans. "Baltar's Escape," "Murder on the *Rising Star*," "The Young Lords" and other middling fare was sold in the buy-through video venue, while the more popular stories such as "Lost Planet of the Gods" remained unavailable until 1997. Perhaps the worst news for *Battlestar Galactica* fans came in 1987: Lorne Greene, Colonial patriarch, father-figure to a TV generation and beloved actor, passed away on September 11.

Resurrection: Into the '90s and Beyond!

Battlestar Galactica survived the '80s drought and began, amazingly, to increase in popularity in the early 1990s. The Sci-Fi Channel reran the series in prime time in 1993-1994 and then during the afternoon hours with *Buck Rogers in the 25th Century* and *Galactica: 1980* in 1996-1997. The year 1993 also saw the advent of *Battlestar Galactica's* 15 "Yahren" Anniversary. A major convention was held in Los Angeles with Richard Hatch and Glen Larson in attendance, but the event was a bust because the hotel where the convention was held turned away guests and visiting celebrities such as John Colicos and Dirk Benedict, claiming that the *Battlestar Galactica* convention was not being held there. When Larson learned of this snafu, he threatened to sue the hotel. A new date for the convention was arranged, and things went markedly better. Although the initial 15 "Yahren" Anniversary did not go down well, serious talk of a *Battlestar Galactica* revival was nonetheless beginning.

Suddenly, renewed interest in *Battlestar Galactica* swept the nation. In 1995, Maximum Press issued a new comic book based on the series. In January 1997, while the *Star Wars — Special Edition* films were blasting the box office, Monogram/Revell reissued all four of its 19-year-old *Battlestar Galactica* model kits. On January 22, 1997, it was announced that *Battlestar Galactica* episodes were going to become available for purchase through Columbia House. The good news just kept rolling in for *Battlestar Galactica* fans: in March 1997, Trendmasters had a line of new *Battlestar Galactica* action figures and spaceship mockups lining toy stores around the country.

Finally, in July 1997, Richard Hatch and Chris Golden's new hardback novel *Battlestar Galactica: Armageddon* was released in book stores nationwide to rave reviews from series fans. At the time of this writing, it appears as if the national movement to revive *Battlestar Galactica* is building steam at full turbo-thrust! The Sci-Fi Channel recently assembled a marathon of episodes called "The *Battlestar Galactica*-thon," and Richard Hatch has reportedly been to the offices of Fox Television and the Sci-Fi Channel to propose a new *Battlestar Galactica* series. Rumor also has it that Dirk Benedict has given Hatch a verbal commitment to reprise the role of Starbuck should the series be made. Although no official news of a revival has reached this author's ears by August 1998, it seems almost inevitable. *Lost in Space* (1998) has been made into a movie, and *Star Wars* fever is also at an all-time high. November 1997 was packed with science fiction releases such as *Starship Troopers* and *Alien Resurrection*, while on TV *Star Gate SG-1* recently premiered. There is also a series called *Earth: The Final Conflict* from the mind of the late Gene Roddenberry in syndication. All of this interest in science fiction movies and television programming can only be good news for *Battlestar Galactica*. If *Star Gate* merits a series, if *Lost in Space* merits a movie, if an idea for a series by the deceased creator of *Star Trek* merits a series, then surely a revised *Battlestar Galactica* is worthy of resurrection as well. Only the future shall tell, however. Perhaps the final chapter of *Battlestar Galactica*'s complex history has yet to be written.

PART II

Battlestar Galactica

Critical Reception

Although this author, like many science fiction aficionados, considers *Battlestar Galactica* to be a "guilty pleasure" (i.e., a program with a great deal of potential, a likable cast and some memorable moments — as well as an equal number of problems), many critics were much less forgiving when it debuted in September 1978. Isaac Asimov (who in 1975 slammed *Space: 1999* in a front-page *New York Times* article), David Gerrold (author of the *Star Trek* episode "The Trouble with Tribbles") and even the Russian newspaper *Izvestia* all came out strongly against the program, asserting respectively that *Galactica* was a *Star Wars* rip-off (cowardly in its main premise) and anti–communist propaganda.

Because of Lorne Greene's presence as Adama, the series was disparagingly referred to far-and-wide in the press as "Battlestar Ponderosa," a reference to Greene's long tenure on *Bonanza*. Despite these daunting critical brickbats, a number of significant mainstream critics and periodicals also came out in favor of the series, including TV commentator Tom Shales and *Newsweek*, which ran a fawning cover story on the show the week of the premiere.

Perhaps it is fair to state that *Battlestar Galactica* received mixed notices from the critical community. Its special effects were universally praised, but its perceived similarity to *Star Wars* was just as often noted.

Battlestar Galactica was probably received worst in the hard-core science fiction community, which felt betrayed by the series' many scientific inaccuracies and derivative premise (which resembled, according to many, *Space: 1999*, *Star Trek*, *Lost in Space*, *Bonanza*, *Wagon Train* and *Star Wars*). Despite the overriding critical disgust, American TV viewers tuned in to the show in record numbers, and *Battlestar Galactica* was immediately a ratings success for ABC. It is a truism in Hollywood that bad reviews almost certainly promise a ratings hit, and this was undeniably the case for *Battlestar Galactica*, a series that (despite its short run) was one of the top 25 series of 1978.

In 20 years, very little has changed for Battlestar Galactica as far as critics are concerned. Today, most sympathetic reviewers, such as Star Trek expert and Sci Fi Vortex panelist Mark A. Altman, remember the series fondly, but consider it a missed opportunity. In 1993, TV Guide referred to the program as a "low point" in science fiction TV history. As efforts to revive Battlestar Galactica pick up steam in the late 1990s, one can expect all the old arguments and debates about the merits of the series to resurface. Below is a sampling of Battlestar Galactica's critical reception the first-time-around the galaxy. Reviews from mainstream and science-fiction critics have both been included to give a full idea of how Battlestar Galactica fared on its maiden voyage:

> For the most part, the characters are given more psychological dimension than the comic-strip cutouts engaged in *Star Wars* and *Galactica* creator Larson has a deft knack for spaced-out humor.... Expensive, ingeniously crafted and singularly fun-filled....— Harry F. Waters, Martin Kasindorf, Betsy Carter, *Newsweek*, September 11, 1978, pages 58–62

> I'm sure the purists blanch at these things, but all television has to be homogenized, so why shouldn't science fiction be? It's amazing that *Battlestar Galactica* looked as good as it did.— Tom Shales, *The Best of Science Fiction Television*, Harmony Books, 1987

> Campy, formulaic, and often as poorly written as the back of a cereal box, *Battlestar Galactica* was also immensely enjoyable, and few shows since have matched it for pure entertainment value.—*Net Trek*, 1995, page 311

> While boasting a charismatic cast and production values still unsurpassed by any sci-fi series today, *Battlestar Galactica* was undermined by repetitive and uninspired storylines....— Lawrence McIlhoney, *TV Zone* Special #17: "The Lost Voyagers of Cult TV," June 1995, page 7

> *Battlestar* was not thought-out particularly well before being rushed onto ABC, and the writing suffered from implausible and often inane plots that were filled with scientific inaccuracies. This is not to say *Galactica* was a bad show. On the contrary, it had some interesting ideas, a capable cast, great special effects and top-notch sets and props. But such things are no substitute for a capable hand at the helm to keep a series steered in the right direction.— William E. Anchors, Jr., *Epilog* #33: "*Battlestar Galactica*," August 1993, page 5

> The galactic negotiations between the people and the Cylons really resembled the U.S.–Soviet SALT talks — not in their actual form but in the

perverted interpretation of the enemies of the treaty from the family of Washington hawks.... Their [*Battlestar Galactica*] inspiration is the pumping-up of military, anti–Soviet hysteria, which in this case is disguised in the modern costume of socio-scientific fantasy.... [A]nti–Soviet symbolism dressed in a transparent tunic of science fiction.— Melor Sturua, *Izvestia*

Star Wars was fun and I enjoyed it. But *Battlestar Galactica* was *Star Wars* all over again and I couldn't enjoy it without amnesia.— Isaac Asimov, "Science Fiction Is More Than a Space-Age Western," Knight-Ridder Newspapers, September 17, 1978

Battlestar Galactica is a black hole of an epic. Aside from its many unpleasant qualities, it lacks what *Star Trek* was smart enough to develop: people.... The old concept of portraying good (human) vs. bad (alien) no longer provides sufficient tension to keep a show alive and that is what *Battlestar Galactica* is heaviest on.—Marvin Kitman, *The New Leader*, "Lost in Space," May 6, 1979, page 22

A strange mix of the flight of the Israelites from Egypt, the *Wagon Train* teleseries and the views of Von Daeniken [sic] whose "God is an Astronaut" slogan the film literalizes ... the superior special effects notwithstanding, make for a charmless clone of George Lucas' paen to the innocent delights of gee-whizz heroics.— Phil Hardy, *The Film Encyclopedia: Science Fiction*, William & Morrow Company, page 339

This lumbering behemoth just doesn't work in any area but special effects. These are zippy and lots of fun, if wholly unscientific and unbelievable.... The wholesale reshuffling of hoary old SF bromides, Egyptian mythology, World War II–type battle scenes and supercilious, unintentionally funny dialogue once again proves that the whole can be no better than the sum total of its parts.— Douglas Menville and R. Reginald, *Futurevisions: The New Golden Age of the Science Fiction Film*, Newcastle Publishing, 1985, page 66

An immediate success, *Battlestar* clobbered the competition and seemed set for a long run. The battles in space, staged by special effects man John Dykstra, winner of an Academy Award for *Star Wars*, were the best ever to soar across a TV screen. But the scripts failed to keep pace, becoming increasingly juvenile, and viewers slowly lost interest.... [A]n expensive failure.— Gene Wright, *The Science Fiction Image*, Facts-on-File Publications, 1983, page 42–43

Perhaps the least likable of all TV SF in its ineptness, its cynicism, its sentimentality and its contempt for and ignorance of science.— John Clute & Peter Nicholls, *The Encyclopedia of Science Fiction*, St. Martins Press, 1993, page 97

Perhaps the most blatant rip-off ever to appear on the small screen. The show ripped-off, naturally, is *Star Wars* which *Galactica* copies in nearly everything but wit and talent.—*Time*, September 18, 1978, page 98

Nine-tenths of the human race have been wiped out and the survivors are fleeing the enemy Cylons.... [T]he premise here is even less honorable: "They're after us! Let's run like hell!"... When the viewing audience began to realize that these people were not going to find a place to stand and fight back, they lost interest. Who can really care about a show that has cowardice as part of its basic format?—David Gerrold, *Starlog*, "Hope—The Human Challenge," September 1979, page 68

Battlestar Galactica proved to be a resounding dud.... The borrowing from *Star Wars* in every detail became so painfully obvious that not even the four-year-old minds for which the series apparently aimed could fail to notice the resemblance.—Harry and Michael Medved, *The Golden Turkey Awards*, Perigee Books, 1980, page 108

... tiresome, totally unimaginative Biblical space opera.... *Battlestar Galactica* was able to recreate the look but not the impact of *Star Wars*.—John Javna, *The Best of Science Fiction Television*, Harmony Books, 1987, page 84

The origins of *Battlestar Galactica* lay only in a hustle for bucks... John Dykstra's special effects are wasted on a wholly mindless plot.—Frederick Pohl, *Scientific Studies in Film*, SF Ace Books, A Grosset & Dunlap Company, 1981, page 278

There is no science background in the show whatsoever. Why don't Viper pilots wear pressurized suits when they fly? What good are those stupid-looking Egyptian helmets? What powers the battlestar and its Viper craft? ... How come they keep running into Earthlike planets out there in the vastness of galactic space? ... [A] million-dollar-an-hour disappointment.—Howard Zimmerman, editor, *Starlog #19*, O'Quinn Studios, Inc., February 1979

The gimmick ... that the group of protagonists is fleeing not from Earth but *to* it—is one that has been utterly beaten to death by now (most notably by that deep space turkey *Battlestar Galactica*)...—Stephen King, *Danse Macabre*, Berkley Edition, December 1983, page 242

Series Overview

The *Battlestar Galactica* series roster is filled with summits and valleys. Quality jumps suddenly, and then spirals rapidly from story to story.

Although there are 24 hours of *Battlestar Galactica* available, the two dozen episodes comprise only 17 individual stories, some of which seem padded out a bit at a length of two hours ("Lost Planet of the Gods," "Gun on Ice Planet Zero," "Greetings from Earth") or even three hours, in the case of "Saga of a Star World." Of the 17 individual adventures, six might be termed good, in the same class as a solid episode of *Star Trek* or *Space: 1999*. These are "Saga of a Star World," "The Living Legend," "War of the Gods," "Greetings from Earth" (all written by series creator Glen Larson), "The Man with Nine Lives" and "The Hand of God" (written by Donald Bellisario).

Four episodes of *Battlestar Galactica* are a step down from the last group in quality, decent shows that are perhaps marginally better than the average hour of science fiction TV — assuming the average is *The Fantastic Journey*, *Star Trek: The Next Generation* or the first season of *Babylon 5*. The stories in this category are "Lost Planet of the Gods," "The Long Patrol," "Baltar's Escape" and "Take the *Celestra*."

The remaining seven episodes, a full 40 percent of the collection, including "The Lost Warrior," "The Magnificent Warriors," "Gun on Ice Planet Zero," "Fire in Space," "Murder on the *Rising Star*" and "Experiment in Terra," are below average, seriously lacking in areas of writing, scientific accuracy and premise.

Part of the problem for *Battlestar Galactica* is that no episodes were written or directed by well-known names in the science fiction field, with the possible exception of "Saga of a Star World" which was directed by Richard Colla (*The Questor Tapes* [1974], *The UFO Incident* [1975], *Something Is Out There* [1988] and "The Last Outpost" in *Star Trek: The Next Generation*'s first season). The original *Star Trek* made extensive use of fine genre writers such as Harlan Ellison, Robert Bloch and George Clayton Johnson, as well as directors such as Gerd Oswald (*The Outer Limits*). *Space: 1999* was also directed by people with expertise in the sci-fi TV field. David Tomblin, who worked on *U.F.O.* and *The Prisoner*, directed some of the best *Space: 1999* stories including "Force of Life" and "The Testament of Arkadia." Yet despite such examples, *Battlestar Galactica* relied heavily on writers and directors who were basically novices with science fiction. The results tend to speak for themselves. Directors Christian Nyby, Jr. (*Ironside*; *Emergency*; *CHiPs*; *T. J. Hooker*; *The Fall Guy*; *Walker, Texas Ranger*), Rod Holcomb, Alan J. Levi, Vince Edwards, Daniel Haller and Ahmet Lateef are not well-known names in science fiction circles, although Haller did go on to direct episodes of *Buck Rogers in the 25th Century* ("Awakening,"

"Journey to Oasis"). Only Donald Bellisario, auteur of *Quantum Leap, Magnum, P.I.* and *J.A.G.*, and Winrich Kolbe, frequent director of *Star Trek: The Next Generation, Star Trek: Deep Space Nine* and *Star Trek: Voyager,* went on to distinguish themselves as important creative voices in the genre after their contributions to *Battlestar Galactica.*

The writing category is grim to consider, because the best work on the series was completed by staff members Larson and Bellisario, although Leslie Stevens (*The Outer Limits, Buck Rogers in the 25th Century*) was tangentially involved in "Gun on Ice Planet Zero." Writer Michael Sloan (*Return of the Man from U.N.C.L.E.*) also contributed some work on "Gun on Ice Planet Zero," but experienced genre scribes such as D. C. Fontana, David Gerrold, Harlan Ellison, Johnny Byrne, Art Wallace, Robert Bloch and Joseph Stefano were all absent. Why? Legend, probably apocryphal, maintains that former *Star Trek* story editor Dorothy Fontana attempted to write an episode of *Battlestar Galactica* in 1978, but was so disgusted by the revision process on the episode ("Gun on Ice Planet Zero") that she gave up, and removed her name from the final show. For whatever reason it occurred, no notable science fiction writers ever created a *Battlestar Galactica* episode. This creative void left *Battlestar Galactica* under the direction of writers who, though obviously well-versed in the conventions of television, seemed unfamiliar with the tenets of science fiction.

Still, 65 million viewers tuned into ABC's *Battlestar Galactica* premiere ("Saga of a Star World") on September 17, 1978. Some of those watchers probably felt they had seen a derivative, TV version of *Star Wars,* but a high number agreed that they had witnessed something quite spectacular and extraordinary: a state-of-the-art space adventure with handsome, expressive leads, incredible special effects, great settings and a vast scope. Judging by the fantastic ratings, even those cynical about the premiere episode came back to sample more *Galactica* in the weeks that followed. Unfortunately, they found that many of *Battlestar Galactica*'s initial strengths dissolved under the weekly pressure and rush of creating a new regular series.

The three-hour premiere, "Saga of A Star World," encompassed the destruction of Colonial civilization, the formation of an outer space wagon train and a rest stop at a deadly leisure planet run by the insectoid Ovions. Then "Lost Planet of the Gods," a sexist but enjoyable sojourn to the "mother" planet Kobol followed. The *Battlestar Galactica* series next veered unexpectedly, settling disappointingly into familiar, wild west–style retreads.

In "The Lost Warrior," Cpt. Apollo had to save a frontier farming planet from a tyrannical, overtaxing local and his Cylon Centurion servant. Predictably, the *High Noon*-style program culminated in a shootout between the Cylon "Red Eye" and Apollo in the street outside a saloon, which came replete with swinging doors. The citizens of the planet wore cowboy hats and boots and carried shotguns.

In "The Magnificent Warriors," a remake of *The Magnificent Seven* (1960), Lt. Starbuck was conned by locals into serving as the sheriff for yet another farming frontier planet, this one menaced by pig-like creatures stealing crops and raping townswomen. The swinging saloon doors, the honky-tonk music and cowboy hats were still in evidence. Even grimmer, "The Lost Warrior" and "The Magnificent Warriors" were shot on the very same Universal back lot set. The episodes aired only a month apart, so the repetition of the much-photographed locale was obvious to any viewer. Later, *Buck Rogers* would also stage episodes on the familiar standing set, particularly "Unchained Woman" (with guest star Jamie Lee Curtis) and "Time of the Hawk."

Even though "The Man with Nine Lives" was a fine episode with a nice guest spot by film great Fred Astaire, it also had fairly obvious Western genre roots. In it, a confidence man not dissimilar to TV's *Maverick* (1957–62) was hunted by strange alien outlaws who were carrying out a blood vendetta. These Borellian Nomen, though at least different from the faceless Cylon Warriors, were clearly modeled on Hollywood's 1950s depictions of American Indians! Pagans with savage laws who spoke in a strange tongue not far removed from pidgin English, the Nomen referred stolidly to their unusual myths, history and folklore. When referring to the power and venom of the "scorpius," and garbed in their robes, these long-hairs seemed kin to the Hollywood stereotype of redskins.

The concept of an "outer space" Western could have proven thematically interesting on *Battlestar Galactica* had it been used for some meaningful philosophical purpose. Indeed, the very same concept had been good enough to motivate many science fiction films including *Moon Zero Two* (1969) starring Catherine Schell (*Space: 1999*) and James Olson (*The Andromeda Strain* [1970]), *Battle Beyond the Stars* (1980) starring Robert Vaughn (*The Man from U.N.C.L.E.*) and George Peppard (*The A-Team*), and the Sean Connery space epic *Outland* (1981). It even showed up as the central tenet of an early '70s Jon Pertwee *Doctor Who* episode entitled "Colony in Space" in Great Britain! Unfortunately, when applied haphazardly to the

Von Daniken *Battlestar Galactica* universe, the Western seemed a cheap and unimaginative gimmick.

Ultimately, the Western stories were rather confusing for attentive, knowledgeable viewers. Was the audience to believe that civilizations capable of space flight and advanced space technology would be unable to protect themselves from rogue savages and cowboys? Why could they not employ force fields, or deploy early warning computer alarms? Why couldn't they bring their laser weaponry to bear? Why had civilizations descended from the 12 Great Colonies reverted to the use of primitive shotguns in less than 200 yahren (years)? These were just a few logical questions about the overused Western premise.

Battlestar Galactica also failed to explain why the *Galactica* was constantly finding human frontier settlements in a new and supposedly unexplored galaxy ("The Long Patrol," "The Young Lords," "Gun on Ice Planet Zero"), when such a big point had been made of the Cylons having destroyed "all humanity in the universe" but for the *Galactica* fleet ("Saga of a Star World"). Another issue of believability involved the unseen ramifications of all these encounters with fellow humans. If the Cylons were hot on *Galactica*'s trail, then the Battlestar was consequently leading the Cylons right to all the surviving human outposts! The people of Equellis, Sectar, Proteus, Attila and the rest would soon be either subjugated or exterminated, thanks to the *Galactica*'s intervention. Why did the *Galactica* never attempt to settle on these worlds, or to recruit humans from them?

The *Battlestar Galactica* "Westerns" ("The Lost Warrior," "The Magnificent Warriors," "The Long Patrol," "The Man with Nine Lives") exposed the true shortcomings of ABC's science fiction series. Ironically, it was not its perceived lack of originality or debt to the recent *Star Wars*. Indeed, in costuming, technology and even in background mythology, *Battlestar Galactica* was quite unique and different from either *Star Wars* or *Star Trek*. Instead, *Battlestar Galactica*'s terminal flaw was its total lack of not only imagination, but of *curiosity* about outer space and the workings of the universe. Glen Larson commented in a *Time* interview that he was seeking to make "space comfortable for the Midwest."[1] That quotation explains a lot of the problems with the series. It was produced to be comprehended and enjoyed by people who did not have even a tiny familiarity with science fiction. It literally was "*Wagon Train* to the stars," a Western transplanted to space without taking into account the unique properties and qualities of that fantastic realm.

Whereas the last big space epic of the 1970s, *Space: 1999*, dramatized incredible, mind-blowing visits to totally alien cultures and worlds in the episodes "Missing Link," "The Guardian of Piri," "Another Time, Another Place," and "The AB Chrysalis," the *Galactica*n fleet never once happened upon worlds or alien inhabitants who were anything but recognizably Earth-like and human. In that sense, even *Battlestar Galactica*'s much praised special effects must be regarded as a dramatic failure, because they were never used to spur or stir the imagination, and to dramatize truly alien civilizations. In a pinch, the fine miniature work could highlight an impressive model like the Eastern Alliance craft in "Greetings from Earth" or the old-fashioned Viper seen in "The Long Patrol," but that was the extent of their usefulness to the series.

Consider for instance the complex miniature landscape of gothic alien machinery and glowing otherworldly orbs that visually dramatized the "The Guardian of Piri" or the various, highly detailed matte paintings of "Mission of the Darians" on *Space: 1999* in 1975–77. Better yet, recall the very alien-looking, crystalline Tholians in *Star Trek*'s "The Tholian Web" or the silicon life form (the horta) in "Devil in the Dark." In those scenarios, special effects illustrated a whole new, exciting realm of existence. Imagination, inspiration and ingenuity created those memorable strange planets and beings. In contrast, *Battlestar Galactica*'s effects were frequently limited to repetitive space battles. The only planets the series visited were farming colonies ("The Lost Warrior," "The Magnificent Warriors"), Cylon bases ("The Living Legend," "Gun on Ice Planet Zero") and Earth-parallels ("Lost Planet of the Gods," "Greetings from Earth" and "Experiment in Terra"). There were no alien metropolises, no fantastic space phenomena, no voyages into non-human societies.

After a short time, the impressive space combat designed by John Dykstra and the oppressive use of stock "battle" footage became incredibly dull. Every time a Viper launched, at least once per episode, the same close-up footage of Starbuck, Sheba, Boomer, and Apollo seated in their cockpits was reused. In space battles, reaction shots of the actors from other episodes were cut in or even printed in reverse ("The Hand of God") so as to appear as "new" footage. These cheap editing tricks considerably lessened the impact of the expensive special effects. Careful viewers knew they were being conned. *Battlestar Galactica*, the most expensive show of all time, relied not on brains, imagination or even new special effects, but on studio settings and "rerun" footage of spaceships swooping and firing their lasers.

Solidifying this perception of weak production values, *Battlestar Galactica* had a terrible penchant for inserting stock footage from unrelated motion pictures into the proceedings. Undoubtedly the intent was to make the series appear more expensive and impressive. "Fire in Space" featured footage from *The Towering Inferno* (or a film like it). "The Magnificent Warriors" and "War of the Gods" stole entire spaceship sequences from Douglas Trumbull's classic *Silent Running* (1972). These jarring "cuts" were not only sloppy, but they actually drew attention away from the drama of the story. And since the spliced-together film stock did not match with the regular series stock, these moments also made the show look cheap — which it most certainly was not!

Scientific accuracy was another frequent stumbling block for *Battlestar Galactica*. "Fire in Space" dramatized a fire burning out of control in the airless void of space. "Gun on Ice Planet Zero" depicted how the *Galactica* was drawn into the sights of a planetbound laser weapon. The question was never asked why *Galactica* did not merely move out of the weapon's range, because the writers apparently did not realize that outer space is a three-dimensional arena. In addition, galaxies and solar systems were continually confused and mistaken for one another ("The Long Patrol," "The Hand of God"). Even more disappointingly, the courageous Viper pilots of the *Galactica* did not wear protective pressure suits in their one-man space fighters, yet they managed nonetheless to survive tearing pressure changes in deep space combat and orbital insertions. On *Space: 1999*, Eagle spaceship pilots almost always wore orange space suits and bulky helmets to protect themselves. That series was obsessed with gravity ("The Metamorph," "The Seance Spectre," "Brian the Brain"), a scientific factor which the writers of *Battlestar Galactica* never took into consideration — if they were even aware of it.

Still, scientific accuracy is a criterion which no TV show passes successfully. Not *Battlestar Galactica*, not *Star Trek*, not *Space: 1999*. To pillory *Battlestar Galactica* simply on its errors in this limited realm is not either fair or valid. *Star Trek* presented a universe where humans and Vulcans, separated by light years, were genetically compatible, and a miraculous transporter could beam people almost anywhere. Had *Battlestar Galactica* offered sterling dramatic stories, no one would have cared much about the faulty science. Unfortunately, such was not the case, and the scientific errors on top of everything else added to the general slipshod feeling of the whole enterprise.

As it grew, *Battlestar Galactica* fortunately escaped the pull of hackneyed space Westerns and scientific error. More often than not, however, it landed in another pit of errors: TV clichés. "Murder on the *Rising Star*" was a predictable "court martial" mystery that unconvincingly put the sterling Lt. Starbuck in legal jeopardy. "Experiment in Terra," "The Young Lords," "The Lost Warrior" and "The Long Patrol" were all essentially the same story: a *Galactica* pilot (either Starbuck or Apollo) lands on a primitive, Earth-type planet and saves primitive humans from a technological threat (either the Cylons or the Eastern Alliance) while his friends worry about him back home. In fact, the *Galactica* hotshot pilots were always crashing their Vipers and being left behind by the fleet. "Gun on Ice Planet Zero," "The Young Lords," "The Long Patrol," "The Lost Warrior" and "Greetings from Earth" all featured scenarios in which a pilot was lost and presumed dead, but then miraculously recovered.

Since "warfare" was the background of *Battlestar Galactica*, one might expect the series to be competent in defining space strategy and fleet counter-punches. Such was not the case. Each time Blue Squadron launched in combat against Cylons, the pilots flew not in tight formation with a cohesive battle plan, but wildly and individually. There was no team work. Each pilot was a hot-dog, choosing targets seemingly at random. A unified battle strategy beyond "you take the one on the right, I'll take the one on the left" was never seen. In "The Living Legend," the best episode of the series, the great Commander Cain's brilliant strategic move was to pull the *Pegasus* out of the fleet and then attack from a different angle. It was hardly inspired strategy when compared to the "Picard Maneuver" in *The Next Generation*, or Kirk's victory over Khan inside the Mutura Nebula in *Star Trek II: The Wrath of Khan*. Brilliant space strategy could have been an area where *Galactica* was really able to break new ground, but it was another missed opportunity.

Despite all these weaknesses, *Battlestar Galactica* never failed to be entertaining. And, to be fair, the series did present some highly involving stories. Perhaps best of all was the aforementioned "The Living Legend" in which the Battlestar *Pegasus*, and her legendary Commander Cain, arrived to aid the ragtag fleet. Interestingly, and rather unexpectedly, a power struggle erupted between cautious Commander Adama and the hot-headed, flamboyant Cain. The character fireworks were well done, and the story was a suspenseful one. There was even a subplot about a love triangle between Cain, Cassiopeia and Starbuck. "The Living Legend" was complex, tense and fun, a superb war drama in space.

Another terrific episode was the two-parter "War of the Gods," in which guest star Patrick Macnee portrayed Count Iblis, a devilish alien figure who grew so popular with the weary Colonial population that he was nearly voted Council President! Only Apollo's determination that Iblis was evil saved the *Galactica* from ruin. The show was mysterious, dark, and fraught with fascinating "galactic" implications. For once, *Battlestar Galactica* had the courage to express curiosity about the cosmos. "War of the Gods" postulated the existence of an advanced super race. Like "The Living Legend" before it, "War of the Gods" was explosive, character-driven drama of the highest TV order.

Even the final episode of the series, "The Hand of God," in which the *Galactica* finally stopped running and attacked a Cylon baseship, was rather rewarding simply because it was different. It was refreshing to see these embattled people stand their ground and fight instead of running all the time. And there were no cowboy hats or saloon doors anywhere. Even more rewardingly, "The Hand of God" took time to develop the relationships between the many cast members. Sheba, Apollo, Boomer and even Baltar seemed more believable and realistically "human" in this installment. "The Hand of God" gave many a viewer reason to hope. It was an exciting hour.

Battlestar Galactica benefits immensely from a very likable cast. Dirk Benedict and Richard Hatch have been unfairly criticized as Luke Skywalker and Han Solo clones for 20 years now but it is simply an untrue assertion. Both actors managed to create original characters of considerable depth in the run of the series. In fact, their sincere performances make even the flimsiest of the stories much more enjoyable.

Despite all of the Alpo jokes he endured from mean-spirited critics, Lorne Greene was also a positive presence. Not unlike Commander Straker in *U.F.O.* (*Battlestar Galactica*'s spiritual ancestor, and another space warfare series), Commander Adama was an obsessed man with a vision and a mission. Frankly, the late and underrated Greene did a terrific job playing him. He too has received much negative criticism, because some people were unable to disassociate him from his role on *Bonanza*. He was thus twice vexed by critics, yet still able to create a figure of immense wisdom. Commander Adama was a believable symbol of strength, preparedness and decency.

Of all the cast, however, perhaps the thoughtful Richard Hatch stands tallest. His Cpt. Apollo was also a decent, caring and loving man. He was a man with integrity, and television can quite simply never have too many of those. Despite disparaging comparisons to Luke Skywalker, Hatch played his part in a most noble, original and uplifting way. When this author thinks of *Battlestar Galactica*, he thinks of Apollo's courage facing down the evil Count Iblis in "War of the Gods," his tenderness with his son Boxey (Noah Hathaway) or his period of mourning after the death of his beloved wife, Serina (Jane Seymour). And, just for the record, Luke Skywalker was a wet-behind-the-ears farmboy, not a trained, seasoned warrior! The two characters are undeniably different in concept and in execution.

Still, Greene, Hatch and Benedict and the rest could have accomplished much more with their parts had they been provided with teleplays that allowed them to grow significantly in unexpected ways. In *U.F.O.*, the audience saw Ed Bishop's Commander Straker lose his marriage, as well as his son, in the tragic "A Question of Priorities" and the sad "Confetti Check A–OK." He faced the possibility of love with duplicitous reporter Jo Fraser in "The Responsibility Seat," and even left his shell and embraced a new friendship in "The Long Sleep."

Likewise, in *Space: 1999* the characters were depicted with broad but meaningful strokes. Sandra Benes (Zienia Merton) longed to have children. Paul Morrow (Prentis Hancock) was still angry over the death of his father. Kano (Clifton Jones) felt a deep personal bond with the personality of Alpha's main computer. And even when the characters did not get to reveal much about themselves, they still had distinguishable personalities and characteristics: Victor Bergman (Barry Morse) was the absent-minded professor, Maya (Catherine Schell) was the playful imp, for example. By contrast to these approaches, *Battlestar Galactica*'s inexplicable stance was to share almost nothing of the characters' inner lives or desires. Apollo's childhood, his school years, his ambitions, wants and needs were never substantively examined by the writers. Athena, the most underused character in the series, ended up being little more than set decoration. She began as a competent bridge officer of importance and a feisty love interest to Starbuck, but by episode 14, "Baltar's Escape," she had disappeared completely from the series.

Similarly, Lorne Greene's well-drawn Adama was woefully underutilized. Here was a courageous leader and noble man who had risen to command a great battlestar, yet the audience knew absolutely nothing of him. What was he like as a young warrior? It is mentioned in "Take the *Celestra*" that he once served as an aid to Commander Kronus, but the episode revealed nothing of how Adama the man felt about that job, or even about Kronus! What did Adama do to earn command of a Battlestar? Why does he hate Cylons so? When did he have time to start a family? In "War of the Gods," the audience discovers the noble leader was once a part of a telepathy experiment on Caprica. How did this affect him? What did he learn from the experience? These are not small questions. Answering such interrogatives would have deflected much of the critical punches aimed at the show.

The most well-developed character on *Battlestar Galactica* was surely Dirk Benedict's Lt. Starbuck, yet all that the audience knew about him was that he was both an orphan and an unrepentant womanizer! Still, "The Long Patrol," "The Man with Nine Lives," "Murder on the *Rising Star*," "Take the *Celestra*" and "The Young Lords" all centered on and promoted acceptance of this character.

In addition to its high-quality regular cast, the *Battlestar Galactica* episode collection, like *Space: 1999* before it, offered a universe of celebrities in guest starring appearances. Popular movie stars Lloyd Bridges, Fred Astaire, Ray Milland, Rick Springfield, Jane Seymour, Britt Ekland, Kirk Alyn, James Olson and Ray Bolger all turned up in the ragtag fleet. TV personalities such as John Hoyt (*Star Trek*, "The Cage"), Paul Fix (*Star Trek*, "Where No Man Has Gone Before"), Ana Alicia (*Falcon Crest*), Ken Swofford (*Fame*), Edward Mulhare (*The Ghost and Mrs. Muir, Knight Rider*), Randolph Mantooth (*Emergency*), Lance LeGault (*The A-Team, Werewolf*), Roy Thinnes (*The Invaders*) and Patrick Macnee (*The Avengers*) showed up too.

Even more impressively, future science fiction TV icons flew aboard the *Galactica* regularly. Anthony DeLongis, the Kazon Magh Culluh in *Star Trek: Voyager* seasons one and two, did two guest shots as a Borellian Noman named "Taba," in "The Man with Nine Lives" and "Baltar's Escape." Frank Ashmore, both Phillip and Martin of *V*, portrayed the villainous Ortega in "Murder on the *Rising Star*." And, if one looks closely, John De Lancie, "Q" of *Star Trek: The Next Generation*, can be seen briefly in "Experiment in Terra"!

If fans watch the *Galactica* collection to see a carefully constructed view of morality, disappointment may ensue. On the morality issue, *Battlestar Galactica* simply has very little to say. There is no blatant didacticism *à la Star Trek* and *The Twilight Zone*. Nor are the episodes designed to express an overall, philosophical thesis like "Collision Course" or "The Testament of Arkadia" in *Space: 1999*. Instead, *Battlestar Galactica* episodes are straightforward, banal action tales designed totally to entertain. It is science fiction as fast food. It never ceased to be enjoyable and entertaining, but *Battlestar Galactica* was shallow from a philosophical standpoint.

As mentioned previously, many stories were just old-fashioned Westerns, and others, when not *cutting in* footage from successful films, were actually *modeled* on successful films! "Gun on Ice Planet Zero" was a remake of *The Guns of Navarone* (1961), while "Fire in Space" was a variation on Irwin Allen's *The Towering Inferno.*

There were rarely agonizing moral decisions to be made, and Apollo, Adama and Starbuck were always presented as being "right" almost *a priori.* They were the stars of the series, and their viewpoints and morality went totally unquestioned and unchallenged. Even the traitor Baltar, a man who betrayed his own race, was never viewed in the context of morality or immorality. He was simply evil, like a silent movie villain. The audience was supposed to hate him because he was "the bad guy." Why did Baltar betray his people? Amazingly, through 17 episodes, the question was never even asked.

Battlestar Galactica's approach to morality was surely a response to the swashbuckling, fun-loving *Star Wars*, but it set the complexity of televised science fiction back a good 15 years. Like the original *Adventures of Superman* of the '50s or even *Space Patrol*, science fiction had simply reverted to mindless action, mock heroics, special effects and phantasmagoria. However, this *a priori* presentation of values also inadvertently created an insidious subtext in *Battlestar Galactica* that has never really been addressed.

All the main characters of the series are high-ranking members of the military. Since these characters are all "good guys," the military mentality quickly became equated with "good" in the eyes of the *Battlestar Galactica* writers, and thus anything non-military, such as the civilian ruling body called the Council of 12, was treated with contempt. Civilians, to contrast the "good" warriors, were treated as stupid buffoons ("Baltar's Escape"), hopelessly naive ("War of the Gods") or simply a cumbersome burden ("The Living Legend")! In *Battlestar Galactica* there was no attempt at defining morality, but there was a blind and blatant worship of the military. In this sense, *Battlestar Galactica* was and is fascist.

Despite all these problems, *Battlestar Galactica* could have grown into something quite good and valuable had it just been permitted the dignity of a second season. The cast was strong, the production values were for the most part slick, and the possibilities of its universe were endless. The mythology of the "Lords of Kobol," for instance, was mysterious and quite unique. And very soon, the writers surely would have realized that special effects and Westerns could no longer hold the attention of viewers. Even by the end of the first sortie, the characters had begun to grow into real people that the audience cared for and liked.

Battlestar Galactica may have initially been inspired by the success of *Star Wars*, but in the end it was no simple rip-off. Lorne Greene, Richard Hatch and the rest of the talented performers assured that fact by creating people notably different from the central characters of *Star Wars*. If only *Battlestar Galactica* had lived to find its dramatic voice. It was canceled April 23, 1979, before the last episode ("The Hand of God") was aired.

Still, even the worst, most banal episode of *Battlestar Galactica* is arguably more entertaining than the best early episodes of the tedious *Babylon 5*, which to this reviewer's eyes remains a hodgepodge of left-over *Star Trek* plots, as well as riffs on long-forgotten *Buck Rogers* episodes such as "Soul Hunter" (a regurgitation of the *Buck Rogers* episode "Space Vampire"). Interestingly, the recent Fox show *Space: Above and Beyond* also aped a lot of *Battlestar Galactica*'s pro-military attitudes and space combat scenes, but its squad of "top gun" pilots was far less appealing than Hatch, Benedict, Jefferson, Lockhart and the other *Galactica* warriors. Still, to understand the present, one must look to the past, and for space combat TV shows *Battlestar Galactica* is the past.

In 1979, *Battlestar Galactica* played theatrically with surprising success in Canada, Japan and even the United States. Modified with "Sensurround," the film was simply a compilation of the opening three hours of the series, this time without commercials. In response to his release of TV episodes as film, Glen Larson received some especially negative and hateful press. One has to wonder where those same angry critics are today, as George Lucas follows in Larson's footsteps by releasing his *Star Wars* films one more time, but with a new gimmick equally as questionable as "Sensurround": new and improved CGI special effects. Apparently Larson was not alone in his desire to "make a buck" off of a science fiction product that had already been seen umpteen times.

Cast and Credits

CAST: Lorne Greene (Commander Adama); Richard Hatch (Cpt. Apollo); Dirk Benedict (Lt. Starbuck); Herb Jefferson, Jr. (Lt. Boomer);

Colonel Tigh (Terry Carter); Maren Jensen (Athena); Laurette Spang (Cassiopeia); John Colicos (Count Baltar); Anne Lockhart (Sheba); Noah Hathaway (Boxey); Tony Swartz (Sgt. Jolly); Patrick Macnee (Voice of Cylon Imperious Leader/Opening Narrator); Jonathan Harris (Voice of Lucifer); Ed Begley, Jr. (Greenbean); David Greenan (Bridge Officer Omega); Sarah Rush (Bridge Officer Rigel); George Murdock (Dr. Salik); John Dullaghan (Dr. Wilker); Jack Stauffer (Bojay); Larry Manetti (Giles); Evie the Chimp (Muffitt the Daggit)

TECHNICAL CREDITS: *Created by:* Glen A Larson. *Produced by:* Donald Bellisario, John Dykstra, Paul Playton, David O'Connell. *Supervising Producers:* Michael Sloan, Leslie Stevens, Glen Larson. *Directors of Photography:* Ben Colman, John Penner. *Associate Producers:* Winrich Kolbe, David Phinney. *Art Director:* John E Chilberg II. *Film Editors:* Robert Kimble, Leon Ortiz-Gil, Larry Strong. *Sound Effects Editor:* Peter Berkos. *Music:* Stu Phillips. *Music Performed by:* The Los Angeles Philharmonic Orchestra. *"Galactica" Theme Written by:* Stu Phillips and Glen A. Larson. *Costume Designer:* Jean-Pierre Dorleac. *Special Effects Coordinator:* John Dykstra. *Special Effects Supervisor:* Universal Hartland. *Production Coordinator:* Peter Anderson. *Special Effects Photography:* Peter Gibbons-Fly, Alex Funke, Keith White. *Unit Supervisors:* David M. Garber, Wayne Smith. *Camera Operators:* Ray Monahan, John Moulds, David Robman, Charles Schulman, David Stipes. *Chief Model Maker:* Bryson Gerard. *Miniature Builders:* Jerry Allen, Nora J. Allen, Sean Casey, Vance Frederkc, Michael Joyce, Phillipe Lantz, Illyanna Lowry, Angelo Mariott, Richard Smiley. *Special Effects Design Supervisor:* David Johns. *Special Effects Illustration and Design:* Dan Gooze, Richard Lasley, Jena Holman, Wendy Vanguard. *Preproduction Art:* Ralph McQuarrie. *Main Title Design:* Wayne Fitzgerald. *Titles and Optical Effects:* Universal Title. *Optical Supervisor:* Robert Hall. *Opticals:* Paul Bolger, Phillip Bills, William Brier, James Burton, Jim Catania, Charles Cowles, Frederick Lagenbach, Ronald Longo, Masaki Norihiro, Eldon Rickman, Richard Ripple, William O'Sullivan, Robert Wilson. *Animation and Rotoscope Design:* Harry Moreau. *Animation Team:* Angela Diamos, Sherry Epperson, Maxwell Morgan. *Special Camera Equipment:* Richard Bennett. *Special Electronic Supervision:* Ray Morgan Elam, George Brennan. *Editorial Assistants:* David Hill, Dennis Kelly, Cory McCrum, Maureen O'Connell. *Production Assistants:* Percy Angress, Bos Bailey, Tim McHugh, George Pryor, Mike Gastaldo. *Test and Display Equipment Provided by:* Tektronix. The

Landram Vehicle is Furnished by Thiokol. Produced in Association with Glen A. Larson Productions; From Universal, an MCA Company

Episode Guide

1. "Saga of a Star World" (Parts I, II and III)
Airdate: September 17, 1978.
Written by Glen A. Larson. Directed by Richard Colla.

SYNOPSIS: In the Seventh Millennium, the Colonial Battlestar Fleet and the Quorum of 12 Colonies prepare for peace with the Cylons. Commander Adama of the Battlestar *Galactica* expresses concern about the treaty, but President Adar has confidence in the Cylon's go-between, the human Baltar. His confidence proves ill-founded, and the robotic Cylons launch a massive surprise attack, devastating the fleet, destroying the twelve Colonies and killing Adama's youngest son Zac.

Adama calls for every surviving civilian ship to be launched at once. Alongside the *Galactica*, freighters, transports and merchant ships of all shapes and specifications flee for deep space. Questioned by the newswoman Serina, Adama names the fleet's destination: Long ago, the Colonial parent race known as the Lords of Kobol wrote of a thirteenth colony, a beautiful world far away. There, on planet Earth, there may be brothers of man who can join the *Galactica* in its struggle against the Cylons.

Once the fleet is underway, many problems arise. Food is in short supply, and Adama's eldest son Apollo and Lt. Starbuck disperse the victuals of the rich and greedy Sire Uri. To reach Carillon, a port of fuel and food, the *Galactica* must also navigate a deadly red minefield called the Nova of Madagon. Once at Carillon, the war-weary Colonials enjoy the luxury of a gambling casino and hotel, but discover a dark secret: Beneath the establishment, insectoid Ovions feast on the humans. The trap is uncovered, but the *Galactica* is left to face an approaching baseship and an imminent Cylon attack.

GUEST CAST: Lew Ayres (Adar); Ray Milland (Uri); Jane Seymour (Serina); Wilfrid Hyde-White (Anton); Rick Springfield (Zac); Bruce Wright (Deck Hand); Norman Stuart (Quorum Member); Geoffrey Binney, Paul Coufos, Chip Johnson (Colonial Warriors); Randi Oakes (Casino Woman); Paula Crist (Ovion Queen); David Matthews (Operative)

COMMENTARY: A promising debut for *Battlestar Galactica*, this three-hour epic installment is fast-moving and ambitious in scope, and it successfully introduces not only the Colonial characters and the Cylon threat, but a whole new galaxy of otherworldly terminology with which viewers would become familiar over the coming weeks.

The show opens with the Cylon attack on the battlestar fleet, and it is marvelously depicted. The destruction of the *Atlantia* is a terrible and thoroughly convincing moment of utter violence. From that spectacular incident on, this opener works well. Of course, it is helped immeasurably by the fact that solid performers such as Jane Seymour, Lew Ayres, Lorne Greene, Ray Milland and Richard Hatch are reading dialogue that in the hands of lesser performers might have sounded hopelessly campy. Fortunately, the actors seem to respect the material, and they play it all straight. One thing no one wanted at this juncture was another *Lost in Space*–style farce. The seriousness pays off, and an overwhelming aura of "doom" hangs over "Saga of a Star World." The destruction of the Colonies seems to unfold with a frightening inevitability, like the fall of Troy.

The Colonial culture of *Battlestar Galactica* is introduced successfully in "Saga of a Star World," not only through the fascinating and colorful costumes of consummate designer Jean-Pierre Dorleac, but also through an interesting linguistic conceit courtesy of Glen Larson. No other science fiction TV show before *Battlestar Galactica* attempted to create an understandable but nonetheless new language for the main characters to speak on a regular and ongoing basis. In a concentrated effort to make the Colonials appear as distantly related but "alien" brothers, Larson peppered their dialogue with strange, unearthly vocabulary. "Microns" were equivalent to "seconds," "centons" were "minutes" and "centares" were "hours." "Yahrens" roughly equaled our Earth "years," and Starbuck didn't smoke "cigars," but rather "fumarellos." Colonial expletives were "frak" and "felgercarb."

All of this terminology made for a rather unique-sounding series, and had *Battlestar Galactica* merely intended to appeal to the lowest common denominator, as many critics have charged, its originators would surely not have complicated the scripts with such creative jargon. In the '90s, sci-fi fans take for granted that aliens such as Klingon speak "real" Klingonese, courtesy of linguists like Marc Okrand, but in 1978 it was not a common occurrence. *Battlestar Galactica*'s attempt to create a Colonial lexicon may today seem campy, but it is surely praiseworthy considering historical context. Of course, one can always wish that it might have been applied a little more evenly throughout the series. At times in the opener, Apollo and other characters shout, "You get the one on the *left* and I'll get the one on the *right*," or refer to "*purple* and *orange*"—designations that seem rather jarring when used in conjunction with "yahrens" and "centons."

In four instances, characters mention "years" rather than yahrens. Adar does so just before the Cylon launch their final attack on the battlestar fleet, and Cassiopeia uses the word while referring to the Gemonese socialator tradition that occurs once only every seven *years*. Starbuck talks about "light *years*" aboard the Gemonese freighter after the destruction of the Colonies, and on the shuttle to Carillon, Serina mentions to Apollo that many warriors may not have worn their uniforms in "*years*." It is a shame these errors could not have been caught before broadcast so the actors could voice-over the word "yahren" during looping.

The running subtext of *Battlestar Galactica*, that many of our Earth myths, folktales and words originated with the Colonials, is introduced in "Saga of a Star World." Thus the 12 tribes of man are named after the 12 signs of the Zodiac. Familiar names such as "Apollo," "Lucifer," "Athena," "Carillon" and "Starbuck" all come from myth or classic literature. The Colonial warriors wear helmets that are distinctly Egyptian in design, yet the culture seems to work together in a Republic-like structure, like many ancient Greek city-states, with the "Quorum of 12" roughly equating to a Senate.

Keeping with the "Star Trekkian" belief that man can get along with all races, various tribes in *Battlestar Galactica* resemble diverse Earthmen, such as Africans and Arabs. Of course, however, it is the WASP (Adama) who senses trouble and is logical enough to protect his people. Additionally, the plight of the *Galactica* (i.e., the cosmic exodus) puts Adama in the biblical role of Moses, and casts the erstwhile Colonials as the ancient Israelites. The Nova of Madagon is the Red Sea that is parted. The defeat through deceit of an enemy in an endless war references not only the Japanese air strike against Pearl Harbor on December 7, 1941, but also the mythic end of the Trojan War in which the Greeks feigned peace with the gift of the Trojan Horse, but in fact brought death and destruction. Their culture destroyed, the Trojans set forth to found a new Troy (Rome), just as the Colonials in *Galactica* flee their territory in search of a new home and a place to fight back and reclaim their superiority.

These many references to myths of various cultures successfully lend a quasi-historical context to *Battlestar Galactica,* and provide a feeling very different from that of *Star Wars,* which bears no relation to any goings-on here on Earth. It is a shame that *Battlestar Galactica* abandoned this rich and intriguing background in upcoming episodes for a view of a universe that more closely resembled the American West than the lands of ancient myth.

Besides its solid guest stars, and welcome peek at an interesting alien yet familiar "human" society, "Saga of a Star World" offers a most commendable fast pace, and plenty of hard-driving action. Moving swiftly from the pathos of Zac's death, to the sneak attack on the fleet, and then to the streets of Caprica, Richard Colla directs the first hour with a steady hand. John Dykstra's space battles are convincing, and every bit the equal of the fine work seen in *Star Wars.* And the actors breathe enough life into the protean characters to make them seem individual and likable. The scene in which Lorne Greene's Adama explores his ruined home and mourns the death of his wife is a sensitive, well-played one. It is an all-too-brief view of the human side of this tragedy. Maren Jensen also shines as Athena in her early scene with Benedict's cocky Starbuck. After the destruction of the Colonies, Jensen's Athena expresses a sort of hopelessness about the future in a wistful, believable and very human manner. Even more impressively, she does it all while garbed in a revealing "flight suit" that has obviously "inspired" Starbuck's attempt at intimacy. Athena is talking about serious issues, while Starbuck is trying to exploit her sensitivity and make advances toward her. It is an adult scene that works on more than one dramatic level, a rarity in the family-oriented *Battlestar Galactica.*

Foreshadowing upcoming stories, the scientific accuracy of this initial *Battlestar Galactica* entry is shaky. The portion of the premiere episode dealing with the minesweeping operation of "The Nova of Madagon" raises some serious questions. Why doesn't the *Galactica* simply fly around the minefield? There is much talk about the *Galactica* having to circle way off-course, and that going through the field is the only option that will not waste fuel, but this is a specious argument. The *Galactica* and her fleet could arc to a point outside the Nova, and arc back on a direct course to Carillon. It could perform this arc on either side (left or right) or above or below the obstacle. It need not stop, turn around and go another way. Space *is* three-dimensional, a concept which would also vex the writers of "Gun on Ice Planet Zero."

Perhaps a more pressing science-based issue is one of motive power. How does the *Galactica* travel so readily to different worlds without the benefit of light speed or faster-than-light drive? In "The Living Legend" and "Experiment in Terra," it is established that the *Galactica* does possess faster-than-light capability, but that the ragtag fleet does not share this ability. Thus the entire trans-galactic migration of the Colonials occurs without benefit of light speed?! If that is truly the case, then the space journey to Earth should take hundreds if not thousands of generations. *Star Trek* solved this problem with the warp drive, and *Space: 1999* solved it with the use of random natural phenomena called "space warps" (the precursor to the wormhole in *Deep Space Nine*). Unfortunately, *Battlestar Galactica* offers no such solution. The Marvel comic book adaptation of the series saw the fleet upgraded with faster-than-light drive, a nice thought that should have been incorporated into the show.

There are other technical problems in "Saga of a Star World." Why do the Vipers have wings? Wings are unnecessary in space! Of course, *Star Wars* spaceships sport wings as well, so *Galactica* is not alone in this scientific error. Why do the Vipers shoot visible jet streams from their engines? Why do the pilots not wear pressure suits (as Eagle pilots did in *Space: 1999*)? The answers to these questions goes back to series creator Larson. It was his goal to make space "comfortable for the midwest." He wanted to make a mainstream show, not a show that would appeal only to the science fiction "techies." Still, these problems effectively disqualify *Battlestar Galactica* from ever attaining a position of true honor in the science fiction TV Valhalla. The very premise of *Battlestar Galactica* has a problem: The Colonial fleet is heading for Earth, but Adama has no idea where it is. In other words, the *Galactica* is just wandering around, hoping that it will find Earth by luck. That is not at all a reasonable or logical assumption considering the vastness of the cosmos.

"Saga of a Star World" has other problems beside those in the scientific realm. From a language standpoint, why is the Cylon leader referred to as The *Imperious* Leader? The word "imperious" is defined as haughty, or arrogant, hardly the terms one would use to describe a revered being and ruler of an entire Alliance! One can only conclude that writer Larson intended the character to be "The Imperial Leader," but felt that was too close to *Star Wars* terminology for comfort.

"Saga of a Star World" is Richard Colla's only contribution to the *Battlestar Galactica* mythos, though he is well-known in science fiction circles as a respected, literate and capable if not inspired filmmaker. He also directed the pilot for the proposed Gene Roddenberrry series *The Questor Tapes* (1974) starring Mike Farrell and Robert Foxworth, as well as the TV specials *The U.F.O. Incident* (1975) starring James Earl Jones, Barnard Hughes and Estelle Parsons and *Something Is Out There* (1988) starring Maryam D'Abo. In addition, Colla contributed his directorial talents to the early *Star Trek: The Next Generation* episode that introduced the Ferengi, "The Last Outpost." Although Colla is credited with directing "Saga of a Star World," he was apparently replaced during filming by an uncredited Alan J. Levi. According to rumors and industry gossip, the change was made because Colla fell briefly behind schedule.

The "military as morality" subtext of *Battlestar Galactica* is never clearer than in this installment. President Adar is depicted as a peace-loving fool easily misguided into leaving the Colonies undefended. The character is appropriately cast, however, since Lew Ayres was well-known as a pacifist and conscientious objector in the era of World War II. Still, the character he plays is misguided (even though many writers have equated the character to Jesus and the final meeting of the Quorum of 12 as the Last Supper of the Twelve Apostles, with Baltar as Judas).

A second civilian, Sire Uri, suggests that the fleeing Colonists should throw down their arms and surrender to the Cylons. He is also shown to be a hedonistic idiot concerned only with his own luxury. Only the military, represented by Adama and the rest of the cast, is depicted as dependable and intelligent. Indeed, if the foolish pacifist President had heeded Adama, the fleet and Colonies would have survived. The Colonial populace itself is shown to be belligerent (i.e., the angry man who badgers Apollo on Caprica), intolerant (the woman who insults Cassiopeia's profession), and concerned only with the next meal. The warriors, on the other hand, display compassion, loyalty, focus and a concentration on the greater good and long-term goals (i.e., the quest for Earth). Taken as a whole, it is a fawning depiction of the military, and a restatement of the hawkish philosophy that man is only secure when backed up by powerful weaponry and the wherewithal to use it. In "Saga of a Star World," Adama is downright paranoid at times (worrying about spies, meeting Col. Tigh in secret in the hangar bay, speaking over secure comm-lines). Yet he is shown to be completely justified in his paranoia: The civilians are (implausibly) working against him — despite the fact that he saved their lives and delivered them from destruction. *Battlestar Galactica* seems to think that martial law is mankind's best hope for survival, a stark contrast to *Star Trek*, which stresses democracy and individual freedom above all else.

When *Battlestar Galactica* arrived on TV on September 17, 1978, a couple of seeming inconsistencies resulted from the broadcast of this episode. In the theatrically released version of "Saga of a Star World," Baltar was executed by the minions of the Imperious Leader following the destruction of the Colonies. On television, he is spared the graphic beheading so that he might return in the following weeks to menace Adama and company. Also of note is the fact that at the time of the premiere, a lot of the press attention focused on the incredible-looking alien delicacies served at the Ovion resort on Carillon. Surprisingly, there is not even one shot of that food in the actual film! What happened? *Newsweek* reported that the director forgot to point the camera down and catch the action.

All in all, "Saga of a Star World" is a solid outing for *Battlestar Galactica*, and actually one of the better entries in the entire series. If one must compare it to *Star Wars*, one can always make the argument that *Battlestar Galactica* steals from different archetypes other than the Lucas film, even while utilizing the same outer space arena. Adama, for instance, is not a retired general (i.e., samurai) like Ben Kenobi, but rather a spacegoing Moses, leading his people away from certain death and disaster. Starbuck is not a smuggler finding his true nobility in duty like Han Solo, but a cocksure young pilot learning about responsibility. In essence, *Battlestar Galactica* is about the annihilation and redemption of a race that has become complacent, whereas *Star Wars* is about an ongoing war with a corrupt Galactic Empire, and the revival of an ancient, noble order called the Jedi. Of course there are similarities between these productions, but they do tend to be surface, superficial ones. Yes, Muffit is cute and robotic just like R2-D2, but the two characters serve vastly different functions within their respective stories. The pepperpot-shaped R2-D2 (derivative in appearance of *Doctor Who*'s Daleks) is a highly advanced machine and data storage device, whereas the canine-shaped Muffit is just a mechanical watchdog, and one far less vocal than either R2-D2 or *Doctor Who*'s popular cybernetic pup K-9. Yes, the Cylons are moderately similar in appearance to the Imperial Stormtroopers of *Star Wars* and both are minions of evil, but Cylons are inhuman machines bent on the annihilation of man, whereas stormtroopers are but human soldiers in white armor serving the needs of a totalitarian government. Again, the concepts are quite different when examined closely, and without an agenda.

One might equally argue that the *Star Wars* saga copies *Battlestar Galactica* in its second installment, *The Empire Strikes Back* (1980). In that Lucas story, the rebels (Colonials?) are forced from their home on an ice planet (shades of "Gun on Ice Planet Zero") by Imperial Forces (Cylons) and forced to flee to space in a ragtag fleet of diverse spaceships (the Colonial Fleet?). Digging even further, Luke loses a comrade in battle who is essentially a "younger brother" to him, named Dack (which rhymes with *Galactica*'s Zac!). Of course, this argument stretches the boundaries of validity, but no more so than does the fatuous claim that *Battlestar Galactica* "stole" from *Star Wars* rather than merely capitalizing on its success. The only thing the two space epics really have in common is John Dykstra's very similar special effects, and lots of fast, illogically winged spaceships. *Battlestar Galactica* exists only because *Star Wars* was such a hit in theaters, but conversely *Star Wars* was such a hit because *Space: 1999* had already pioneered all of its amazing special effects techniques on TV! Maybe Gerry and Sylvia Anderson should have filed a lawsuit, too! In science fiction circles, it is always difficult to declare who copied whom, but one can fairly say that *Battlestar Galactica* seized the opportunity created by the success of *Star Wars* while simultaneously telling its own distinct story.

2. "Lost Planet of the Gods" (Parts I and II)
Airdates: September 24, 1978, and October 1, 1978.
Written by Glen A. Larson and Donald Bellisario.
Directed by Christian Nyby, Jr.

SYNOPSIS: A deadly plague incapacitates the *Galactica*'s warriors, leaving Apollo and Starbuck to train a group of raw recruits, including Apollo's wife-to-be Serina and his sister Athena. An additional problem develops when the *Galactica* is faced with a strange void, a vast area of darkness ahead in deep space. Adama believes this strange phenomenon is actually the hallowed path to the legendary planet Kobol, the parent world from which Colonial culture sprang eons ago. After several days of travel in the void, the *Galactica* is led out of darkness by a brilliant white star which appears at the height of the joining ceremony of Apollo and Serina. Soon, a small dead planet is detected near the lonely star, and Adama realizes that they have indeed found the legendary world of Kobol. He descends to the planet with Apollo and Serina to decipher the hieroglyphs found in the pyramid tomb of the Ninth Lord of Kobol. Before Adama can find the way to Earth, he is confronted unexpectedly by an old enemy, and Apollo is faced with a tragic loss.

GUEST CAST: Jane Seymour (Serina); Sheila DeWindt, Janet Louise Johnson, Jennifer Joseph, Millicent Crisp (Female Warriors); Janet Lynn Curtis (Sorell); Bruce Wright (First Guard)

COMMENTARY: The second episode of *Battlestar Galactica*, in which the fleet is left in the hands of "novice" female warriors, is sexist rigmarole in its first half, but strong and compelling drama in its final hour.

The none-too-subtle subtext of "Lost Planet of the Gods" is that the civilian Colonial fleet is in deep trouble if it must depend on *women* warriors to defend it. What an incredible step backwards for women in science fiction television! These female trainees are portrayed as unprofessional, foolish and hopelessly whimsical — yet incredibly gorgeous. The usually competent and thoughtful Serina, instead of concentrating on Apollo's important training lecture about space combat, whispers seductively in his ear that she loves him. This is hardly appropriate or adult behavior considering the circumstances and the importance of Apollo's words. Cadet Bree, a young, long-haired blond, acts like a ditzy Valley Girl throughout training. Worst of all, the episode has the audacity to garner laughs from the fact that Athena inadvertently destroys Starbuck's Viper in a battle simulation! This last bit of so-called "comic" business is especially offensive since Maren Jensen's Athena has already been established as not only a capable shuttle pilot, but as a high-ranking bridge officer on the *Galactica*. Like Starbuck or Apollo, she is a *trained* warrior. Accordingly, she should command the respect of not only other *Galactica* crew members, but also of her warrior compatriots, Starbuck and Apollo. It is strange, backwards and disconcerting to find such rampant sexual discrimination in the far reaches of another galaxy!

Thus, for all of its special effects advancements, *Battlestar Galactica* is philosophically less-advanced than the previous sci-fi blockbuster of the 1970s, *Space: 1999*. In that series, Helena Russell (Barbara Bain) was the second most important character and chief medical officer of Moonbase Alpha. In the second season, Catherine Schell's Maya was allowed to fire laser guns, pilot Eagle spacecraft and engage the alien enemies in physical combat, without rebuke from the men around. In other words, the women were fully and equally integrated into the action in *Space: 1999*, unlike the condescending gender attitudes described here. Fortunately, with the addition of Anne Lockhart's Sheba to the series in "The Living Legend," *Battlestar Galactica* would take a more progressive stance about female competence in combat.

Fortunately, the final portion of "Lost Planet of the Gods" grows more interesting, and far less inflammatory, as Cpt. Apollo and Serina are joined briefly in marriage and then head off with Commander Adama to explore the ruined city of Eden on Kobol. The Cylon attack on the pyramid, and the Egyptian-style set design inside the tomb, are both strong and believable. Further verisimilitude is attained by the nice work of the *Battlestar Galactica* second unit, who shot some atmospheric footage at the ruins of Luxor in Egypt to cut-in with the main unit studio work done in California. The name of the city, "Eden," is significant, of course, since Eden is the first home of Man according to the Bible. In *Battlestar Galactica*, Eden is a city on the mother world Kobol, again the first home of Man in the universe.

Baltar's unexpected arrival in the ruins, claiming that he has been waiting months to escape from the Cylons, also adds some shades of gray to the unfolding galactic drama. For a moment he is almost believable in his protestations of innocence. Many fans have speculated that it is actually Baltar's intent in "Lost Planet of the Gods" to double-cross the Cylons and eventually defeat them. Even Lucifer reports that he is unsure who is to be escorting whom to Cylon space by Baltar's way of thinking. The fact that Baltar's motives and schemes can be interpreted in more than one way makes this facet of "Lost Planet of the Gods" an interesting subplot. Things are not usually so uncertain in the black-and-white world of *Galactica*.

Finally, the death of Serina is a 20-Kleenex tearjerker. Jane Seymour, star of *Dr. Quinn, Medicine Woman* (now appearing on a cable network), does a more-than-competent job in making Serina a truly three-dimensional person, but obviously the talented actress never intended to stay with the series. In fact, the role of Serina developed in a way she had never expected when she accepted the role in early 1978. In November 1980, the actress told interviewer Alan Brender in *Starlog* #40 that she originally played a character similar in strength and courage to Jane Fonda in *The China Syndrome* (1978), a character at one time named "Lyra." In addition, Seymour's unseen version of Serina was very sick and actually dying of some form of interstellar cancer! The dying character spent most of her time in the pilot/miniseries worrying about who would take care of her son Boxey. Seymour was understandably dazed and confused when all of Serina's touching backstory and tragic dialogue was unceremoniously cut out of "Saga of a Star World."[2] Still, after accepting an increase in payment for her services, she came back for one additional two-hour episode. It is a shame Seymour did not stick with the series, because her presence deepened the reality of Apollo's character greatly. Seymour is familiar to genre fans not only for her role as the fortune-teller "Solitaire" in *Live and Let Die* (1973), but for her memorable performance in the romantic time travel story *Somewhere in Time* (1980), a well-regarded genre project co-starring Christopher Reeve and directed by Jeannot Swarcz.

George Murdock also appears in "Lost Planet of the Gods" as the compassionate Dr. Salik, a character who would reappear several times throughout the season (notably in "Fire in Space" and "Greetings from Earth"). Murdock is a full-fledged sci-fi veteran thanks not only to his work in *Galactica* but also to his performance as Admiral Hanson in "The Best of Both Worlds," the popular Borg invasion cliffhanger of *Star Trek: The Next Generation*. His most unusual genre role was perhaps that of "God" in the 1989 feature film *Star Trek V: The Final Frontier*. Out of the genre, he portrayed Lt. Scanlon on *Barney Miller* (1975–82). Murdock has been seen lately on episodes of *The X-Files* such as "The Red and the Black," where he was dealing, ironically, with alien colonists.

For the science fiction record, *Buck Rogers in the 25th Century* (1979) opened its maiden season with an episode very similar in content to *Battlestar Galactica*'s "Lost Planet of the Gods." "Planet of the Slave Girls" saw the Earth Directorate warriors incapacitated by serious food poisoning (a kin to the plague in this *Galactica* story). This meant that the planet Earth was defenseless from a villain called Kaleel (Jack Palance), and that Earth had to rely on untested novices for defense. Among the untested pilots were (gasp!) women! The sexist ploy was even more despicable on *Buck Rogers* because one of the lead characters, Wilma Deering, was a female fighter pilot herself.

3. "The Lost Warrior"

Airdate: October 8, 1978.
Written by Donald Bellisario and Herman Groves.
Directed by Rod Holcomb.

SYNOPSIS: While leading a Cylon force away from the fleet, Apollo's Viper runs low on fuel and the warrior lands on a remote farming world called Equellis. On this forgotten frontier planet, where rough-and-tumble cattle raisers called "Oviners" live off the land, Apollo meets a lovely woman, Bella, and her overeager son Puppis. They tell him about tyrannical local thug LeCerta and his evil metallic Cylon Warrior henchman,

"Red Eye," who for nine yahrens have demanded that the poor farmers pay a regular tribute. When Bella's brother is murdered by a malfunctioning Red Eye, Apollo takes matters into his own hands and faces his opponent in a quick-draw competition outside the local saloon.

GUEST CAST: Kathy Cannon (Bella); Claude Earl Jones (LeCerta); Lance LeGault (Bootes); John Timko (Puppis); Rex Cutter (Red Eye); Red West (Marco); Jay Donohue (Jason)

COMMENTARY: The first in a tiresome and unfortunate series of trite space Westerns, "The Lost Warrior" is perhaps the perfect example of *Battlestar Galactica*'s lack of curiosity about the universe. Instead of exploring a strange new alien world and alien civilization, the viewer is rewarded only with the clumsy transfer of inappropriate wild west clichés into outer space. That the Equellis Oviners of a distant galaxy wear American West–style cowboy hats and boots, and spend time drinking booze and listening to a honky-tonk electric piano in a saloon replete with swinging doors, is nothing short of a betrayal. More than $1 million was spent on each episode of *Battlestar Galactica* and this half-baked retread society was the best the art director and writer could come up with? Was literally all of the money going to the space battles?

The Western setting is a bastardization of *Battlestar Galactica*'s Von Däniken-esque premise. The series as a whole postulates (for the most part rather effectively) that the distant twelve Colonies and Earth's ancient cultures (Atlantis, Lemuria, the Toltecs, the Mayans and the Egyptians) have the same root, extraterrestrial source. This is a perfectly acceptable premise because the origins of those Earth cultures is somewhat of a mystery to modern man, or at least a point for debate among historians. The American West, a society that existed scarcely a hundred years ago, is not at all the same thing. We all know the economics, the politics, the cultural underpinnings and societal causes for the look, dress and lifestyle of this well-documented time period. There is no mystery to be exploited there — it is all recorded fact. So for *Battlestar Galactica* to run across an Old West society in another galaxy and suggest there is a common, ancient connection in Earth's history (like the pyramids of Egypt) is both ridiculous and unbelievable in the extreme.

The Western setting was also a bad decision from a publicity standpoint as well. The series was already being hailed far-and-wide in the press as *Battlestar Ponderosa* because of Lorne Greene's longtime association with

Bonanza and because of the *Wagon Train* premise. "The Lost Warrior" merely reinforces the notion that *Galactica* is a Western retread with rockets instead of horses, and lasers instead of six-shooters. Unfortunately, "The Lost Warrior" would not be the last *Galactica* Western. Swinging saloon doors and all would return in "The Magnificent Warriors."

The American West–style culture of Equellis begs several questions of internal consistency. Firstly, why would not the outposts of the Great Colonies look a little more advanced than the backwater life depicted on Equellis? The glimpse of Caprica seen in "Saga of a Star World" was a technological paradise, an artful near-future style metropolis that seemed to blend the neon best of the Big Apple with the amazing pyramids of Ancient Egypt. At least some of that fabulous technology should have gone out into space with the pioneers who settled Equellis. After all, they must have arrived there via space transport, and any culture capable of constructing interstellar spacecraft could erect a more advanced society than that seen in "The Lost Warrior." Why would intelligent people, even the toughest and most adventurous pioneers, choose to live in an environment thousands of years more primitive than the culture they grew up in?

"The Lost Warrior" story fails from other logical standpoints as well. Why are the Oviners aware of the Great Colonies, but unfamiliar with Cylons? The Great War has been going on for 1,000 years! Is the Equellis colony that old? And how has Equellis escaped the attention of these two forces, despite the fact that starships seem to crash there with alarming regularity? (Starships of Apollo, Bella's husband and Red-Eye all crashed in a nine "yahren" period!)

Disturbingly, "The Lost Warrior" also fits into another favorite science fiction subgenre or cliché that this author calls "The Single Mother in Jeopardy Syndrome." This predictable, oft-repeated story always involves a single mother, her young child, an isolated house and a terrible threat to the family's safety. Into town (or onto the planet) rides the hero of the series. He is always a handsome, sensitive male. An unspoken respect and attraction grows quickly between the hero and the mother just like it does between Apollo and Bella in "The Lost Warrior," and for a time the hero serves as a surrogate father to the child (Apollo and Puppis). Soon, however, domestic bliss is broken, and the hero just barely succeeds in defeating the nearby threat to the makeshift family before offering it a tender goodbye.

In "The Lost Warrior," the makeshift family is menaced by the evil Cylon Red Eye. In the *Buck Rogers in the 25th Century* second season episode "The Satyr," another Single Mother in Jeopardy story, stalwart Buck Rogers arrives on a planet to save a lonely widow and her son from an attacking Satyr. In the *Galactica: 1980* episode "The Return of Starbuck," Lt. Starbuck protects an alien woman and her infant son from Cylons. This syndrome was a favorite fall-back for lazy sci-fi writers in the 1970s and 1980s, and was also seen on *Planet of the Apes* in "The Legacy" (1974), and in an episode of *MacGyver* which guest-starred *Star Trek: The Motion Picture*'s Persis Khambatta. It even recurred as late as 1985 in *V*. In "The Wildcats," it was Marc Singer's resistance fighter Mike Donovan who saved the single mother and her daughter from the evil of the alien Visitors. Over and over again, it is the same, tired formula.

In addition to these two notable clichés, "The Lost Warrior" started the unfortunate trend on *Battlestar Galactica* of having cast members briefly marooned on alien worlds. It happened to Starbuck in "The Long Patrol," "The Young Lords" and on *Galactica: 1980* in the aforementioned "Return of Starbuck." It happened to young, impulsive Cree in "Gun on Ice Planet Zero," and it happened to Cassie (Cassiopeia), Apollo and Starbuck when their Vipers were smashed on Paradeen in "Greetings from Earth." The overdependence on this story element was probably the main continuing problem *Battlestar Galactica* faced during its short run. The primary question of the week was always, "Who is going to have to be rescued this week?" Why couldn't an inventive writer or producer conceive a different way to involve characters in a planetbound story?

With all of this criticism, one must wonder if there is anything good about "The Lost Warrior." Perhaps there is. There are two very well-written scenes that take place on Equellis. In the first, Apollo and Bella talk about guns, and how they have both lost their most important loved ones because of guns. In the second tender scene, Apollo talks truthfully and starkly to Puppis about how it felt, how it scared him, to kill Red Eye. These sincere character moments are highlights in a show where the costume, sets and concepts are derivative. Richard Hatch's performance is heartfelt, and already he has individualized Apollo as a sensitive, literate and gentle man. Critics who complained that Apollo was a bland Luke Skywalker clone must either have (a) never watched the series after the initial three hours or (b) been crazy. By the time of "The Lost Warrior," Richard Hatch's Apollo had shown more genuine heart, more sincerity and more individuality than Mark Hamill's Luke Skywalker did in all three *Star Wars* films. Such is the nature of TV; it allows more time for intimacy. *Battlestar Galactica* took advantage of this opportunity, and so did Hatch. Perhaps that is why Apollo is still so well-loved today, 20 years after *Battlestar Galactica*'s cancellation.

Another positive facet in "The Lost Warrior" is the glimpse into the Cylon mentality. Red Eye shows irritation and impatience with humans in this tale. He also reveals that he can sense that Apollo wants to kill him. Whether this is a malfunction peculiar to Red Eye, or an ability of the Cylon race as a whole is uncertain. However, it is fair to say that Red Eye is the most developed Cylon Centurion until the friendly "Cy" appears in the "The Return of Starbuck," the final episode of *Galactica: 1980*.

Veteran character actor Lance LeGault makes his first appearance on *Battlestar Galactica* in "The Lost Warrior" as the doomed Uncle Bootes. He would be used to better and far more menacing effect in his two performances as the leader of the Borellian Nomen in "The Man with Nine Lives" and "Baltar's Escape." He has also appeared on *Star Trek: The Next Generation* as the Klingon captain of the sleeper ship *T'Ong* in the second season adventure "The Emissary." He later menaced Dirk Benedict as the recurring villain Col. Decker in *The A-Team*.

4. "The Long Patrol"
Airdate: October 15, 1978.
Written by Donald Bellisario.
Directed by Christian Nyby, Jr.

SYNOPSIS: On the first patrol outside the Cyranus system, Starbuck loses his ship, the prototype Recon Viper #1, and is incarcerated at the medieval establishment Proteus Prison. He soon discovers he is the only "original" sinner in the ancient prison: All the other inmates are descendants of criminals who were sent there decades, even centuries, ago. The prisoners believe that the war with the Cylons is still raging, and that the alcohol they are forced to produce is sent to grateful Warriors across the Cyranus system. Starbuck's task is not only to share the truth, escape from Proteus Prison, recover his stolen Viper and return to the *Galactica*, but to solve the mystery of the "Silent One," an astronaut from Earth who may have once dwelled in his cell.

GUEST CAST: Ted Gehring (Croad); Tasha Martell (Adultress); Sean McClory (Assault); James Whitmore, Jr. (Robber); Cathy Paine (Voice of C.O.R.A.); John Holland (*Rising Star* Maitre d'); Nancy DeCarl (Robber's Wife)

COMMENTARY: Despite the fact that Universal's back lot, particularly its standing "Western village set" (seen also in "The Lost Warrior" and later in "The Magnificent Warriors"), is used again in "The Long Patrol" to depict Robber's ramshackle asteroid home, this episode is a distinct improvement over the previous story, perhaps because there is at least a modest attempt to dramatize a bizarre and interesting culture. In addition, the opening minutes of the show are devoted to humor and character-building — a welcome touch after all the space battles.

The unusual Proteus Prison is definitely a place worth visiting for *Battlestar Galactica*. All the inmates there are descendants of the original sinners, but have somehow adjusted to the idea that this is where they will live and where their children will live for a long time. This is a unique concept that has not been seen frequently in other science fiction television, and it makes for a moderately inventive centerpiece to the episode. One has to wonder, however, why these people have chosen a life of imprisonment. Such a decision seems to go against the basic tenets of human nature, so perhaps *Battlestar Galactica* was commenting slyly on the power of tradition. In Proteus Prison, tradition is so ingrained in the inmates that they cannot even open their cell doors and escape. If such was indeed the intent of the writer, it is certainly an interesting and valid point to make. Tradition, after all, is often illogical or nonsensical, yet it is a powerful force in the lives of many people.

Proteus Prison is seen not to be a "Western" jail or set (like Robber's home) but rather a far-off extension of familiar Colonial Technology. The Enforcers wear distinctive uniforms, carry lasers and fly spaceships, so there is obviously a technological infrastructure supporting the culture rather than just a vague "Old West" motif as in "The Lost Warrior." Hence Proteus is more believable and better dramatized, too. There is a nice combination of location shooting (the Amgrosia docks) with a matte painting of the medieval-style fortress/prison in the background.

Logistically, however, *Battlestar Galactica* is again on shaky ground. The Colonial Culture is shown in various episodes to be somewhat obsessed with its own history. Commander Adama recalls the cause of the Cylon/Colonial conflict in "Saga of a Star World" and cites ancient myth about the thirteenth colony in "Lost Planet of the Gods." Yet in the span of only 700 yahren, the Colonies have completely forgotten about the extra-galactic Proteus Outpost. Does this seem at all likely or in keeping with Colonial record-keeping precedent, especially since the average lifespan of a Colonial is 200 yahren? Taking the long lifespan into account, Proteus has not been isolated *that* long. Certainly it disappeared in what would be considered a technological or information age, one complete with spaceships, and during the Cylon War.

Proteus Prison would not be the last penal asteroid in science fiction television to transform into a bizarre, degraded society. During the short reign of Colin Baker as the sixth *Doctor Who*, the errant Time Lord discovered the twisted world of Varos. In "Vengeance on Varos," the descendants of the prison guards also lorded it over the descendants of inmates, as in "The Long Patrol."

The opening portions of "The Long Patrol," wherein Starbuck woos both Athena and Cassiopeia aboard the *Rising Star*, are very funny, and well-played by the cast. Jovial, fun-filled moments like this enliven the embryonic characters significantly and are, tellingly, often more interesting than the main plots of many *Battlestar Galactica* episodes. After "The Long Patrol," Starbuck's attraction to Athena would mysteriously vanish, and he would settle on Cassiopeia as the only target for his affections. Although one is reluctant to criticize the cocky lieutenant's bow to commitment, his decision had the effect of locking out Maren Jensen's Athena from many interesting subplots. It is clear from Athena's significance in "Saga of a Star World (i.e., "the locker scene") and "Lost Planet of the Gods," as well as from early publicity photos of the show which inevitably featured Greene, Hatch, Benedict and Jensen, that she was intended to be a primary mover-and-shaker in the series. But after "The Long Patrol," in which Jensen has several nice scenes with Benedict and Laurette Spang, Athena's presence is limited mostly to the *Galactica* bridge. She becomes a latter-day Lt. Uhura: a glorified technician rather than an important human being. Although a subplot in "Fire in Space" involves Athena, by then her significance to the series was minimal since Spang and Anne Lockhart had become the more "important" females.

In addition to featuring an interesting culture on Proteus and highlighting character interplay, "The Long Patrol" continues the trend of revealing "bits" of data about planet Earth. In "Lost Planet of the Gods," Adama found hieroglyphs in the tomb of the ninth lord of Kobol. In "The Long Patrol," Starbuck is incarcerated in a cell filled with drawings not only of Earth's solar system, but of wildlife such as deer and, amazingly, a white unicorn. This scene nicely creates a feeling of "forward" momentum in the series, and refocuses the viewer on the object of *Galactica*'s quest: Earth. This is especially important because the urgency of the premise is maintained; the *Galactica* must go on, ever forward, to their destination. *Star Trek: Voyager* (1995–) faltered badly in its second season because there was no sense whatsoever of urgency or mission. The lost Federation vessel just seemed to be stuck in Kazon space, going forever in circles and taking its time. This is one instance where *Star Trek* could have learned from *Battlestar Galactica*'s example.

Some spectacular new miniatures are introduced to *Battlestar Galactica* in "The Long Patrol." The enforcer's Sixth Millennium Viper, an older model of the Colonial starfighter, is a great design that is masterfully evocative of a technology long past for the *Galactica*n people. It has a long snout like the standard Viper but a less graceful, clunky wing design and pulsar guns built right into the central hull rather than perched on wings. The model moves convincingly and is supplemented by a raspy sound effect which suggests the ship does not cut through the stars as efficiently as the "modern" Viper.

Robber's freighter, another new miniature, is also shown. It is a bulbous, blocky thing that successfully reminds the viewer of an old jalopy. These are the first new ship designs seen since the premiere episode of the series.

Tasha Martell, who appears briefly in "The Long Patrol" as the criminal "Adultress," appeared on the famous *Star Trek* second season premiere, "Amok Time." She played Spock's treacherous betrothed "T'Pring." The delightful but sarcastic computer C.O.R.A., voiced expertly by Cathy Paine, is perhaps a precursor to *Knight Rider*'s K.I.T.T. (another Glen Larson creation.) Unfortunately, C.O.R.A. would not reappear in the short run of the series. Were *Battlestar Galactica* to be revived today, it would be a good idea to have a similar flight control computer in each and every Viper, in case a warrior is incapacitated in combat.

There is one blooper in "The Long Patrol" worthy of mention. At the close of the episode, Robber and his family share a meal with Adama and his brethren. When they all start to discuss Earth and the prisoner who once drew pictures of that mythical world in Starbuck's cell, Robber declares that his father told him about that prisoner, "The Silent One," *years* ago. Of course, he should have said "*yahrens*" ago.

5. "Gun on Ice Planet Zero" (Parts I and II)
Airdates: October 22, 1978, and October 29, 1978.
Written by Donald Bellisario, Leslie Stevens
and Michael Sloan. Directed by Alan Levi.

SYNOPSIS: Baltar's baseships herd the battlestar's convoy through a tight space corridor, and force it into range of a deadly laser pulse weapon which has been constructed on a mountain peak of an inhospitable ice planet. Realizing that every ship in the fleet could be destroyed by the weapon, Adama sends a team of Warriors and experienced convicts to destroy it. The Colonials brave the frozen conditions and encounter a colony of human "clones" created by human genius Dr. Ravashol. He is also the creator of the laser pulsar that now threatens to destroy the *Galactica* convoy. As time runs short and destruction looms in space, Apollo must convince Ravashol to help him, protect a stowaway Boxey, deal with the disloyalty of the convicts and mount a daring mission on the pulsar weapon. At the same time, Starbuck has a personal score to settle with the Cylons, who have captured cadet Cree.

GUEST CAST: Christina Belford (Leda); Britt Ekland (Tenna); Dan O'Herlihy (Ravashol); Richard Lynch (Wolfe); James Olson (Thane); Roy Thinnes (Croft); Denny Miller (Ser-5-9); Alan Stock (Cadet Cree); Curtis Credel (Hals); Walt Davis (Vickers)

COMMENTARY: Essentially a no-brainer, "Gun on Ice Planet Zero" is another ludicrous *Battlestar Galactica* story padded interminably to two hours. Particularly devastating to the production is the cheap, cobbled-together look of the drama caused by the oppressive and inappropriate editing of stock footage into the proceedings. Perhaps the only noteworthy element of the production is the number of prominent guest stars. Sex symbol Britt Ekland, Mary Goodnight of *The Man with the Golden Gun* (1974), plays an exceedingly good-looking clone and Dan O'Herlihy, the OCP corporate president of *Robocop* (1987) and Grig of *The Last Starfighter* (1983), appears as her creator, Ravashol. Also present are James Olson of sci-fi epics *Moon Two Zero* (1969) and *The Andromeda Strain* (1970), Richard Lynch of *Bad Dreams* (1987) and the *Star Trek: The Next Generation* episode "Gambit," Roy Thinnes of the series *The Invaders* (1966–68) and the Gerry and Sylvia Anderson film *Journey to the Far Side of the Sun* (1969), and Christine Belford of *Banacek* (1972–74) and *Empire* (1984). Belford was also a final contender for the role of Col. Wilma Deering in Glen Larson's *Buck Rogers in the 25th Century*. Although she eventually lost that role to Erin Gray, Belford did play opposite Gil Gerard as Col. Marla Landers in the *Buck Rogers* episode "Vegas in Space."

Despite these high-quality performers, this is one instance where it is fair to say that there are frankly too many guest appearances in one story. Not one of these fine actors or actresses manages to make much of a lasting impression. Instead, they all seem to be competing for a close-up moment! The final result is that the ex-cons, who should be the most volatile and dynamic characters on the screen, seem totally interchangeable. The audience never learns to care about them, and so even Leda's noble self-sacrifice at the climax carries very little emotional weight. And, discouragingly, virtually every scene Britt Ekland participates in is little more than a special effects gimmick, a split-screen shot supposed to feature many of her clones. Because it is never made clear to the audience whether it is following the "same" Ekland being, or one of her many clones, there is no emotional connection made with her performance either. Of all the guest stars, Roy Thinnes fares best. At least his Croft is allowed to show nobility, grief and loyalty — human characteristics denied the cardboard cut-outs "Thane" or "Wolfe."

Production values are surprisingly and blatantly weak in "Gun on Ice Planet Zero." Avalanche and "authentic" frozen location footage is cut into the show awkwardly, but it is not film (or film stock) compatible with the *Battlestar Galactica* production. More likely, it is from some unmemorable Universal film such as *Avalanche* (1978). One million dollars were spent per episode, and *Battlestar Galactica* resorts to stock footage the first time it has to depict a planet other than a Western frontier town. It is shameful.

All of the "snow" footage with the principal *Galactica* actors was shot indoors on a large soundstage with a smooth, flat ground and white papier-mâché rocks. It is an obvious and unconvincing illusion. *Space: 1999* also did a story on a snow world entitled "Death's Other Dominion" (1975), but that planet was much more believable in appearance because there were no papier-mâché rocks in evidence anywhere. On *Battlestar Galactica*, the white painted, papier-mâché rocks resemble those tacky objects frequently seen on the original *Star Trek*, a full ten years before production of *Battlestar Galactica*! However, it is interesting that George Lucas' sequel to *Star Wars*, 1980's *The Empire Strikes Back*, takes place largely on a snow world too. Who was ripping-off whom at that point, one might rightly ask? *Star Trek VI: The Undiscovered Country* also boldly went where *Battlestar Galactica* had gone before in 1991: to a frozen asteroid and subterranean shelter (in this case called Rura Penthe).

While tangentially on the subject of *Space: 1999*, it is appropriate to note that in the Charles Crichton–directed episode "Death's Other Dominion," the ice world encountered by the Alphans was called Ultima Thule. That *1999* story is nicely referenced by Boomer in Part I of "Gun on Ice Planet Zero," when he asserts to Starbuck that he completed rigorous snow training on "Ice Planet Thule."

Making the many shifts from stock footage to studio footage and papier-mâché rocks all the more jarring is the fact that an optical snowstorm is superimposed over "real" location footage, but frequently left out from the studio scenes! Additionally, more stock footage from an earlier *Battlestar Galactica* is peppered through the show as well. The Ice Planet is identified through dialogue and computer readouts as an asteroid, but dramatized visually through stock footage of the planet Carillon from "Saga of a Star World." Sloppily, when Starbuck's snowram (a redressed landram) shoots down a strafing Cylon disc on the *icy* surface of the planet, the film editor cuts to the explosion of the baseship near Carillon, also from "Saga of a Star World." This is an especially bad cut since the rocky, mountainous outcroppings of Carillon, *a desert planet*, can be viewed for a few seconds. The many space-battle sequences in "Gun on Ice Planet Zero" are also reruns (though some familiar sequences are printed in reverse to throw off attentive special effects watchers). The battles on display here had been seen twice: in "Saga of a Star World" and "Lost Planet of the Gods." In fact, all the space dogfights are so repetitive that they actually detract from, rather than add to, the show's appeal.

There are other careless errors permeating "Gun on Ice Planet Zero," creating the impression that the show was rushed together in a haphazard fashion. In the final portions of Part II, a female *Galactica* bridge officer declares that they will be in range of the pulsar cannon "within *moments*." Of course, the Colonies do not measure time in minutes, they measure it in *centons*! Also, the floors of the subterranean Theta caves are completely smooth and flat even though the walls and ceiling are rocky — a common flaw of "studio-made" caves (as witnessed by the same flaw in *Star Trek*'s "The Devil in the Dark").

While discussing the problems of this episode, some mention must be made that the very premise of "Gun on Ice Planet Zero," that *Galactica* cannot circumnavigate one planet in the whole, gigantic galaxy, is blatantly ridiculous. Perhaps it played well in the midwest, but for science fiction fans it was simply unacceptable. There is no reason to believe that the *Galactica* could not have avoided that system altogether had it chosen. Actually, since the *Galactica* is supposedly capable of light speed ("Experiment in Terra"), why couldn't it merely accelerate through the pulsar corridor in the blink of an eye and destroy the mountaintop gun with one of its potent missiles (seen in "The Living Legend" and "The Hand of God")? Obviously, the premise of "Gun on Ice Planet Zero" was never seriously considered or thought-out by producers and writers on the *Battlestar Galactica* team. All they wanted was a sci-fi version of the popular action film *Guns of Navarone*, or a futuristic *The Dirty Dozen* (1967). Unfortunately, what they got was a preposterous, thematically empty sloppily edited pile of hokum. Some clichés just cannot be translated successfully to outer space.

It should be noted that "Gun on Ice Planet Zero" was released by MCA on videocassette in 1997 to great enthusiasm. Suncoast Video and other video retail stores have reportedly been unable to keep the video in stock for any length of time because of its popularity.

6. "The Magnificent Warriors"
Airdate: November 12, 1978.
Written by Glen A. Larson.
Directed by Christian J. Nyby, Jr.

SYNOPSIS: After a Cylon attack destroys two Colonial agro ships and damages a third, seed must be procured from an agricultural outpost on the planet Sectar if a food shortage is to be avoided. Hounded by Siress Belloby, an obnoxious woman who has an energizer to trade for Sectar's foodstuffs, Adama leads the important mission only to find that the town of Serenity has its own problem: It is being ravaged by pig-like alien savages called the Boray. When Starbuck is tricked into serving as Serenity's constable and Belloby is captured by Nogow, leader of the Boray, Adama realizes he has more immediate concerns than feeding his space fleet.

GUEST CAST: Barry Nelson (Sire Bogan); Brett Sommers (Siress Belloby); Eric Server (Dipper); Dennis Fimple (Duggy)

COMMENTARY: "The Magnificent Warriors" is another fairly uninspired space Western set on a frontier planet, just like "The Lost Warrior" and portions of "The Long Patrol." This one, however, is not a riff on *High Noon*, but on *The Magnificent Seven* and Akira Kurosawa's *The Seven Samurai*. Like "The Lost Warrior," swinging saloon doors, cowboy attire and Western-style architecture are featured in "The Magnificent Warriors." This raises a question. With virtually no new space battle effects since the premiere, and three episodes set wholly on the Universal Studios back lot and utilizing Western costumes, where was *Battlestar Galactica*'s one million per episode being spent? Certainly not in the depiction of those spectacular agroships seen here, footage lifted directly from 1972's Douglas Trumbull production *Silent Running*.

Still, before getting mired down in more Old West clichés, "The Magnificent Warriors" opens with some charming and surprisingly witty scenes involving Commander Adama and Siress Belloby. Adama dislikes Belloby intensely, but she is obviously hot for him. As Adama tries to escape her attention, she becomes more and more difficult to shake. This is the kind of fun character interaction that could have jump-started the series had it been applied a little more frequently. Recalling the playful, bantering nature of Kirk, Spock and Bones on *Star Trek*, Col. Tigh and Apollo take great delight in Adama's romantic plight here. Lorne Greene proves that he is an adept comedian, and he shows the audience a side of the solemn Commander Adama that is rarely revealed. "The Magnificent Warriors" is also Greene's only opportunity to take Adama off the battlestar and into planetbound action, and he seems to enjoy the chance to do something different. Of course, a Western planet was a natural setting for the long-time *Bonanza* veteran.

Good science fiction TV shows "cultivate" dedicated fandoms, cults and admirers through the tact with which they advance complex philosophical ideas and thought-provoking moral issues. *Battlestar Galactica*'s "The Magnificent Warriors" is essentially another black-and-white battle between easily delineated lines of good and evil. The *Galactica*ns are good. The Borays are evil. They fight. Good wins. The End. In other words, there is nothing at all to distinguish this episode (or "The Lost Warrior," for that matter) from a 1960s TV western. Actually, that remark is an insult to old Westerns, since programs such as *Gunsmoke* and *Bonanza* did feature compelling moral battles at times. Anyway, it is sad that the producers of *Battlestar Galactica* felt obligated to treat the vast universe as an arena limited to six-shooters and horse thievery.

All that established, the crop-stealing Boray are perhaps the most interesting non-human beings to appear on *Battlestar Galactica* since the Ovions in "Saga of a Star World." The makeup on these pig creatures is fairly convincing for the era; later in 1979, Mattel would release an action figure of these alien marauders. A Boray would also show up in the background of the *Buck Rogers* first season episode "Unchained Woman" starring Jamie Lee Curtis. Returning as well in that installment of the Gil Gerard series is the Universal back lot western set seen here, in "The Lost Warrior" and in "The Long Patrol"—and even Apollo's snappy white tunic from Equellis.

"The Magnificent Warriors" is also full of typical *Battlestar Galactica* production carelessness. Editing is again mercilessly choppy. At one point, Cylon ships race beyond Blue Squadron. Someone asks Boomer how many of them he saw. He says, "I count six!", but the film editor inexplicably cuts to a green computer (Tektronix) display clearly displaying *five* fighters. Since Boomer ostensibly read his information directly from his tactical computer, one has to wonder if the lieutenant can count. In the same sequence, a black "hook" or "tail," a device used in the motion control process for miniature movement, can be clearly seen attached to the back end of the swooping Cylon raiders. As glaring as that error is here, it is even worse in the premiere of *Galactica: 1980* ("*Galactica* Discovers Earth"), where the unsightly fin is visible five or six times for several seconds at a clip.

Matters of story logic and internal consistency fare no better in "The Magnificent Warriors." Adama wastes time trying to get an energizer from Belloby because the *Galactica*'s energizers have Colonial markings on them. Fine. But are viewers to believe that a race advanced enough to build ships the size of the *Galactica* cannot erase, paint over or burn off markings on the side of a portable generator? The "marking" argument put forward by Adama is merely a weak excuse on the part of writer Glen Larson to bring the obnoxious Belloby into the proceedings.

How is one to judge "The Magnificent Warriors"? The opening sequences are charming and humorous, as is Starbuck's plight as constable of Serenity, and the Boray are convincing villains. Yet at its core, the story is nothing but recycled elements of old movies (just like "Gun on Ice Planet Zero"). *Doctor Who*, the long-lived British cult series, frequently reinterpreted old films in novel ways (Mummy movies in "Tomb of the Cybermen," *The Time Machine* in "The Daleks" and *Rebecca* in "Black Orchid"). Yet that series found logical, inventive and humorous means by which to transport the accoutrements of those plots to new worlds and times. *Battlestar Galactica* seems merely content to land its people on one wild west world after the other. At least when *Star Trek* encountered Earth cultures in space (Nazis in "Patterns of Force," Indians in "The Paradise Syndrome," Romans in "Bread and Circuses" and gangsters in "A Piece of the Action"), it did not repeatedly visit the *same* era. *Battlestar Galactica* would have been far more enjoyable had it shown a little diversity in story locale. Six stories of the series had been telecast by the end of "The Magnificent Warriors," and three of those involved the Universal back lot's Western trimmings.

Another problem with "The Magnificent Warriors" concerns continuity. "The Long Patrol" established that the *Galactica* was entering a new galaxy (beyond the Cyranus solar system) where no colonist had gone before. Yet in "Gun on Ice Planet Zero," the *Galactica*ns are not surprised to find human life on the ice planet, and in "The Magnificent Warriors" no one is surprised to find a community so far out, despite the belief that Man has never been this deep into space. Bogan even recognizes the warriors as Colonials, tying his culture to the Colonies. In the next episode, the same error would repeat. The family stranded on Attila in "The Young Lords" would also be aware of the Great Colonies even though the fleet is in a new galaxy, where supposedly no humans have been before. What gives? Were the episodes filmed or shown out of chronological sequence? Should "The Magnificent Warriors" have occurred before the events of "The Long Patrol"?

Barry Nelson, who plays the duplicitous "Bogan" in "The Magnificent Warriors" with quite a bit of devilish charm, is notable in genre history because he also portrayed James "Jimmy" Bond in a TV presentation of "Casino Royale" a few years before Sean Connery assumed the mantle of 007 in the Cubby Broccoli film series. Also of note to trivia buffs is the fact that this *Battlestar Galactica* episode is the only one to feature a sort of information age "data screen" over an initial view of the planet Sectar. This data informs the viewer of the planet's name, its quadrant and the startime. It is a rather nice technique, and an interesting visual alternative to *Star Trek*'s oral voice-over "captain's log." For some reason, the planetary data screen never recurs.

"The Magnificent Warriors" was not the last sci-fi production to appropriate *The Magnificent Seven* premise. Roger Corman's *Battle Beyond the Stars* (1980), saw Richard Thomas recruiting galactic mercenaries Sybil Danning, Robert Vaughn, George Peppard and Brent Spiner for a battle to save the peaceful planet Akira (named after *Seven Samurai* director Akira Kurosawa) from the villainous Sador (John Saxon) and his monstrous mutants.

7. "The Young Lords"
Airdate: November 19, 1978.
Written by Don Bellisario, Frank Lupo and
Paul Playton. Directed by Donald Bellisario.

SYNOPSIS: Lt. Starbuck's Viper is damaged during combat, and he crashes on a swamp world called Attila. After the Cylons pursue him through a muddy river, Starbuck meets a family of wild children who hope to rescue their imprisoned father from Spectre, an early model IL Cylon, and his garrison of centurions. As Starbuck grows close to the eldest daughter, Miri, he also learns that her brother Kyle plans to sell him to the Cylons. After a failed prisoner exchange and a Cylon double-cross, Starbuck and Kyle work together to rescue his father and bring down Spectre's regime.

GUEST CAST: Charles Bloom (Kyle); Bruce Glover (Megan); Audrey Landers (Miri); Adam Man (Nilz); Brigitte Muller (Ariadne)

COMMENTARY: "The Young Lords" is essentially the same simple tale of good vs. evil highlighted in any number of *Battlestar Galactica* episodes. In fact, it is very much a play-by-play repeat of "The Lost Warrior." A *Galactica* pilot crashes on a distant, primitive world (this time it is Starbuck; in "The Lost Warrior" it is Apollo). There, he teaches a child/children (Puppis in "The Lost Warrior," Kyle, Miri and the rest in "The Young Lords") a lesson about adulthood while his friends on the battlestar worry and mount a rescue mission. Then, the warrior defeats the Cylons (Red Eye in "The Lost Warrior," Spectre's garrison in "The Young Lords"). The seventh episode of *Battlestar Galactica* is thus a thinly-disguised remake of the third episode! The only variations between the two episodes, guest stars and settings, are totally superficial.

Despite the overused premise, the location work in "The Young Lords" is nothing short of breathtaking. Starbuck's difficult escape into the muddy swamp with the chrome Cylons in pursuit, wading knee-deep in the murky water, is well-choreographed and exciting. It is rewarding and somewhat terrifying to see these hulking robot monsters in a real-life setting instead of inside typical studio sets. The convincing appearance of the Cylons stomping through the river, in slate gray daylight, probably accounts for the visceral visual impact of that scene. The rest of the episode is less successful, enlivened only briefly by the unexpected comic banter between, of all characters, Baltar and Lucifer.

It is certainly a delight to listen to the sarcastic voice of Lucifer (Jonathan Harris, Dr. Smith on *Lost in Space*) as he taunts the charismatic, scene-chewing John Colicos about Spectre. It is also rather ironic that Harris should voice an insufferable robot, since he is so famous for despising the famous "bubble-headed booby" robot on that Irwin Allen series.

The end of "The Young Lords" is also unrewarding and poorly conceived. Kyle and Miri's family elects to stay behind on Attila — alone.

Perhaps that is an acceptable solution for the father, Megan, who is a little bit over the hill, but what about Kyle, the teenage boy growing into manhood? And what of Miri, the teenage girl blossoming quickly (oh so quickly!) into womanhood? Sooner or later, their hormones are going to kick in at light speed. Realistically speaking, they are not going to have any outlet for their physical needs — except each other! That scenario would certainly make for a unique episode of *Battlestar Galactica*— perhaps an outer space riff on *The Blue Lagoon* (1981)? A more logical and satisfying conclusion would have seen the family returning to the fleet with Starbuck. Aside from the above-mentioned "implications" concerning Kyle and Miri, why would any family choose to remain alone on a planet when the rest of humanity is high-tailing it out of the galaxy permanently? How long will it be before the Cylons return to Attila in force?

Continuing the James Bond connection, actor Bruce Glover appears in "The Young Lords" as Megan, the family patriarch. He played the homosexual killer Mr. Wint in 1970's *Diamonds Are Forever*. This makes him the fourth guest star on *Battlestar Galactica* after Jane Seymour ("Lost Planet of the Gods"), Britt Ekland ("Gun on Ice Planet Zero"), and Barry Nelson ("The Magnificent Warriors"), to be associated with the exploits of agent 007.

Adding further evidence to this author's assertion that the special effects of *Battlestar Galactica* were frequently made less special by their oppressive repetition is the battle which opens "The Young Lords." But for one or two shots of a Viper's damaged underside, it is all stock footage. Again, one has to wonder where that magical million dollars per episode was being spent.

Of interest to fans watching *Battlestar Galactica* for its mythical references and historical qualities, "The Young Lords" is jam-packed with interesting references. It features the second appearance of a unicorn. The first such animal was seen in a wall painting in Proteus Prison in "The Long Patrol." Seen in the flesh here, it is a beautiful animal that serves as Kyle's steed.

The youngest girl in the Attila family is named Ariadne, a name from the Theseus/Minotaur myth of Ancient Greece. In myth, Ariadne was the daughter of King Minos, who was forcing young Athenians to die in the labyrinth at the hands (horns) of the monster called the Minotaur. Theseus romanced Ariadne, and discovered the secret of the labyrinth, killing the Minotaur. He then left Ariadne behind on the island of Crete. In *Battlestar Galactica*, Ariadne is a young girl with very few distinguishing features, but in a sense she is left behind by the heroes at the end of the story, so perhaps there is a little of the myth present. From modern, pop-culture myth comes the name "Miri." Miri was also the name of a young girl played by Kim Darby in the early *Star Trek* episode "Miri." Young Miri fell in love with Cpt. Kirk, just as young Miri here seems to have a bit of an attachment to Lt. Starbuck. The name "Spectre," of course, continues the tradition of giving Cylons evil-sounding names (i.e., "Lucifer").

With seven episodes and 11 hours behind it, it is fair to say that *Battlestar Galactica*'s progress completely stalls with "The Young Lords." "The Long Patrol," by a hair the best of the early episodes after the two-hour installments, at this point looks suspiciously like a fluke. By featuring so many needlessly repetitive, hackneyed Westerns, movie rip-offs and fairy tales, *Battlestar Galactica* does nothing to earn itself the respect of the science fiction fan. Fortunately, with upcoming episodes such as "The Living Legend" and "War of the Gods," the series would start to find its way to a few quality stories.

8. "The Living Legend" (Parts I and II)
Airdates: November 26, 1978, and December 3, 1978.
Written by Glen A. Larson. Directed by Vince Edwards.

SYNOPSIS: On long range patrol, Starbuck and Apollo encounter Sheba and Bojay from the battlestar *Pegasus*, a sister ship lost two yahren ago after a battle involving the fifth fleet. In command of the *Pegasus* and Silver Spar Squadron is Cain, Sheba's father and the greatest military commander in Colonial history. The fleet rejoices when it learns that Cain and the *Pegasus* have survived, but Starbuck is less than happy to learn that Cassiopeia and Cain were once lovers.

To Adama, Cain's arrival signals that his fleet will be well-protected at last. But Cain, an individualist rather than a team player, has other notions. With *Galactica*'s assistance, Cain believes he can conquer the Cylon city Gamorray and build a home for humanity there. While Cain and Adama debate the merits of their respective strategies, the *Galactica* fleet runs perilously low on fuel, and Baltar closes in with three baseships. With few options remaining, Cain opts for a provocative battle strategy that might leave only one battlestar and crew intact.

GUEST CAST: Lloyd Bridges (Commander Cain); Rod Haase (Tolan); Junero Jennings (*Pegasus* Bridge Officer)

COMMENTARY: The fourth multi-part episode of the season, Glen Larson's "The Living Legend" is without a doubt the strongest episode of the *Battlestar Galactica* collection. Invigorated by strong character conflicts and fireworks, as well as a charismatic command performance from Lloyd Bridges, this episode demonstrates what the series could have been had the crisp writing of the pilot been repeated. "The Living Legend" is a rip-roaring, exciting war drama with strong, likable people, moderately believable (if not inspired) battle tactics and realistic but divergent philosophical points of view.

"The Living Legend" is undeniably exciting. Three baseships and a gaggle of Cylon fighters press the *Galactica*, until Cain's battlestar triumphantly joins the fray. This tense battle sequence feature excellent cross-cutting (from Baltar to the *Galactica*, to the Cylon fighters, and finally to a terrific shot of the approaching *Pegasus* as seen through the cockpit of Baltar's fighter). The scene even highlights humor as a Cylon Centurion suggests to Baltar, who is again gloating about the *Galactica*'s destruction, that he should "really take a look at the *other* Battlestar." It is a fun moment in an exciting scene. And, it is better than most combat sequences in the series because the overall tactics and movements of vessels are spelled out. Everyone has a plan here, and ships are not just rocketing and weaving all over the place in a free-for-all. Putting an individual face to the Cylon battle group for the first time, Baltar orders his overwhelming armada to destroy the *Galactica* landing bays so its pilots cannot land or refuel. Adama, meanwhile, must wait patiently for Cain while the *Galactica* takes a beating. By contrast, Cain waits for the right moment to spring his trap. Because the dynamics of the battle are well delineated, it is more interesting and suspenseful than the fighter dogfights featured so often.

Even better, the Colonial military does not speak as one unified voice in "The Living Legend." Instead, Commander Cain and Commander Adama hold vastly different opinions, both of which are treated with respect by writer Larson. Usually in *Battlestar Galactica*, any view which opposes Adama's is ridiculed or treated with disrespect. Not so here. In fact, a large portion of the viewing audience probably felt that Cain might be right in his assessment of the tactical situation. After all, Cain is the more attractive, flamboyant and "Kirk"-like Captain, eager to fly in and kick chrome butt. Adama is seen in much less glamorous terms as a man who would prefer to avoid a fight if at all possible. In the end, Adama's caution is warranted. Had the *Galactica* and the *Pegasus* gone off on some mission of glory against Gamorray, the Cylons would have decimated the

Civilian fleet. That "The Living Legend" permits this discourse about military policy and highlights two opposing philosophies in an adult, thought-provoking manner demonstrates that the program was finally growing up. This is a far more realistic and three-dimensional debate than the one-sided battles against the Council of 12 that were frequently featured on the program in episodes such as "Saga of a Star World," "Baltar's Escape" and "Greetings from Earth."

Lloyd Bridges of *Sea Hunt* (1957–61) fame guest stars as Commander Cain, and he succeeds in profiling a charismatic leader very different from the solemn Adama. Ironically, back in 1964 Lloyd Bridges was producer Gene Roddenberry's first choice to play the captain of the starship *Enterprise* in *Star Trek*. Having already appeared in a less-than-adequate science fiction film called *Rocketship X-M* (1950), Bridges turned down the role. Finally, nearly 14 years later, he is given the chance in *Battlestar Galactica* to command a spaceship, and he is certainly up to the challenge. Unlike Lorne Greene's Adama, who wears the blue uniform of the bridge crew, Bridges' Cain always sports the tan jacket of the Colonial Warriors, nicely suggesting his preoccupation with combat and war and differentiating the nature of the two leaders.

Anne Lockhart joins the regular cast of *Battlestar Galactica* as Sheba in "The Living Legend," and she is an extremely affable actress. Though perhaps not as elegant as Jane Seymour's regal Serina, Lockhart's Sheba nonetheless deflects some of the shouts of space sexism that had been raised by viewers, especially in regards to the first part of "Lost Planet of the Gods." At last a woman is shown to be a capable warrior. In "The Hand of God," Sheba would also show a more sensitive side to her character, becoming a three-dimensional person. After the cancellation of *Battlestar Galactica*, Lockhart, daughter of *Lost in Space* star June Lockhart, went on to guest star in the *Buck Rogers* 1980 episode "A Dream of Jennifer" as a dead ringer for Buck's long-lost 20th century girlfriend. She also appeared in the low-budget science fiction film *Troll* (1986) directed by John Carl Buechler.

Continuing the *Battlestar Galactica* tradition of throwing in mythical references left and right, "The Living Legend" writer Glen Larson provides a plethora of names that have a specific meaning outside the universe of *Galactica*. The *Pegasus* is, of course, named after the white, winged horse of Ancient Greek myth. In a nice bit of symbolism, the warriors of Silver Spar Squadron have gold, winged horses emblazoned on their Viper helmets, instead of the eagles seen on Blue Squadron headgear. "Cain" is a familiar name from the Old Testament. In the Bible, Cain was the first son of Adam and Eve, the man who slew his brother Abel out of jealousy. Although there is no "Abel" in "The Living Legend," Commander Cain does betray a spiritual brother, Adama, by deliberately fouling an important mission to retrieve the fuel of Cylon tankers. If Adama truly represents "Adam," then he should be a father-figure to "Cain" instead of a brother, however. Lastly, Sheba is yet another biblical-sounding name and reference. "Sheba" was the name of the Kingdom in first century B.C. Yemen, or Arabia. The Queen of Sheba ruled the Sabaeans, and brought spices and riches to the splendorous court of King Solomon, the wisest of Israelite kings. There does not appear to be a direct connection between the character "Sheba" and the name's mythic origin.

The name "Gamorray" seems to be a modification of "gamma ray," "Gamorrah" or "Gamera," as in the flying Japanese turtle, and is often pronounced differently by actors within the same scene. John Colicos calls the planet (phonetically) **Gah**-mor-ay, with the heaviest accent on the first syllable. This is also how Lloyd Bridges and Lorne Greene pronounce the word. Performing voice-over duties for Lucifer, Jonathan Harris pronounces the word "**Gam**-ma-ray."

With "The Living Legend," *Battlestar Galactica* proves that it is capable of integrating interesting, clashing philosophies, adult character interaction, suspense and fine special effects. It is the perfect war drama because it questions all the old military truisms about battle, glory and victory, yet simultaneously celebrates the satisfaction of a clever and successful strategy. There are many human emotions at work amidst the epic backdrop (Sheba's jealousy of Cassiopeia, Starbuck's jealousy of Cain, Cain's egotism, Tigh's feelings of inadequacy to "the living legend" who replaces him on the bridge of the *Pegasus*, and Adama's anger at being betrayed). Had "The Living Legend" been the recipe for more *Battlestar Galactica* episodes, the sound and fury of the series would have found a much more mature and interesting context. Instead *of Wagon Train* in space, it could have been *From Here to Eternity* in space.

9. "Fire in Space"

Airdate: December 17, 1978.
Written by Jim Carlson and Terrence McDonnell.
Directed by Christian Nyby, Jr.

SYNOPSIS: During a vicious attack, one Cylon fighter rams the *Galactica* bridge as another strikes the hangar bay, causing it to catch fire.

Adama is badly wounded, and the attack traps Athena, Boomer, Boxey and Muffit in a rejuvenation center. With much of the *Galactica* on fire, Apollo, Starbuck and Sheba modify their Vipers to put out the flames with boraton spray, but the effort has no effect, and the conflagration continues to rage. Before facing critical open-heart surgery, Adama warns Col. Tigh that he must blow a hole in the *Galactica's* hull to smother the fire — but that course of action could also destroy all life on the *Galactica* permanently!

GUEST CAST: Jeff McKay (Fire Engineer); William Bryant (Fire Leader)

COMMENTARY: Widely regarded by critics and fans alike as the single worst episode of *Battlestar Galactica* because of its scientifically flawed premise, Jim Carlson's and Terrence McDonnell's "Fire in Space" is nonetheless an involving and tense hour. Though the fire threat is a hopelessly contrived one, the bulk of the episode's running time is wisely spent on welcome examples of character-building.

For once, the series finds time to focus on Athena and Boomer, two underutilized characters in the *Battlestar Galactica* family. In "Fire in Space," Athena acts as a natural leader, and even administers first aid to a wounded warrior. She is decisive, pragmatic and competent, further proof that the series was trying to undo the damage done by the sexist "Lost Planet of the Gods." And to the delight of Athena fans, Maren Jensen actually gets to mouth dialogue that is not technobabble!

Herb Jefferson, Jr.'s, Boomer is deepened as a person too, revealing his juvenile delinquency on Caprica as well as his natural command abilities. One has to wonder, though, why a black character is saddled with a childhood of sketchy morals and petty crimes. Boomer's delinquent history smacks a bit of racism. Why couldn't the white Starbuck, an orphan and cocksure womanizer, have been a hovercar thief, instead of Boomer? Are the writers of *Battlestar Galactica* trying to tell the audience that even in the furthest reaches of space, black-skinned humans will have a predilection to commit crimes? This character moment, though interesting, has some ugly implications.

Even the stolid and conservative Col. Tigh is highlighted in "Fire in Space" as he assumes command of the Galactica and faces some very tough decisions. This gives the talented Terry Carter another opportunity to show the layers of this interesting, serious officer. Many great moments in

Battlestar Galactica come from Col. Tigh. His frustration in "The Living Legend," his anger at the Council in "Baltar's Escape" and his weariness in "The Hand of God" are just a few such well-acted moments. Carter brings this interesting military man to life in memorable, quiet fashion, and hopefully Tigh will be included in any *Battlestar Galactica* revival. Although he is a less-flashy soldier than Adama, Apollo, Sheba or Starbuck, Tigh is among the most realistic "humans" in *Battlestar Galactica* because he shares opinions, displays doubts and has a sense of humor.

The "fire" gimmick of this story, ridiculed by so many, is actually just a dramatic hook to learn more about all three of the aforementioned series characters, and thus it is somewhat forgivable from a narrative standpoint. After all, virtually every outer space TV program and movie, with perhaps the exception of Kubrick's *2001: A Space Odyssey*, features fires in space in one sense or another. In *Star Wars*, the Death Star blows apart in flames at the conclusion of the film. In *Star Trek,* it is usually a Klingon bird of prey that is flaming out of control (*The Undiscovered Country* and *Generations* are just two examples). But regardless of the context of spaceship design or of competing productions, fire is fire, and space is space. If fire in space is accepted in one setting (such as *Star Wars*) as "dramatic license," then it is acceptable in *all* settings — even in the much maligned *Battlestar Galactica*. Therefore, all the critical sneering at *Battlestar Galactica* for "Fire in Space" is little more than intellectual snobbery from critics who are already predisposed not to like the program. Where were the complaining critics during the booming, fiery explosions of *Star Wars*?

Even if one is a hard-line science fanatic, and not predisposed to believe that fire is acceptable in *Battlestar Galactica* if it is okay in *Star Wars*, consider this explanation: In "Fire in Space," the fire ignites not in space, but inside a landing bay, a locale where surely there *is* air to burn. *Nowhere* in "Fire in Space" is the fire actually seen burning *outside* the confines of the landing bay, in airless outer space. Maybe that explanation helps a little bit.

In fairness to *Battlestar Galactica*, *Star Trek* of all generations has frequently used the same style of "accident" or "disaster" story as "Fire in Space" to tell stories about characters surviving difficult internal situations. In the fifth season *Star Trek: The Next Generation* episode "Disaster," Cpt. Picard was stuck in a turbo-shaft with three obnoxious children while Keiko, trapped in Ten Forward (a rejuvenation center of a sort), delivered a baby. "Civil Disorder" on *Star Trek: Deep Space Nine* was a similar type of disaster story set on the Cardassian space station. On *Star Trek:*

Voyager, the main characters were trapped in the holodeck (yet another rejuvenation center) as the ship was balled up like a sphere of tin foil in "Twisted." Perhaps then, "Fire in Space" is actually representative of another subgenre of science fiction television: the disaster movie. Perhaps "Sub Smash" on *U.F.O.* (1970) in which Ed Bishop's Commander Straker is trapped in a sinking submarine and fighting claustrophobia, and "The Trap" on *Planet of the Apes* (1974) with astronauts and apes stuck beneath an earthquake-ridden San Francisco, could also qualify in this genre. Therefore, "Fire in Space" is certainly not without precedent, and should not be singled out for critical disdain. At least *Battlestar Galactica* used the plot two decades ago, not in the '90s as did *The Next Generation, Deep Space Nine* and *Voyager.*

On the other hand, one totally lame plot element of "Fire in Space" mars the episode more than the outer space conflagration. In the world of *Battlestar Galactica,* water is apparently called "boraton." The Vipers are loaded with "boraton" liquid, and the pilots fire it like laser beams at the burning landing bay. In space, there is absolutely no way that water could be used in the same fashion as a laser beam! Assuming it does not freeze instantly in the cold of space, water would disperse in zero gravity, not be propelled forward in a stream. Remember the Klingon blood floating around the interior of a battle cruiser under siege in *Star Trek VI: The Undiscovered Country?* That is precisely how water should look in a zero-g environment. Also, how are Viper turbo lasers modified to become space "fire hoses"? Are these two devices truly compatible? Are Vipers large enough to carry gallons of water? This element is perhaps the hardest to accept in "Fire in Space."

More significant than these scientific blunders are the special effects blunders in "Fire in Space." The first such blooper occurs as Cpt. Apollo tracks the Cylon ship headed at ramming speed for the *Galactica* bridge. Apollo fires his bright red lasers, misses the Cylon ship, and the special effects show several crimson blasts of light emanating from Apollo's Viper and *connecting* with the bridge of the battlestar. In other words, *he* has shot the ship! Essentially, Apollo has done more damage than the Cylons, since he has just roasted the *Galactica*'s command center with a volley of turbo lasers! This is exactly the scenario that Starbuck teased Athena about in "Lost Planet of the Gods" — continuing to spray laser beams once a pilot has locked on a target and it has evaded him or her! Surely, these opticals should not have been added to this sequence at all. Apollo's Viper should have pulled up when he realized he could not fire at the Cylons without damaging the *Galactica.*

Also disturbing are the many close-ups of the *Galactica* landing bay on fire (shown from the aft position, i.e., from Sheba's point of view). The ship itself and even the fire look terrific, but behind the *Galactica* a special effects technician has neglected to add *stars* to the composite. Space is pure black, a velvet drape instead of a dotted land of stars. More damaging than this notable omission, the film editor of "Fire in Space" cuts to the *wrong* special effects sequence when the Cylon rams the landing bay. What is shown to viewers is not the creation of the initial fire, but rather the explosion on *top* of the *Galactica* when Starbuck and Apollo blow the hull. This shot should be the episode's climax, but through editorial sloppiness it shows up at the beginning of the episode instead, when the explosion on top of the *Galactica* makes no sense in the context of the teleplay. The same shot also appears again at the climax. If all of this is not depressing enough, there is stock footage galore in this episode, apparently from *The Towering Inferno*. Once more, bad or rushed special effects and lousy editing practices undercut the success of an expensive hour of *Battlestar Galactica*. Some may claim that these flaws are only noticeable on repeat viewings, but *Star Trek* and other science fiction shows tend to either survive or die based on "repeat" viewings. It was only in multiple viewings that *Star Trek* became incredibly popular. Clearly, in the case of *Battlestar Galactica*, the much-lauded optical effects are sabotaged by their inappropriate placement in the final edit!

Finally, there are many lapses of situational logic throughout "Fire in Space." A piece of flying shrapnel lodges in Adama's heart following the attack on the bridge. If this is so, why does he have no visible wound when Tigh finds him hurt on the deck? Why no blood (not even a trickle from his mouth)? Secondly, Tigh states dramatically that if the second energizer on the *Galactica* goes out, the ship will have no power. This line suggests the ship possesses only two energizers. That assertion seems to contradict the information relayed in "The Magnificent Warriors," which suggested there are energizers operating all over the battlestar. If there were only two energizers all along, then Tigh's suggestion to Adama to trade one energizer to Serenity for seed in the aforementioned episode was not very bright — it would have crippled the *Galactica*!

Also, Tigh handwrites a note to Boomer at one point in "Fire in Space." There is a close-up of the note and it is in recognizable English, in *cursive*. Of course, the Colonies are not from Earth and should therefore not write in English, much less modern cursive. In "Lost Planet of the Gods," it was established that the mother culture of the colonies on

Kobol wrote in "hieroglyphic" symbols. Where, all of a sudden, did English cursive come from? And where did Tigh get an "ink" pen, while in the rest of the series documents are transcribed by light pen (as in "War of the Gods" Part II) or dictated directly into the computer from a hand-held microphone? Wouldn't a computer print-out with Tigh's message (in hieroglyphs, not English) have been more appropriate to the production considering the extra-galactic context of *Battlestar Galactica*? Again, these are not nitpicks. These are serious issues of consistency that deserve to be addressed. Sometimes the producers of *Battlestar Galactica* seemed to believe that it was acceptable to change premises every week because the viewer would not remember what happened the week before. That is an insulting belief. This author and many others watched the show religiously because we wanted to like it, to be blown away by a science fiction show as powerful as *The Outer Limits, The Prisoner, Star Trek* or *Space: 1999*.

So is "Fire in Space" a tense, dramatic example of the space disaster sub-genre popularized by recent *Star Trek* spin-offs, or is it a poorly conceived and executed mess? Probably both. It is a great example of what author Stephen King calls a "moron" movie (or TV show), i.e., a production that somehow manages to entertain despite all kinds of problems. In the case of "Fire in Space," perhaps it is the sincerity of the performances that make the show memorable. The breathlessness of the premise, and the fast pace might help too. Perhaps "Fire in Space" perfectly captures why *Battlestar Galactica* is so often deemed a guilty pleasure. Its stories are often ludicrous, yet told in the most sentimental and sincere manner, and filled with likable performers. It may be unknowing and ignorant, but it is also *innocent*. It is just fun, plain and simple.

10. "War of the Gods" (Parts I and II)
Airdates: January 14, 1979, and January 21, 1979.
Written by Glen A. Larson. Directed by Dan Haller.

SYNOPSIS: After several Colonial patrols have vanished without a trace following frightening encounters with ghostly lights in space, Apollo, Sheba and Starbuck find the wreckage of a colossal spaceship marring the surface of a barren world. They are then met by the ship's regal sole survivor, Count Iblis, who asks to return home with them. Iblis soon seduces Sheba and wins over the hearts of the Colonial people by performing miracles, but Adama and Apollo remain wary of the mysterious visitor. Even though he has delivered Baltar to the fleet and stimulated food growth on the agro-ship, Iblis is not at all what he seems. Adama fears that the stranger is a malevolent fallen angel who has broken his people's laws — and who even now is being observed by the strange lights in space.

Apollo, Starbuck and Sheba return to the world where Iblis was found, believing that the secret of his real identity lies in the wrecked ship. Iblis materializes, and his nature soon becomes all-too-clear. When Apollo is struck down by Iblis, the young captain's last chance for survival rests with the strange lights in the sky.

GUEST CAST: Kirk Alyn (Gemonese Man); Patrick Macnee (Count Iblis); Norman Stuart, John Williams (Council Members); Paula Victor (Gemonese Woman); Olan Soule (Carmichael); Paul Coufos (Pilot); Bruce Wright (Guard)

COMMENTARY: "War of the Gods" is an involving, well-told story about the long competition between good and evil. It succeeds as drama because of some surprising implications about the nature of the crashed ship on that distant planet and because, for once in *Battlestar Galactica*, the face of evil is so charismatic: Patrick Macnee.

For nearly 20 years, *Battlestar Galactica* fans have wondered and debated about the mysterious ship that Sheba, Apollo and Starbuck gaze into during the climax of the "War of the Gods" with such surprise and horror. Significantly, the camera never follows them inside that strange craft. Still, it is clear that whatever they see inside is incredibly shocking. The text of the episode, however, cleverly reveals the nature of the life (or death) inside that ship. This author's assertion is that the crashed ship is actually Cain's missing battlestar, the *Pegasus*, from "The Living Legend"!

There is much textual evidence supporting this hypothesis. Immediately before the *Galactica*ns visit the planet, Sheba states that with Bojay and her father missing, she has nobody important in her life. This dialogue puts the memory of Cain and the *Pegasus* squarely in front of the viewing audience. Why bother to make this point at all, unless it is significant to the outcome of the plot? Surely by now, viewers are well-aware that Sheba is Cain's daughter, so this important line of dialogue is not just a "helpful" reminder. On the contrary, it is there to foreshadow the climax.

Then, upon landing on the planet and observing the crash, Apollo specifically notes that something as big as a "battlestar" must have crashed there, again alluding to the only other battlestar known to be out this far in space, the missing *Pegasus*. Finally, at one point during the first part of the episode, Iblis promises Sheba with a twisted smile that she shall "see her father again soon." When Sheba does attempt to gaze into the crashed vessel, she is stopped short by Starbuck and Apollo, who warn her that she does not want to look inside. The only thing that could explain their strange behavior is that they are protecting Sheba from the pain of seeing her slain father. Then, when it is obvious Sheba is still swayed by Iblis, Starbuck suggests that maybe she "should" see the interior of the craft. In other words, the only way to break Iblis' spell over Sheba is for her to see that the person she cares most for in the world, her father Cain, has been killed by Iblis.

The novelization of "War of the Gods" by Glen Larson suggests that the crashed ship is merely filled with the corpses of beings who resemble demons. This is an unacceptable solution for two reasons. The first is that Apollo and Starbuck react with abject horror when they peer into the ship. Would two seasoned warriors really react to an alien corpse in this manner, one different from humans but no more disturbing or frightening than the insect-like Ovions or the pig-like Boray? Secondly, Iblis has already revealed that his people do not truly die. He states, "Death is just the beginning." How does this explanation jibe with a score of dead demons on that ship? How can they be dead, a state which Iblis' people are incapable of experiencing? Besides, the philosophic thrust of "War of the Gods" is that Iblis can hold sway only over those who freely give themselves to him. That is the danger: follow Iblis and end up dead, like the people in that crashed ship! If the ship is filled only with dead demons, they were equals, *not* subjects, of Iblis, and the dramatic point about willingly selling one's soul is lost. Why did the other demons die, while he survived? Did his compartment of the ship have a passenger cockpit airbag? If the people on the crashed ship were humans (other Colonials, for instance), then the terror of this episode becomes tangible. The crew of *Pegasus chose* to follow Iblis, and they paid for that decision with their lives. The people of the *Galactica* just narrowly avoid the same mistake.

There are other implications to suggest that the destroyed ship is actually the *Pegasus*, mainly that the craft's battleship gray coloring and door archway design resembles closely that of a Colonial battlestar. Yet according to "official" fan mythology and the novelization by series creator Larson and writer Robert Thurston, the crashed vessel is not the *Pegasus*, but rather an "angel" ship full of horned, hoofed demons. These creatures,

"Diabolos," are supposedly of the same race as Count Iblis. Apollo and Starbuck hide Sheba from seeing a demon corpse because they are afraid it will frighten her. Some fans believe this footage was actually shot, but that ABC censors removed it because they felt it was not appropriate for the 8:00 P.M. family time slot. Other fans maintain the scene was never shot at all, and the wrecked ship was intended to be a mystery all along.

Regardless of whether the ship is or is not the *Pegasus*, this is one of the few *Battlestar Galactica* episodes that can be interpreted in more than one way. It is not only a change of pace, but actually a relief to have some subtlety in the often banal TV world. This complex mystery alone may explain the continued popularity of this episode. Along with scores of fans, Richard Hatch considers "War of the Gods" one of his favorite episodes.

Patrick Macnee shines as the evil Count Iblis. Playing "pure evil" to its limit, he proves to be a charismatic villain. His individual brand of evil, a contrast to the faceless Cylon automatons, works well on this outer space series. Apollo and Adama, *Galactica*'s two most heroic and noble faces, both repeatedly clash with this representative from a superior race, and the amazing thing is that "Iblis" wins one encounter after the other. Only the interference by Iblis' people saves the *Galactica* from suffering permanently under the devil's dominion. Count Iblis is so popular a nemesis among *Battlestar Galactica* fans that he was featured repeatedly in the new *Battlestar Galactica* Maximum Press comics released in 1995. Macnee is the fifth *Galactica* guest star connected in some way to the world of James Bond. He played the lovable but doomed "Tibbet" in Roger Moore's final outing as 007, *A View to a Kill* (1985). He is also remembered, of course, for his role of John Steed in *The Avengers* (1963–1970) and his cameo as Sir Eton-Hogg in *This Is Spinal Tap* (1982).

One surprisingly subtle touch in "War of the Gods" is the notation by Baltar that he recognizes Iblis' voice as belonging to the Cylon Imperious Leader! It is a chilling moment when Baltar realizes the Leader's voice was transcribed into machine language more than a thousand yahren earlier, and therefore that Iblis himself must be ancient. Of course, this scene was added because the actor Macnee voices the Imperious Leader for the series, as well as portraying Iblis in this episode. This connection of two evils nicely suggests that evil has but one face (or voice), and that Iblis has been stirring trouble for many generations. Perhaps he is even responsible for the downfall of the original, organic Cylon beings.

Most fascinating of all, "War of the Gods" informs viewers where all humanity's shared myths of angels and devils originated. The "lights" are angels, and Iblis is a renegade angel known as Mephistopheles. He is symbolic of the Devil, Satan, the Prince of Darkness. In fact, Iblis should be called Lucifer, but that name was already in use in *Battlestar Galactica*. Interestingly then, the very spiritual *Battlestar Galactica* in "War of the Gods" asserts that gods are not supreme beings at all, but advanced humans with long life-spans. This belief mirrors the anti-religious, pro-humanistic philosophy of *Star Trek* and its many spin-offs.

The special effects work in "War of the Gods" is stunning as well. Besides the coruscating light spheres that bounce around the fleet, the blue angel mothership miniature is perhaps the most impressive and spectacular ship design in the series. Each time it arrives on the scene, it is accompanied by its own majestic theme music, a kind of religious chorus that adds to the grandeur of the effects. For TV miniature work, this vessel is absolutely extraordinary. Strangely, some critics have complained loudly that by featuring this huge blue "angel" spaceship, *Battlestar Galactica* is actually attempting to rip-off Steven Spielberg's *Close Encounters of the Third Kind* (1977) and its chandelier-like mothership. This is not a fair assertion. The ship in *Galactica* is distinctly different in design from the mothership, and it houses not aliens looking to make peaceful contact, but angels monitoring their own kindred. The plots of the respective productions are also enormously different, although aliens in both are responsible for abductions of fighter crafts.

All of this praise by no means indicates that "War of the Gods" is perfect drama or science fiction. As always, there are a few problems that should be reported. The first is that Apollo and Starbuck repeatedly tell Adama that they could not investigate the crash of the mystery ship because of high radion levels (i.e., radioactivity). They mention at least twice that they are willing to return to the planet with protective suits and detecting equipment so they can search the ship. However, when the duo returns to the planet, protective suits and special equipment are nowhere in evidence. Why did they not bring the necessary gear? Also, Count Iblis is reported to be on Agroship 9 at one point in "War of the Gods," but in "The Magnificent Warriors" there were only *three* agroships in the fleet. Indeed, seed was so important in that adventure because two of the three agroships were destroyed by Cylons! Did the *Galactica*, between episodes six and ten, have time to construct and "flower" eight new agroships? Other than these strange continuity oversights, the episode holds together fairly well, and is significant for introducing the Colonial sporting event called "Triad" to the series. In

Triad, two competing teams of two men attempt to throw a silver ball into the *Galactica*n equivalent of a basketball hoop: a round hole in the wall, high above the triangular arena. The contestants in this game wear skimpy clothing, knee pads and bike helmets. In addition to being an insight into the athletic life of the fleet, the game also showed off the sterling physiques of actors Dirk Benedict and Richard Hatch through its revealing uniforms. Triad would re-surface in "Murder on the *Rising Star*."

If all *Battlestar Galactica* episodes had featured the fascinating implications and charismatic personal battles seen in "War of the Gods," *Battlestar Galactica*'s story quality might not be an issue for debate today. With this story, and also "The Living Legend," it seemed that the series was truly hitting its stride. Delightfully, the eleventh story, "The Man with Nine Lives," would also be a good one. In December 1978 and early 1979, things were truly looking up for the series for the first time. A plateau of high quality had finally been reached.

11. "The Man with Nine Lives"
Airdate: January 28, 1979.
Written by Donald Bellisario.
Directed by Rod Holcomb.

SYNOPSIS: Starbuck, Apollo, Boomer and Jolly shuttle to the luxury liner *Rising Star* for a three-day furlough, but they run afoul of three Borellian Nomen, zealous members of a strange religious sect. The Nomen have initiated a "blood hunt," and are hot on the trail of the wily Chameleon, an elderly con-man who claims to be Starbuck's long-lost father! The Nomen pursue Chameleon and Starbuck to the *Galactica*, where Chameleon plans to authenticate his claim with the help of a genetic tracer. When Starbuck and Chameleon are alone in the landing bay, the Nomen prepare to strike.

GUEST CAST: Fred Astaire (Chameleon/Cpt. Dmitri); Anthony DeLongis (Taba); Robert Feero (Bora); Anne Jeffreys (Siress Blassie); Lance LeGault (Maga); Dan Barton (Ducket Taker); Patricia Stitch (Broadcaster Zara); John Holland *(Rising Star* Maitre d')

COMMENTARY: "The Man with Nine Lives" is a compelling hour which involves high personal stakes for Starbuck and some strong character moments for Apollo, Boomer and Cassiopeia. Rewardingly, the episode also succeeds in introducing unique villains to *Battlestar Galactica* series, even if they are based in part on societal and Hollywood stereotypes about Native American Indians.

Like Native Americans, the Borellian Nomen exist uneasily on the fringes of a purportedly "democratic" society, and they pride themselves on a noble history of bravery and courage (they alone survived in rough desert conditions on a world called "Vega"). Like Native Americans, many of whom live on land "reservations" in America today, the Nomen of *Battlestar Galactica* reside separately from the rest of the fleet population, on their own isolated freighter.

And finally, the Nomen share with American Indians a code of honor that is always taken very seriously. However, the Nomen presented in *Battlestar Galactica* are very interesting not for the numerous similarities to Native Americans, but because they are apparently the basis of the "new" Klingon philosophies and principles which dominate in the *Star Trek* spin-offs of the 1980s and 1990s, particularly *The Next Generation* and *Deep Space Nine*.

Recall that in the original *Star Trek* series, the Klingons were swarthy human lookalikes who despised honor and had virtually no ethics whatsoever. In the words of *The Making of Star Trek* (an official book co-authored by *Star Trek* creator Gene Roddenberry while the show was still on the air), "Their only rule in life is that rules are meant to be broken by shrewdness, deceit or power. Cruelty is something admirable, honor is a despicable trait."[3]

It was not until 1987 and the introduction of the noble Worf (Michael Dorn) on *Star Trek: The Next Generation* that the Klingons changed significantly in demeanor. Honor, a heretofore "despicable trait" became paramount to the ethos of this new alien race. Physically, the new Klingons of post-*Galactica* years closely resemble the Borellian Nomen. In *Star Trek: The Motion Picture* (released in 1979, soon after *Battlestar Galactica*), the once-human Klingons now had exaggerated foreheads, long hair and heavy beards. This shift in Klingon appearance and values has never been explained by any *Star Trek* production.

In later *Star Trek*, such as *The Next Generation* and *Deep Space Nine*, the revisionist Klingons adhere rigidly to a strange code of honor, just as the Nomen do in *Battlestar Galactica*'s "The Man with Nine Lives." For further evidence of this assertion, compare the racial philosophy underlying the text of the following two passages. The first is spoken by the

Nomen leader, Maga, on *Battlestar Galactica* in 1979. The second is from *Star Trek: Deep Space Nine*, "The Way of the Warrior" in 1995. Although the words are by no means identical, the underlying ideals reveal a high degree of similarity. Consider this: Do the following passages reveal the Klingons of the *Next Generation* to have more in common with the "honor is despicable" original Klingons of the '60s show, or the *Battlestar Galactica* Nomen?

> It is you have insulted me, twice.... You must answer to the code. Your name will be stricken from the roster of the Nomen.... Do with him as you wish; to me he no longer exists" [from *Battlestar Galactica:* "The Man with Nine Lives"].

> For as long as I live, you will not be welcome anywhere in the Klingon Empire. Your family will be removed from the High Council, your land seized and your house stripped of its titles! You will have nothing! [from *Deep Space Nine:* "The Way of the Warrior"]

In addition to their newly shared physical qualities and unswerving belief in themselves as outstanding warriors, the Nomen and the "new" Klingons share other traits: They view human beings as "weak," and they believe strongly in revenge. Indeed, the threat of "The Man with Nine Lives" is that the Nomen are on a "blood hunt." Similarly, Klingons have frequently launched missions solely for the purpose of revenge in stories such as "Reunion," wherein Worf kills Duras, a man who has disgraced his family name.

Significantly, Klingons and Nomen also pride themselves on their mutual abilities to intimidate and frighten other races. In "The Man with Nine Lives," one Nomen tells another, "You are a warrior of the code. Your very name strikes like a Scorpius at the heart of others." In *Star Trek: The Next Generation*'s "Heart of Glory," the same qualities are reflected by Klingon warriors trying to incite Worf to mutiny. The Klingons and the Nomen are both the ultimate "bad-asses": warriors who live by a strict code of ethics and who scare timid human beings to death.

The unfortunate fate of the young Nomen Taba, played by Anthony DeLongis (Kazon Magh Culluh in *Star Trek: Voyager*), is also strongly echoed by Worf's fate in *The Next Generation*'s third season story "Sins of the Father" (1990). In that tale, Worf's honor is challenged, and his sash is unceremoniously ripped off in front of other Klingons, just as Maga cruelly and publicly rips off Taba's sash in this episode of *Battlestar Galactica*. Additionally, Worf faces discommendation from the Klingons, a punishment wherein he is to be ignored by his people. They literally turn their backs on him. That is identical to what occurs with Taba in "The Man with Nine Lives"! His name is stricken from the Nomen code, and he is isolated from his people. The characteristics of the races could not be more similar.

If there are no other reasons to remember *Battlestar Galactica* today, this similarity of "honorbound" alien races is surely a compelling one. *Battlestar Galactica*'s Borellian Nomen are unquestionably the spiritual ancestor of modern *Star Trek* Klingons! That is perhaps *Battlestar Galactica*'s most lasting impact on the world of science fiction television — and make no mistake, it is a significant one. Of course, there is no direct evidence of a "steal," and this writer does not assert theft on the part of *Star Trek* producers and writers. However, it is common knowledge that while preparing *The Next Generation* in 1986, Roddenberry carefully reviewed other science fiction productions of recent vintage.[4] This is why Data and Tasha Yar are reminiscent of Bishop and Vasquez in James Cameron's *Aliens*. This is why the Picard-Crusher relationship is identical — from rank, position and the "lost in space" dead husband, to Dr. Russell and Commander Koenig in *Space: 1999*. This may also explain why the new Klingons are more like the Nomen of *Battlestar Galactica* than original *Star Trek* Klingons, and why the Borg are modifications of *Doctor Who*'s Cybermen.

One of the major problems of *Star Trek*, which has now lasted 30 years, is that to continue successfully from generation to generation, it must assimilate (like the Borg Collective) ideas from other contemporary TV series and films. It is ironic that in the 1980s and 1990s, it features an altered Klingon race that is the polar opposite of Gene Roddenberry's original vision and appears to be based instead on *Battlestar Galactica*. Remember, according to Roddenberry, co-author of *The Making of Star Trek*, the original-series Klingons considered honor despicable! What changed? Was it simply that when putting *The Next Generation* together, the concept of Klingons changed into something akin to the Nomen of *Battlestar Galactica*?

It is also ironic that *Star Trek: Voyager* is now telling stories such as "Sacred Ground" which seem to affirm the *Space: 1999* philosophy of the universe, that some things just "cannot be explained" by science. This was a plot device ("the mysterious unknown force") reviled by *Star Trek* fans in the 1970s. Now, apparently, it is acceptable. Perhaps these assimilations of other series ideas are only natural. *Star Trek* is the big fish of televised science fiction. It has earned that position through decades of endurance. Perhaps it is only right that it devours in part or whole the concepts of smaller fish such as *Space: 1999* or *Battlestar Galactica*. What is so troubling about this is that many modern Trekkers have overlooked *Star Trek*'s assimilation of *Space: 1999* and *Battlestar Galactica* concepts, and railed against these other series as "inferior." That begs the question: if *Space: 1999* or *Battlestar Galactica* are so inferior, why are both programs so influential to the characters, concepts and races seen on *Star Trek: The Next Generation*, a series with nary an original bone in its body?

Besides showing the world the clear antecedent of modern Klingons, "The Man with Nine Lives" is a joy for two other reasons. The first is that there is not a space battle or a Cylon to be found anywhere. The special effects are given a much-needed rest, and the dramatic narrative is allowed to drive the show. The second plus is the welcome concentration on character issues. Starbuck gets to find himself a father, argue with his best friend Apollo, and even contemplate marriage to Cassiopeia! Also, Starbuck's history as an orphan is revealed for the first time. The fleet infrastructure is well-defined in "The Man with Nine Lives" too. The viewer sees IFB (Inter Fleet Broadcasting) transmissions, watches a "*Galactica* Recruitment" commercial, learns of various fleet ships (the orphan ship, the livestock ship, the *Borella*) and even sees some *Galactica* "art" in the form of the *Rising Star*'s weird dance performance. On top of it all, Fred Astaire is a delightful presence as the tricky Chameleon. Somehow, this actor seems immediately comfortable in the world of *Battlestar Galactica*. He makes the transition to words like "yahrens" and "cubits" with a smooth, practiced grace. He perfectly captures the essence of a character who is related to Benedict's mischievous Starbuck. All these factors make "The Man with Nine Lives" one of *Battlestar Galactica*'s finest and most enjoyable hours. The kiddies may not have liked it (no Cylons, no space battles), but for once there is a story of some substance for adults to latch onto.

12. "Murder on the *Rising Star*"
Airdate: February 18, 1979.
Written by Donald Bellisario, James Carlson and
Terrence McDonnell. Directed by Rod Holcomb.

SYNOPSIS: Starbuck is accused of murdering the sarcastic Ortega, a rival on the Triad courts. Unfortunately, Starbuck is to be prosecuted by the fleet's most accomplished lawyer, Opposer Solon. Acting as Starbuck's defender, Apollo sets out with Boomer to clear his friend's name. The only clue involves a strange character called Charybdis, a man who may have been involved with Ortega — and Baltar!

GUEST CAST: Frank Ashmore (Wing Sgt. Ortega); Brock Peters (Chief Opposer Solon); Patricia Stitch (IFB Broadcaster Zara); W. K. Stratton (Barton); Luman Ward (Palloni); Jeff MacKay (CPI Komma)

COMMENTARY: "Murder on the *Rising Star*" is *Battlestar Galactica*'s rather tepid version of the old sci-fi TV standby, the legal jeopardy/court martial drama. It offers nothing new or interesting to this tiresome subgenre, or even the universe of *Battlestar Galactica* in general. Seen on *U.F.O.* (1970) and *Star Trek* (1966) respectively as "Court Martial," and on *Buck Rogers in the 25th Century* in 1980 as "Testimony of a Traitor," this subgenre is also a mainstay of modern era *Star Trek*. The series regular accused of murder has been seen in *Star Trek: The Next Generation* as "A Matter of Perspective" with Commander Riker as the suspect, on *Star Trek: Deep Space Nine* with Dax as the suspect in "Dax" and Worf as the suspect in "Rules of Engagement." It has even been seen on *Star Trek: Voyager* as "Ex Post Facto" with Robert Duncan McNeill's Tom Paris fingered as a possible murderer. "Murder on the *Rising Star*" is no more or less innovative than these other show, but perhaps equally dull. The "court martial" subgenre is basically an admission on the part of writers that they have no new sci-fi concepts to explore, only old *Perry Mason* (1957–66) plots to rehash. The "court martial" subgenre is perhaps the most contrived of all TV clichés because it is a foregone conclusion that the series regular is innocent. Because of this knowledge, there is no tension, and the show merely wastes 48 minutes. Does any viewer truly believe that Starbuck, Riker, Dax, Worf or Paris are guilty of cold-blooded murder? It is doubtful, unless one is extremely gullible, or has never watched a television show before. Still, the makers of *Battlestar Galactica* should not feel guilty for trotting out this hackneyed premise. Since *Star Trek* is still employing the scenario as late as 1996, 17 years after "Murder on the *Rising Star*," *Galactica* does not look like the worst offender.

Since the central premise of "Murder on the *Rising Star*" holds little drama or suspense, there is very little going on in the story. It is filled mostly with continuity problems and protestations from Starbuck that he is an innocent man. The continuity and logistical errors are hard to take. Where, for instance, is Chameleon? He was just introduced as Starbuck's long-lost father in the previous episode, "The Man with Nine Lives," yet when his son's face is all over the *Inter Fleet News* as a murderer, he is conspicuously absent. Did he leave the fleet? Did he die? Why not even a hand-written note delivered to Starbuck, saying he is thinking about him? One thing that the makers of *Battlestar Galactica* never seemed to understand is that they could not just introduce new characters and developments one week and then suddenly forget about those developments the next. Consistency and continuity are highly prized by science fiction fans, and when they do not get it they turn off the television or switch channels to something less offensive!

The conclusion of "Murder on the *Rising Star*" is also far-fetched. Apollo establishes Charybdis' motive but not, importantly, his presence on the *Rising Star*. How did Charybdis steal Starbuck's gun, kill Ortega, replace the gun, and escape totally unseen, especially with Chulla walking around? Since this question of logistics is unanswered, the episode does not even hold together as a mystery. This is not to say that the show is terrible. It is an average and competent hour of television drama. "Murder on the *Rising Star*" could be an episode of *Perry Mason*; *Diagnosis: Murder*; *Murder, She Wrote*; *Walker, Texas Ranger* or another humdrum dive into murder mediocrity. There is just nothing here to distinguish "Murder on the *Rising Star*" as notable science fiction.

Although Colonial legal precepts are spotlighted in this episode, they are seen to be too similar to America's 20th century judicial system. Adama gets to sit in as judge, and even say that Starbuck's defense is "highly irregular," that wonderfully clichéd line of all TV and movie judges. Otherwise, opposers equal prosecutors and protectors equal defense attorneys. It is all just a little too on-the-nose. The show might have been truly interesting if the Colonial legal system had been based on Ancient Egyptian precepts or Old Testament notions of law instead of contemporary U.S. law. Of course, to build a story around those ideas, the writers might have had to do some research other than watching old *Perry Mason* episodes.

In a short run of 17 episodes, "Murder on the *Rising Star*" is the fourth episode to feature a central role for Lt. Starbuck. (The others are "The Long Patrol," "The Young Lords," and "The Man with Nine Lives.") Although it is delightful to see much of Dirk Benedict's charming Starbuck, it seems some of this time (especially the weak "The Young Lords") might have been better utilized concentrating on Adama, Boomer, Athena, Jolly or Tigh, five characters who rarely shared a central role in the *Battlestar Galactica* stories.

Genre fans will recognize Opposer Solon as actor Brock Peters, the versatile performer who voiced Darth Vader on NPR's radio broadcast of *Star Wars* and played Charlton Heston's corrupt boss in *Soylent Green* (1973). He has also been seen in two *Star Trek* movies as Admiral Cartwright (*The Voyage Home* and *The Undiscovered Country*). And, in 1995, he appeared in the *Star Trek: Deep Space Nine* episode "Paradise Lost" as Cpt. Sisko's father. His character's name in *Battlestar Galactica* is significant for those devotees pursuing the series' mythical and historical strands. The Greek archon Solon (circa 600 B.C.) was one of seven wise men of Ancient Greece. He is remembered for ending enslavement as a means to pay debt, and for splitting the Athenian population into four classes based on wealth. He was a wholly "positive" figure in history, yet in *Battlestar Galactica* Solon is a hard-nosed lawyer occupied with anti-Starbuck rhetoric. Perhaps a better name for the character would have been Draco, considering Opposer Solon's draconian approach to law.

Frank Ashmore, who plays murder victim Ortega, is a science fiction cult favorite for his portrayal of two Fifth Columnist Visitors in both the *V* miniseries and regular series. First he was Martin, Diana's assistant in *V* and *V—The Final Battle*. Later, he returned to the weekly program as Phillip, Martin's brother, to investigate the murder of a Visitor leader, Charles. Ashmore has also appeared in other science fiction productions such as *Parts: The Clonus Horror* (1979), a movie recently skewered by *Mystery Science Theater 3000*.

Lastly, "Murder on the *Rising Star*" offers one other name of mythical origin: Charybdis. In Homer's *The Odyssey*, Charybdis was a deadly threat around which the clever Odysseus had to navigate his ship. On one side was Scylla, and on the other was Charybdis, a treacherous whirlpool which sucked in unsuspecting sea vessels. In *Battlestar Galactica*, Starbuck is framed by Charybdis, and Apollo has to "navigate around" him to save his friend. And at the end of the story, Apollo is trapped in his vessel (the shuttle) between two villains, Baltar (Scylla?) and, of course, Charybdis. Clever.

13. "Greetings from Earth"
(Special two-hour presentation)
Airdate: February 25, 1979.
Written by Glen A. Larson.
Directed by Ahmet Lateef.

SYNOPSIS: An alien spaceship housing six humans is recovered, and hopes run high in the fleet that this is finally a contact with the lost thirteenth tribe. Unfortunately, the human family aboard the small ship reveals that it hails from "Terra," not Earth. Additionally, the family is being pursued by an enemy as ruthless as the Cylons: the fascistic Eastern Alliance. Over the protests of the Council of 12, Starbuck, Cassiopeia and Apollo ferry the family to the distant planet Paradeen. There, Apollo hopes to find records of Earth that will reveal its location. Led by the vicious Commandant Leiter, the Eastern Alliance pursues the *Galactica*ns to Paradeen in a heavily armored destroyer. After surviving an incursion into Paradeen's abandoned city, Starbuck and Apollo defend the family from the Eastern Alliance. Still, there is an unknown saboteur at work: Someone has smashed the Colonial Vipers!

GUEST CAST: Lloyd Bochner (Commander Leiter); Ray Bolger (Vector); Kelly Harmon (Sarah); Murray Matheson (Geller); Randolph Mantooth (Michael); Bobby Van (Hector)

COMMENTARY: The first part of *Battlestar Galactica*'s thirteenth episode, "Greetings from Earth," ranks with the best episodes of the short-lived series, finding a slot somewhere close to the highs of "The Living Legend," "War of the Gods" and "The Man with Nine Lives." "Greetings from Earth" Part I is taut and involving, and there is actually a complicated moral issue at stake. Apollo feels that the people on the ship should not be interfered with, but the Council feels differently. The same debate is carried on by feuding doctors Salik and Wilker. The crux of the issue revolves around interference and responsibility. If the *Galactica* does interfere, they are responsible for the lives of the Terran ship's crew. But, do they have the right at all to interfere in the lives of others, even if interference does promise new information and new hope for the Colonials about Earth? Rewardingly, this ideological struggle is enunciated quite expertly and the argument is an involving and emotionally charged one. This is the kind of complexity that was missing from "The Lost Warrior," "The Young Lords" and "The Magnificent Warriors."

Although Apollo is again shown to be correct in his opinion and values, at least the other members of the military (and therefore *Galactica*'s family of regulars) are allowed to differ in a thoughtful rather than condescending manner. Boomer's speech detailing the *Galactica*'s voyage thus far is not only well-written and sincerely delivered by Herbert Jefferson, Jr., but it puts the series in perspective, and almost makes the earlier space Westerns forgivable by explaining that all the races encountered thus far have been offshoots of the Colonies, not alien civilizations. Another perspective is expressed through Maren Jensen's Athena, who compassionately teaches the children of the *Galactica* about the visitors, who (they hope) are from Earth. This is something *Battlestar Galactica,* even in its abbreviated run, always managed exceptionally well: It learned from its mistakes. It changed. Viewers cried sexism over "Lost Planet of the Gods," and in response Sheba, a competent female warrior, was introduced as a regular. Viewers cried foul at the insipid space Westerns and cardboard frontier civilizations of early shows, and the producers responded by having Boomer and Athena debate this point themselves. Although there were errors and missteps, someone was paying attention.

Unfortunately, the second part of "Greetings from Earth," which settles down on Paradeen, is less effective. The two androids, Hector and Vector, are embarrassing in appearance (they have painted white faces like old vaudevillians). Also, they act in a most decidedly juvenile and campy manner, singing, dancing and telling silly jokes. The "great" city of Paradeen is merely stock footage of a modern American city that is reused in "Experiment in Terra," and all throughout the *Buck Rogers in the 25th Century* TV series as New Chicago. The family shuttle of "Greetings from Earth" would later be appropriated by the *Buck Rogers* production team as well. It appears as *Ranger III* in "Awakening," and as Buck's shuttle in the second season stories "The Crystals" and "The Satyr."

The presence of the Eastern Alliance in "Greetings from Earth" may have been an attempt on the part of the series producers to liven up their product a bit. By this time, Nielsen ratings had taken a dip, and efforts were being made to pump up the series. Though the neat-looking, chrome Cylons were adequate villains (and popular with children), they lacked a human, individual face. They were not very interesting in an adult drama, especially since they could not ever hit their targets during battle! Since Baltar was captured by the Colonial fleet in "War of the Gods," the Cylons had no individuality whatsoever after episode ten. That is why they did not appear in episodes 11 through 16 (almost a third of the series). The makers of *Battlestar Galactica* had learned with Patrick Macnee's Count Iblis in "War of the Gods" and the fascinating Nomen in "The Man with Nine Lives" that individual, charismatic foes played better on the series, and made the episodes much more compelling. Accordingly, a new human foe with an individual face was introduced. However, the weapons and technology of the Eastern Alliance are shown in "Greetings from Earth" to be far more primitive than the equipment of the Colonials, making them less than a dramatic foe. The Eastern Alliance forces would reappear in the next episode, "Baltar's Escape," as well as in "Experiment in Terra," again with little impact. In execution, the Eastern Alliance baddies were not really much more interesting than the faceless Cylons. Although they were human in appearance, they were stereotypical space Nazis right down to their clipped style of speaking, their black Gestapo-style uniforms and handguns that resembled Nazi lugers.

The title "Greetings from Earth" is also supposed to be an attention grabber. Yet this episode has nothing whatsoever to do with Earth, instead focusing on the planet "Terra" (not to be confused with Earth!). There are no "Greetings from Earth" in this story whatsoever. Still, the episode is interesting because the series finds a new race in space — also human. Since even the angels in "War of the Gods" were but evolved humans, this discovery raises some questions. *Battlestar Galactica* seems to speculate that there are very few non-human aliens of any considerable intelligence in outer space. Consider that the Ovions and Borays are based on lower-life forms: insects and pigs. Even the Cylons, once reptiles (another lower life form), have adopted human shape because it is practical! Why the preponderance of humans in *Galactica*? Was it merely because the writers had no imagination about the cosmos, or was the series attempting to differentiate itself somehow, to find a niche? It was clearly not an "alien" encounter show like *Star Trek* (with silicon life in "Devil in the Dark," crystalline life in "The Tholian Web" and non-corporeal life in "Errand of Mercy") or *Space: 1999* (with space brains and cosmic entities dwelling inside black holes, as well as monsters and humans). What, then, was *Galactica*'s corner? Was it intended foremost as a war drama set against the backdrop of space? Or perhaps its central thesis is that man is linked to other humans across space, some behind us in technology ("Greetings from Earth") and some of us far ahead ("War of the Gods"). Whatever the reason, episodes like "Greetings from Earth" make *Galactica* moderately distinctive in the science fiction Valhalla.

Randolph Mantooth, star of *Emergency* (1972–1977), guest stars as Michael in "Greetings from Earth." Also present is Ray Bolger of *The Wizard of Oz* (1939) as the android Vector. Portraying the "space Nazi" is Lloyd Bochner, an imposing actor who perfectly captures the egotism and arrogance of the Eastern Alliance.

"Greetings from Earth" also introduces the miniature of the Eastern Alliance Destroyer, one of the most fascinating and best-detailed vehicles in the series. It appears to be built in part from a model kit of a U.S. F-15 jet attack fighter, but it is sufficiently redressed (with an arrowhead command center) to suggest a futuristic technology that, while advanced, is not quite up to Colonial standards. The *Galactica* viewer would be granted an even better view of this interesting ship in "Baltar's Escape" when the craft is rolled into the landing bay.

14. "Baltar's Escape"
Airdate: March 11, 1979.
Written by Donald Bellisario.
Directed by Winrich Kolbe.

SYNOPSIS: The Eastern Alliance soldiers, Baltar and the Borellian Nomen join forces to escape confinement on the Prison Barge. Meanwhile, Commander Adama learns that the Council of 12 intends to retire him and revoke martial law. When Baltar captures Boomer, Sheba and the entire Council, Adama is left with no choice but to negotiate with the traitor. As Adama turns himself and the interfering Siress Tinia over to Baltar as hostages, Apollo and Starbuck formulate a dangerous rescue mission involving two disassembled Cylon Centurions.

GUEST CAST: Lloyd Bochner (Commander Leiter); Ina Balin (Siress Tinia); Anthony DeLongis (Taba); Robert Feero (Bora); John Hoyt (Sire Dombra); Lance LeGault (Maga)

COMMENTARY: Another solid action-adventure, "Baltar's Escape" is a fun (though not inspired or thoughtful) hour of television. It closely resembles one of those old Marvel comic epics where suddenly all of Spiderman's enemies escape from jail at once and the hero must face Green Goblin, Dr. Octopus and Dr. Doom at the same time. On *Battlestar Galactica* however, it is the Borellian Nomen from "The Man with Nine Lives," the Eastern Alliance commandant and soldiers from "Greetings from Earth," and the villainous Baltar who form the challenge to the stalwart Colonials.

The main point of interest in this empty-headed action story is the unflattering depiction of the civilian government. As in "Saga of a Star World," "War of the Gods," "Greetings from Earth" and others, the civilian forces of the fleet are treated as complete boobs who are absolutely incapable of making even the most simple decision. Here, they improbably wish to form a treaty with the nefarious Eastern alliance. The Council is even ready to declare peace, the same mistake that was made at Caprica. This reveals the civilian government not only to be stupid and short-sighted, but forgetful as well.

"Baltar's Escape" reveals for the first time that the fleet has been suffering under martial law since the destruction of the Colonies in "Saga of a Star World." Strangely, this state of affairs is considered *good* by both the writers of the episode and by Apollo and Starbuck. The efforts of the civilian government to restore freedom and individual rights are seen as a negative thing, a misguided notion. Why? And why must all Council members be portrayed as idiotic, sniveling cowards? As usual, *Battlestar Galactica*'s vision is a distinctly fascist one, but it is more obvious in "Baltar's Escape" than in any other adventure. It is also especially ironic when put in the context of this story. Adama goes on at length in the episode about how the Enforcers of the Alliance are militaristic tyrants who squash freedom. Yet what about the warriors of the Colonial fleet? They too seek to maintain military law. All attempts by civilians to enact new laws or make new policy are mercilessly ridiculed, if not sabotaged! In effect, the Eastern Alliance and the Colonial Fleet are not run all that differently!

The Borellian Nomen reappear in "Baltar's Escape" and prove again that they are undeniably the legitimate predecessors to modern, revisionist Klingons both in appearance and demeanor. Besides considering themselves the greatest warriors in the galaxy and advising Baltar expertly in military strategy, here they stop their own hearts and feign death. It is a nifty trick — one that the half–Vulcan Mr. Spock used on more than one occasion in the original *Star Trek*.

Pulling all the villains together in this story is John Colicos as Baltar. As always, Colicos is a dynamic screen presence and an interesting performer to watch. He is one of the few Hollywood actors who can exude menace one moment, and then abruptly shift to comedy. Though Baltar is never really the most well-rounded character in *Battlestar Galactica*, he is one of the best performed. Ironically, even Colicos himself did not know what motivated the villainous Baltar. He told *Starlog* interviewer Peter Bloch-Hansen his secret in making Baltar so interesting, while knowing virtually nothing about his background or motives, in issue #138 (January 1989). "When in doubt, be enigmatic,"[5] he declared. Well, whatever works! Rumor has recently sprung up in *Battlestar Galactica* fandom (1997) that Colicos' has been tapped by Glen Larson to perform the voice of Baltar in a new animated production of *Battlestar Galactica*.

Winrich Kolbe, who ably directed "Baltar's Escape," has directed numerous episodes of *Star Trek: The Next Generation*, *Star Trek: Deep Space Nine* and *Star Trek: Voyager*, including the final TV voyage of Jean-Luc Picard and company: "All Good Things." He is a capable director and, though "Baltar's Escape" lacks any specific subtext or complex meaning, his work here is still competent and successful. "Baltar's Escape" is an easily digested adventure that is neither memorable or unusual. Although it is not as strong as "The Living Legend," "War of the Gods," or "The Man with Nine Lives," at least it is not another Western, nor is it predictable and clichéd. "Baltar's Escape" is not a bold step forward for the series — nor is it a step backwards.

Star Trek fans should recognize the man who portrays Sire Dombra. He is John Hoyt, who portrayed Dr. Phil Boyce in the first *Star Trek* pilot "The Cage," filmed back in 1964. Hoyt also appeared as a friendly alien opposite Sally Kellerman and *Space: 1999*'s Martin Landau in th*e Outer Limits* episode "The Bellero Shield." Lance LeGault, who recurs here as a Borellian Nomen, would return to the science fiction TV genre in the *Buck Rogers in the 25th Century* second season premiere "Time of the Hawk."

15. "Experiment in Terra"
Airdate: March 18, 1979.
Written by Glen A. Larson.
Directed by Rod Holcomb.

SYNOPSIS: While trailing the escaping Eastern Alliance Destroyer, Apollo is diverted by the alien angels and greeted by a being called "John." John has an important mission for the young captain: He must save Terra from nuclear annihilation before it is too late. Apollo is given the identity of a Nationalist pilot, Charlie Watts, but even Charlie's girlfriend Brenda does not believe his crazy story of an Eastern Alliance ruse. While Apollo addresses the Terran Praesidium, the *Galactica* races to Terra at light speed in hopes of preventing the destruction of another human colony.

GUEST CAST: Melody Anderson (Brenda); John DeLancie (Nationalist Soldier); Logan Ramsey (Moore); John MacLean (President); Edward Mulhare (John); Nehemiah Persoff (Commander); Ken Swofford (Max)

COMMENTARY: Glen Larson's "Experiment in Terra" is the final piece of the "Terra" trilogy, which began with "Greetings from Earth" and continued with "Baltar's Escape." It is also the only example of gunboat diplomacy evident in *Battlestar Galactica*'s episode roster, although the gunboat diplomacy story is a common one in *Star Trek* ("The Apple," "A Taste of Armageddon," "Return of the Archons" and "A Piece of the Action," to name but a few). At the end of this episode, the Terrans have clearly decided to annihilate their planet, yet the *Galactica* arrives and blasts Alliance nuclear weapons out of the sky—thus undercutting the Terran's freedom to choose their own destiny. Since the *Galactica*, unlike the starship *Enterprise*, has no non-interference Prime Directive, apparently its crew feels it is permissible to leap into the fray at this time. Besides, they literally have the angels on their side, although Adama is not aware of that. In "Experiment in Terra," there is little or no debate about the *Galactica*'s (or the angel race's) right to interfere in the affairs of another society. At least in *Star Trek*, Spock, Bones and Kirk debated such issues before deciding to interfere!

"Experiment in Terra" is a strange hodgepodge of ideas. Apollo's plight in Charlie's body, and the presence of the angel called John, are both treated as subjects for humor of the *Topper* variety, while the subject matter at the center of the plot, the annihilation of all human life on Terra, is hardly a laughing matter. Besides the uneven tone, "Experiment in Terra" fails to explain enough about the details of John's advanced powers. The angel can appear to Apollo outside of the lightship, but not to the Terrans. Why? Additionally, why do the angels pluck Apollo out of the cockpit of his Viper and make him look like Watts? Why do they not instead pluck Watts himself off of Luna 1, and send him back to help his own people? Chances are that Watts could deal with things more effectively than Apollo, since he is more familiar with the culture and people of Terra. With the world teetering on atomic oblivion is there *really* time for Apollo to bicker with ghosts (John), continue Charlie's affair with Brenda, learn a Terran lexicon, deliver a speech to the Western Praesidium *and* save the planet? Perhaps "Experiment in Terra" should have been a two-part episode so it would not feel as hurried. Lastly, if these angels are protecting the human forces of good and light throughout the universe, why did they permit the destruction of the Colonies at the hands of Cylon death machines? Where were John and the others when Caprica was on the verge of destruction? Or, mysteriously, is the cosmic exodus of the *Galactica* to Earth part of the angel race's grand scheme? If so, perhaps that should have been stated within the text of "Experiment in Terra."

Charlie Watts' fate is also a point of inconsistency in "Experiment in

Terra." Early on, John informs Apollo that Watts will soon escape from his prison on Luna 1. However, later in the show, the president is assured by his aide that Watts is dead because all life has been destroyed on Luna 1. From Max's report to Brenda, the audience knows this latter statement to be true. Is Watts dead, or will he escape unharmed as the all-knowing John asserts? A little clarity on this issue would have been nice.

The notion of a superior force guiding humanity to a preordained fate is an acceptable science fiction idea that has worked before on television, particularly in the first year of *Space: 1999* ("Black Sun," "The Testament of Arkadia"). In that series, it was established that a cosmic intelligence of unknown appearance and motive was using the Alphan space colony to bring life back to certain dead planets and areas of the universe. In *Battlestar Galactica*, the cosmic force (at least the one seen in "Experiment in Terra") is played for laughs, and is very human in appearance. This group of angels resemble the heavenly troupe of *It's a Wonderful Life* (1946) more than thoughtful, believable superiors. No wonder Count Iblis took off on his own! In fact, the existence of Count Iblis brings up more questions. If he is a member of John's race, a fallen angel, why can *he* be seen by Colonists outside the lightship? Obviously, there is very little consistency between "War of the Gods" and "Experiment in Terra."

Still, "Experiment in Terra" is not without merits. It is a stronger show than many early *Battlestar Galactica*s, including "The Lost Warrior," "The Magnificent Warriors," "The Young Lords" and "Fire in Space." The characters are well-established now, and the story features a kind of slick, "go for broke" breakneck pace. It is definitely not a step backwards for the series. Best of all, Richard Hatch confidently and movingly delivers a stirring speech in "Experiment in Terra." It could well be called the Apollo Manifesto or "The *Battlestar Galactica* Thesis." The point is, not surprisingly in context of the series' military tone, that *real*, lasting peace can only be achieved through a strong military presence. Only the threat of superior firepower can insure peace and deter the enemies lurking "out there." It is a rather unforgiving and discouraging right-wing philosophy of life, but one that has gained adherents since Ronald Reagan's enormous defense spending apparently initiated the economic collapse of the Soviet Union. In *Battlestar Galactica*, one senses that this hawkish philosophy exists mostly to justify the actions of the main cast of *Galactica*, not because of any deep thought or general world view. The cast represents the military, and the military are the good guys, plain and simple.

Edward Mulhare, who guest stars as the angel John, was a regular on

Knight Rider and *The Ghost and Mrs. Muir* (1968–70). The latter credit is the most important since in that late 1960s series he was also playing an interfering, non-corporeal life form! Melody Anderson, the confused Brenda, is also no stranger to science fiction. A year after her performance in "Experiment in Terra," she played legendary space heroine Dale Arden in Dino DeLaurentiis' production of *Flash Gordon* (1980). Nehemiah Persoff, the Supreme Commander of the Eastern Alliance, would later appear on the *Star Trek: The Next Generation* third season adventure "The Most Toys."

There is one other important guest star in this episode. You may not recognize his face at first but you will certainly recognize his voice. Look closely at the Nationalist Guard who approaches Starbuck's Viper with a troop of soldiers about halfway through "Experiment in Terra." He is John DeLancie, "Q" on *Star Trek: The Next Generation*. Perhaps "John" was not the only interfering, God-like entity on Terra after all. Maybe "Q" was there too!

The scene with Dirk Benedict and John DeLancie occurs in a familiar setting to genre buffs as well. It is Vasquez Rocks, the site where "Arena" was shot for the original *Star Trek* and where "Who Watches the Watchers" was shot in 1990 for *The Next Generation*. Vasquez Rocks is an overexposed film and TV location because it has been used so frequently to double as other worlds. It was even the butt of a great joke in *Bill & Ted's Bogus Journey* (1991). Its use in *Battlestar Galactica* is not distracting, however, since the sequence set was shot at night. Only the momentary light flare of an explosion makes the trademark Vasquez mountain briefly recognizable.

Of some interest to faithful *Battlestar Galactica* followers is the fact that in "Experiment in Terra," Adama pulls the battlestar out of the fleet at light speed to rescue Apollo. This the only time in the series the *Galactica* leaves her wards behind. The action was justified since the Cylons were thought gone at last by this point in the journey. They had not appeared since "War of the Gods." Still, Adama has usually insisted that the fleet be defended at all costs, so his decision here seems a little out of character.

16. "Take the *Celestra*"
Airdate: April 1, 1979.
Written by Jim Carlson and Terrence
McDonnell. Directed by Dan Haller.

SYNOPSIS: While celebrating the career of *Celestra*'s Commander Kronus, Starbuck spies his long-lost love, Aurora, in a crowd. After following her back to the *Celestra*, Starbuck learns that Kronus is not quite the selfless hero he is cracked up to be. With his harsh first officer Charka, Kronus exploits the working people of his productive industrial ship. Starbuck and Apollo become embroiled in a mutiny on the *Celestra* led by Aurora, and lock horns with the villainous Charka.

GUEST CAST: Ana Alicia (Aurora); Paul Fix (Kronus); Nick Holt (Charka); Richard Styles (Hermes); Randy Stumpf (Damon); James R. Parkes (First Mutineer); Michael Horsley (Second Mutineer); Ted Hamaguchi (Third Crewman); Robert Murvin (Duty Officer)

COMMENTARY: An unexpected and surprisingly engaging story of a futuristic labor revolt, "Take the *Celestra*" nicely demonstrates where a little imagination and a bit of curiosity might have taken this promising sci-fi series. Over 20 hours of *Battlestar Galactica* had already been produced by the time of "Take the *Celestra*," yet this is the first episode to take a look at what life is like on a ship in the ragtag fleet other than the *Galactica*. On the industrial ship *Celestra*, the truth turns out to be quite awful, and the story is an interesting one that raises many moral issues.

In particular, stern old Commander Kronus is fascinating. He is clearly a hard-liner and a strict disciplinarian. He is a difficult person to like. At the commander's promotion reception, Tigh attempts to make a toast to Kronus, but is nastily silenced by Kronus himself, who suggests tactlessly that the colonel is due for duty on the bridge. It is an awkward moment, but one which reveals Kronus' total lack of generosity and kindness. This unflattering depiction of Kronus is the only instance in the series where a martial, military point-of-view is looked on in a less than positive manner. Kronus, though obviously a committed officer who feels he knows the best way to command, causes a backlash on the *Celestra* with his heartless methods. His people consider him to be a cruel slave driver, and they rebel against him. Although the morality of his methods is never pointedly addressed, Kronus symbolically pays for his draconian philosophy by dying at the end of the story. Mitigating the power of this depiction somewhat, "Take the *Celestra*" tries to suggest that Kronus was unaware of the extent of Charka's cruelty, but that is no excuse. A commanding officer is deemed responsible for the behavior of his crew. In this case, Kronus' obsession with discipline and achieving results led him to overlook inhuman atrocities.

Despite their early disdain for Kronus, Aurora's people willingly join hands with him to fight the evil Charka at the conclusion of the story, suggesting that though Kronus may have been misguided, he is still one of the good guys. In other words, the military is again taken off the hook! The real baddie is obviously the villainous Charka, who has ruthlessly duped the military (and Kronus) and seized power. *Battlestar Galactica* again offers in Charka a sneering, purely evil character instead of a multidimensional one. At least in this story, Charka is given a motivation for his actions: He feels he has been passed over for command of the *Celestra*. If it was good enough motive for Iago in Shakespeare's *Othello*, it is good enough for Charka in *Battlestar Galactica*.

Of the main characters, Laurette Spang's Cassiopeia registers the strongest in "Take the *Celestra*." While Starbuck acts like an adolescent boy with raging hormones, Cassiopeia is played by the talented Spang as a mature, understanding adult who is not out to "possess" anyone, least of all a womanizer who does not want her. One wonders what she sees in the fickle Starbuck, especially in this tale, wherein he tosses her aside to start something up with Aurora. The end of "Take the *Celestra*" is something of a dramatic cop-out, with Starbuck returning to Cassie only after it has been established that nothing can occur between him and Aurora. While Spang's performance is superlative here, *Battlestar Galactica* terminology takes it on the chin as she alternately refers to concert reservations as "tickets." They should always be called "duckets."

There are a few other problems in "Take the *Celestra*" as well. Has Kronus been awarded a promotion by Adama without an investigation of the life and morale on his ship? And in another weird moment, Apollo tells Starbuck to look good for the spit-and-polish Commander Kronus. He orders Starbuck to button his jacket and look presentable. What makes this strange is that Apollo's jacket is also unbuttoned, and he makes no attempt to make *himself* presentable to Kronus. These little inconsistencies are outweighed by a number of positives, however. Finally, something is learned of Adama's past (he served under Kronus on the Battlestar *Rycon*). Also, Sheba and Cassiopeia share a tender talk about Starbuck. As usual, the characterizations and relationships in *Battlestar Galactica* show sentimentality and verisimilitude.

Ana Alicia would return to romance Starbuck's spiritual descendant, the warrior Dillon (Barry Van Dyke), in one of the final episodes of *Galactica: 1980* ("The Space Croppers"). She also joined Gil Gerard in the *Buck Rogers in the 25th Century* first season episode "Vegas in Space" (1979). Paul Fix, Commander Kronus here, portrayed Dr. Mark Piper in the 1965

Star Trek pilot "Where No Man Has Gone Before." This makes him the second *Enterprise* medical officer to visit the battlestar. John Hoyt, Dr. Boyce in "The Cage," appeared as Council member Dombra in "Baltar's Escape."

The *Celestra* itself had been seen already in many episodes of *Battlestar Galactica*, but always at a distance. It is shown close-up here, and from a variety of angles. It is revealed to be a highly detailed, believable miniature. It is most certainly not an attractive vessel, but rather an ungainly sort of space carrier or tug. It looks just like a no-frills electronics ship should: bulky and utilitarian. The *Celestra* is equipped with a rotating communications dish on its dorsal side and a huge docking bay to the fore that is lit with a blue light. It is a very well-designed effect, and a believable spacecraft given the nature of the Colonial fleet.

"Take the *Celestra*" also continues the tradition (begun with episode 11, "The Man with Nine Lives") of starting each story with Commander Adama's "State of the Fleet"–style report. In various episodes, this speech focuses on morale, unresolved plot points from previous episodes, and the nature of the solar systems through which the *Galactica* is traveling. Even better, this welcome literary technique always points ahead with tantalizing bits of information about Earth. Like the prison cell painting of Earth's solar system discovered by Starbuck in "The Long Patrol," or the coordinates provided by the angels in "War of the Gods," these references to Earth kept the series pointed in the right direction while simultaneously reminding viewers of the *Galactica*'s ultimate goal. This is why the first series seems so cohesive and urgent, as opposed to the often lackadaisical-seeming quest of the *Voyager* starship on *Voyager*. When a starship stops to examine every nebula or asteroid belt, its mission to get home is easily forgotten.

By this point, Athena, Boxey and Muffit seemed to have been dropped. They do not appear at all in "Baltar's Escape," "Experiment in Terra," "Take the *Celestra*" or even the final episode of the series, "The Hand of God." What happened to these characters? Why were they dispatched? Maren Jensen's Athena, in particularly deserves better than this.

"Take the *Celestra*" may not be a brilliant hour of television science fiction, but it does reveal new sides of colonial life. It also fulfills the *Wagon Train* premise of a "new adventure on every ship in the fleet" that was promised by series creator Larson. Aside from the look at life on the *Celestra* and the information about industry and electronics in the fleet, this episode also reveals the pomp and circumstance of Colonial Medal Ceremonies.

Those perspectives, as well as the continued lack of Cylons, make this a unique contribution to the series. It stands as one of the better *Battlestar Galacticas* alongside "The Living Legend," "War of the Gods" and "The Man with Nine Lives." This positive assessment of the episode is not, however, shared by many fans of *Galactica*. In a recent Internet poll, "Take the *Celestra*" came in dead last in the *Battlestar Galactica* roster, below "Gun on Ice Planet Zero," "Fire in Space" and even "The Lost Warrior." It probably fared so badly because it did not feature the Cylons, the Eastern Alliance, Baltar, the Nomen or any other popular *Galactica* villains. Also, it did not take place on a new planet, or specifically further the quest for Earth. To some fans, the latter failing probably makes "Take the *Celestra*" seem rather unimportant. On the contrary, "Take the *Celestra*" goes a long way towards exploring the conditions in the ragtag fleet on the journey to Earth. This was an interesting avenue to explore, and even if the episode has its weak points, at least it was an attempt to do something different.

17. "The Hand of God"
Airdate: April 29, 1979.
Written by Donald Bellisario.
Directed by Donald Bellisario.

SYNOPSIS: While on a double date in the *Galactica*'s astronav post, a "celestial chamber" used by spacefarers in the ancient days of cosmic flight, Apollo, Sheba, Starbuck and Cassiopeia detect a signal on an unused gamma frequency. Apollo believes that the transmission, which displays an old-fashioned ship landing on a craggy planet surface, originates from Earth! When a hidden Cylon baseship is detected on the edge of the solar system, Commander Adama suspects the signal is a new ruse. Tired of running from the Cylons, the *Galactica* crew enlists the aid of Baltar, who has been promised freedom for cooperation, and mounts a daring attack on the baseship.

COMMENTARY: The final hour of *Battlestar Galactica* is strong and memorable enough to make even the casual series fan long for a second season, even after 20 years. Virtually everything from performances and dialogue to special effects and humor seem to blend together perfectly in "The Hand of God" for almost the first time in the short run of the series.

There is direct evidence of Earth at last, giving fans hope that the "shining quest" will soon carry the *Galactica* and her people to a safe haven. Even more delightful, in "The Hand of God," the Colonials grow tired of running and decide to fight back. What an inspiring thing it is to see Adama turn to Tigh and order the attack on the baseship. These characters have suffered for so long that it is a positive, life-affirming thing to see them transform from victim to aggressor! Even John Colicos' despicable Baltar redeems himself, saves the fleet and is set free. And, after the loss of Serina in "Lost Planet of the Gods," the thoughtful Cpt. Apollo at last embraces life again and embarks on a romantic relationship with Sheba, while the Starbuck/Cassie involvement evolves and deepens as well. Gloriously, the Cylons are finally dispatched as a continuing villain, too. With all this dramatic material flying about, "The Hand of God" has enough plot and character development to cover almost an entire season. If every show had been as exciting and suspenseful as this one. *Battlestar Galactica* could have been the *Star Trek* of the 1970s instead of just another lost science fiction opportunity. "The Hand of God" ranks with "The Living Legend" and "The War of the Gods" as one of *Galactica*'s most compelling and enjoyable hours.

The teleplay for "The Hand of God" by Donald Bellisario is well-written, and it is filled with humorous and deep moments. Both Tigh and Adama make a point to ask Apollo and Starbuck what they were doing up in the celestial chamber with Cassie and Sheba, a cute moment acknowledging that people in the *Galactica* universe *do* think about sex. There are also veritable tidal waves of emotional farewells to Starbuck and Apollo from Cassie, Boomer and Sheba, and a mention of Serina for the first time since "The Lost Warrior."

Finally, the uplifting conclusion of "The Hand of God" puts a temporal context on the *Battlestar Galactica*'s voyage. Now that the United States Moon landing (the weird gamma signal) has been integrated into the series, it is clear that the events of *Battlestar Galactica* must take place after Earth-time 1969. Of course, how far ahead of 1969 is still up for debate, as long as one ignores the dreadful *Galactica: 1980*.

Although space battle footage is again recycled in "The Hand of God," notably from "Saga of a Star World" and "The Living Legend," the stock footage is nicely balanced by fresh footage of a gas giant planet and a wonderful special effects moment that depicts Apollo inside the celestial temple. In a single, lovely shot, the camera moves in for the *Galactica* hull and focuses ever tighter on the "flower bud" of the chamber. Inside, a rotating chair and a figure (Apollo) are clearly visible as the warrior sits surrounded by stars. The moment early in the show when Apollo lowers the metal casing of the chamber to reveal the vastness of outer space is also spectacular. Indeed, this is one of the few times that *Battlestar Galactica* actually captures the beauty of the cosmos in a meaningful way.

For the last several years, actor Richard Hatch has been fighting a noble (but uphill) campaign to revive *Battlestar Galactica* in its original form. If reports can be trusted, he has been to Fox Television, Universal Studios and even to the Sci-Fi Channel to propose a resurrection. Any such *Battlestar Galactica* revival would, of course, totally discount the follow-up series *Galactica: 1980*, in which it was established that Cpt. Apollo had died and that Boxey had grown up and been transformed into "Troy." That is a good thing, because Apollo is simply too strong a character to let go, especially with Lorne Greene now deceased. At age 50 and in command of the *Galactica*, Apollo would be even more interesting to watch today. He could be accompanied by a more mature Col. Starbuck on the bridge.

Until the revival gets out of the launching bay, "The Hand of God" ends the 17-episode *Battlestar Galactica* collection. The series made some terrible blunders with space Western stories, with scientific inaccuracies and TV clichés, but upon close viewing, it is also revealed to be a sentimental and sincere series. By the end of it all, Adama, Boxey, Apollo, Starbuck, Cassie and Sheba all seemed to be real, caring people. Viewer's hearts went out to these travelers who had seen so much horror and disaster. Even though the human, emotional moments came few and far between, the cast was strong enough and sympathetic enough to pull off a victory even in the face of all the harsh criticism and indecisive writing. The people of *Battlestar Galactica* will always be more real, more interesting and less perfect than the superheroes of *The Next Generation*, the politically correct ciphers of *SeaQuest DSV* or the cardboard *Trek* inspired cut-outs of early *Babylon 5*.

This author would like to see *Battlestar Galactica* live again on TV in a more intelligent, more philosophical and more thought-provoking form. A new series could focus on the reality of life in the fleet under martial law. Internal political struggles could be played out, and character growth could continue along the terms defined in the 1978 series. *Battlestar Galactica* was clearly edging in those directions by the end of its first season anyway. Just imagine what might have happened had the series been granted a second season, especially with Isaac Asimov as head writer?

When fans decry *Battlestar Galactica* as a *total* failure, they fail to remember that *Star Trek: The Next Generation*'s first year was, politely put, a disaster. Its second year was none too good either. It was not until the third season that the series truly hit its stride with viewers by offering solid, well-told stories. After a dreadful second season, and an incredibly good fourth season, *Star Trek: Voyager* looks to be following the same pattern.

Battlestar Galactica never shared the same opportunity to grow and develop as *The Next Generation* and *Voyager* have, despite the fact that its ratings were considerably higher. It is quite possible that had these other shows not flashed the well-known *Star Trek* name before their individual titles, they would not have survived the first season either. Still, *Battlestar Galactica* in its initial run provided some rip-roaring adventures for children of all ages. It may not have always been especially complex, thoughtful or meaningful, but it was a heartfelt adventure. And Richard Hatch, Lorne Greene, Dirk Benedict, Laurette Spang, Terry Carter, Maren Jensen and the rest of the cast deserve kudos for highlighting beautiful, noble humanity in the midst of all the "spectacular" special effects and indifferent writing.

Additionally, one cannot deny that *Battlestar Galactica* filled a very important need when it aired in the late '70s. Fans were hungering for more *Star Wars*, but the follow-up films came once only every three years. *Battlestar Galactica* offered the same kind of swashbuckling adventure and special effects as the *Star Wars* productions, and made that long wait between sequels much more tolerable. *Galactica* was a guilty pleasure all right, but it filled a void created by the absence of new *Star Wars* movies and new *Star Trek* or *Space: 1999* episodes. Today it is a nostalgic reminder of the '70s and of the long stretch between *Star Wars* and *The Empire Strikes Back*.

PART III

Galactica: 1980

Galactica: 1980 arrived on ABC in January 1980 and was gone from first-run broadcast television by August. Barely a blip on the national consciousness, the series relied heavily on *Battlestar Galactica* special effects footage and on stock sitcom, superhero and cop-show situations. Although Lorne Greene and Herb Jefferson, Jr., returned for *Galactica: 1980*, they were woefully underutilized. Most of the action was handled not by *Battlestar Galactica* veterans, but by shallow Apollo and Starbuck clones Troy and Dillon, as well as by a troop of prepubescent *Galactica* children who had developed "super" powers thanks to Earth's gravity. Seen today as a "nightmare" series in more ways than one, *Galactica: 1980* was created by Glen A. Larson, the talent behind *Battlestar Galactica*, and thus a little harder to completely negate than many fans might wish. Although just about everyone who watched the series would rather forget it, the fact remains that the *Battlestar Galactica* and her fleet did complete their "shining quest": They found Earth, albeit briefly, in *Galactica: 1980*.

Critical Reception

Critics and fans are unanimous in their hatred of *Galactica: 1980*, and for good reason. The series could have transported viewers anywhere in the known universe as well as through the dark and mysterious corridors of time. It could have explored Colonial culture or intelligently portrayed a culture clash between barbaric Earthlings and advanced humans from another galaxy. Instead, it opted to feature car chases ("*Galactica* Discovers Earth," "The Night the Cylons Landed"), sitcom-brand humor ("The Super Scouts"), precocious space children ("Spaceball") and heavy-handed "relevant" themes ("The Super Scouts," "The Space Croppers"). It did not take long for angry critics to realize that they were watching an inferior hodgepodge, a bad sequel to a series that had its own ups and downs to contend with. The critics responded accordingly — with venom!

Make no mistake, *Galactica: 1980* is *not* a "guilty pleasure." There is nothing remotely pleasurable about the series at all. It is like watching a train wreck or a plane crash. With special effects stock footage spliced in seemingly at random, bland performers at center stage and poorly written stories, *Galactica: 1980* is an excellent candidate for the worst science fiction series of all time. That estimation has not changed since 1980, and the show is as universally despised today as it was two decades ago. The sampling below represents the critical consensus:

> If *Galactica* fans were expecting the worst when the sequel arrived in 1980, they certainly weren't disappointed. Nearly every episode was written at a dramatic level best suited for children, with the stars spending most of their time explaining all sorts of inane subjects.... Overall, *Galactica: 1980* is a fairly awful series geared only to the most fanatical of *Galactica* enthusiasts. — William E. Anchors, Jr., *Epilog #33: "Galactica: 1980,"* August 1993, page 8

> The stories were a complete waste of time. *Battlestar Galactica* at least had a few interesting attempts. But what I see in *Galactica: 1980* is a studio amortizing its set and its name. This is television as a merchandising ploy. — Michael Cassutt, *The Best of Science Fiction Television*, Harmony Books, 1987

> ...an embarrassing, child-oriented mess in which Earth had been found and all semblance of logic and drama abandoned. — Lawrence McIlhoney, *TV Zone* Special # 17: "The Lost Voyagers of Cult TV," June 1995, page 5

> The series was a mess, thrown together so haphazardly that it couldn't even attract diehard *Battlestar Galactica* fans. — John Javna, *The Best of Science Fiction Television*, Harmony Books, 1987

Series Overview:

Galactica: 1980 flew for only ten short weeks, six stories in all. It had been designed by Larson as an "earthbound" series instead of an outer space one. The series' primary gimmick was to re-use the extensive and costly special visual effects of *Battlestar Galactica* while at the same time tell "cheap" stories on Earth about Colonial incursions into 20th century American culture. It was felt that the mix of Earth action and outer space special effects would make the series more accessible to middle America than even the original, highly rated *Battlestar Galactica* had been. The original scheme was to offer a variation on the theme of Robert Wise's *The Day the Earth Stood Still* (1951), about advanced aliens bringing peace and wisdom to Earth while at the same time facing danger from "primitive" 20th century man. It did not quite work out that way, however. *The Day the Earth Stood Still* never became mired down in silly humor, car chases and gimmicks, as *Galactica: 1980* was wont to do.

Since *Galactica: 1980* was on the air for such a short time, it is hard to determine what interesting or unusual flourishes the series might have developed had it lasted longer. On the basis of "what's on screen," there is precious little of quality to discuss in *Galactica: 1980*. From a visual standpoint, the series was pure retread. The Colonial costumes of Jean Pierre Dorleac returned, as did a few of the *Galactica* interiors. Notably, the expensive bridge set was not reconstructed; stock footage from various *Battlestar Galactica* episodes was inserted instead whenever a bridge scene was required. This caused its own set of problems since various original crew members such as Omega and Rigel could frequently be seen in the quick cuts. Of course, these characters had miraculously not aged even one day in the 14 "yahrens" since the events of *Battlestar Galactica*. One corner of the bridge was eventually reconstructed: the communications center to the immediate right of the main viewing screen. This was basically a rectangular room no larger than a hallway, and it featured only one measly control panel. It lacked the neat Tektronix gimmickry of the *Battlestar Galactica* bridge and looked rather primitive.

The visual effects were mostly retreads as well. In "*Galactica* Discovers Earth," the first Viper approach to Los Angeles was actually footage from "Gun on Ice Planet Zero." In "The Super Scouts," an attack on the Gemonese freighter was from various early *Battlestar* episodes. In "The Space Croppers," the attack on the agro-ships was from "The Magnificent Warriors" and the footage of the Imperious Leader was from "Saga of a Star World." Even some of the youngest children watching *Galactica: 1980* were probably aware that they were watching repeat footage rather than new special effects work.

When new special effects were required by the stories of *Galactica: 1980*, they tended to be clumsy. The flying motorcycles of "*Galactica* Discovers Earth" were "augmented" by bad rear-projection work. The startling Cylon attack on Los Angeles in the same episode was nothing more than scenes from the movie *Earthquake*, with Cylons superimposed over crumbling buildings. When Troy and Dillon's Viper broke down in "Spaceball," a sloppy editor merely "paused" *Battlestar Galactica* Viper footage. The only episode that featured new visuals (a new Cylon attack craft) was "The Night the Cylons Landed."

If the special effects, costumes and props were all retreads, so were, unfortunately, the characterizations. Kent McCord, Barry Van Dyke and Robyn Douglass all worked hard to make the series successful, but they played ciphers rather than people. Kent McCord played Cpt. Troy, a grown-up Boxey. He was patient, considerate, generous and determined — in other words, an exact duplicate of Apollo! Van Dyke's Dillon was a Starbuck knock-off: a cocky, womanizing hot-shot pilot. Douglass' character was, bizarrely, a copy of *Superman*'s Lois Lane. She was a confident reporter, bound and determined to get her story. At the same time, however, she was a friend of aliens with superpowers. These characters might have succeeded despite their clichéd origins had the stories provided background about them. How did Troy feel about the death of his father (Apollo) and mother (Serina)? What happened to Muffit? On what ship in the fleet had Dillon been raised? How was he chosen to become a warrior? What about Jamie's life? Did she have an interesting past — any past at all? The characters were all blanks — bland blanks, to be precise.

One new character was not bland: Dr. Zee. Portrayed by Robbie Rist (*The Brady Bunch*) in "*Galactica* Discovers Earth" and by Patrick Stuart (not to be confused with Patrick Stewart of *Star Trek: The Next Generation* fame) in the remainder of the series, this character was termed "a genetic mutation" by Larson's pilot teleplay. He was a super-advanced and super-snobbish alien. The series never provided a background for this character until the very last show aired: "The Return of Starbuck." Ironically, the unusual Dr. Zee was probably the most-hated of all *Galactica: 1980* characters. Generally, know-it-all teenage male geniuses do not do well in sci-fi. Dr. Zee and *Star Trek: The Next Generation*'s Wesley Crusher (Wil Wheaton) are despised because of their arrogance, and because they tend to be the characters who most regularly "save the day." The problem with this is that these geniuses manage in both shows to make the adults (all of them either trained Colonial Warriors or Starfleet officers) look hopelessly incompetent. In *Galactica: 1980*, the arrogant Dr. Zee rules over the wise Adama with an iron hand. It is neither fun nor entertaining to see the great Commander Adama, the one man responsible for the survival of the fleet, reduced to taking orders from an English-accented brat.

The returning characters, Adama and Boomer, had little of value to do in *Galactica: 1980.* Since no bridge set had been constructed for the great Battlestar, Lorne Greene had no set on which to act! Instead, he appeared in Dr. Zee's throne room, or in the communications cubicle/closet when necessary. Most of the action took place far away, on Earth. Boomer suffered too: He was the *Galactica* Colonel by this time, and like Adama should have been stationed on the bridge. Since the series had no bridge, Boomer was "homeless" as well.

All of these shortcomings might have been overcome had *Galactica: 1980* featured some interesting stories. After "*Galactica* Discovers Earth," the three-part premiere, science fiction concepts were for the most part abandoned. "The Super Scouts" was a comedy about *Galactica*n children trapped on Earth. "Spaceball" featured the *Galactica*n children (again), this time trying to save a baseball camp for underprivileged children. This has the distinction of being perhaps the most inconsequential hour of science fiction television in history. "The Night the Cylons Landed" featured about 30 minutes of a good plot: Cylons crash on Earth and race to a radio station to bring down the Cylon fleet. Unfortunately, the show ran for two hours. The remainder of the running time was spent on car chases, superheroics and ill-conceived attempts at comedy as the Cylons are mistaken for Halloween night party-goers. "The Space Croppers," the fifth story, relied again on gimmicks (invisibility) and trite conflicts between unimportant "warring" Earth families. Only the last episode ("The Return of Starbuck") was a quality show. Featuring Dirk Benedict as a guest star, the episode not only revealed Lt. Starbuck's fate, it also presented for the first time an inkling of Dr. Zee's unusual heritage. It was the only satisfactory show of the bunch.

What made *Galactica: 1980* more disappointing was the fact that all episodes of the series but one ("The Space Croppers") were penned by Glen A. Larson, the creator of *Galactica: 1980* and *Battlestar Galactica*. It was his concept that fueled this sequel, and yet even he could do nothing with it! Considering that Larson also wrote "Saga of a Star World," "The Living Legend," "War of the Gods" and "Greetings from Earth," all fine episodes of *Battlestar Galactica*, the low quality of his *Galactica: 1980* outings is especially difficult to understand. The series highlighted competent if not inspired TV directors such as Daniel Haller, who had directed several episodes of *Buck Rogers* including "Awakening" and "Journey to Oasis" and who would go on to direct episodes of the Lee Majors series *The Fall Guy* (1981–86). Also aboard were Sigmund Neufeld, Jr., another *Buck Rogers* veteran ("Vegas in Space," "Cruise Ship to the Stars" and "Twiki is Missing"), Barry Crane, director of the *Buck Rogers* episode "Mark of the Saurian," and Ron Satloff, frequent contributor to *Hunter* (1984–1991.) Larson's producing partners were also intelligent, resourceful talents. Many years after *Galactica: 1980*, producer Frank Lupo created the well-regarded *Werewolf* (1987) horror series for Fox television. With all of this talent in evidence, *Galactica: 1980*'s total incompetence is mystifying.

The most damning problem with *Galactica: 1980* is that it does not even seem to jibe with the events of *Battlestar Galactica*. The last episode of the first series ("The Hand of God") featured a transmission of the Apollo 11 landing. Boomer stated that this gamma transmission could have been floating around the cosmos for hundreds if not millions of years. At the very least, the existence of the transmission indicated that in Earth time, at least, the outer space series was taking place *after* 1969. *Galactica: 1980* begins 14 yahrens (years) after the last episode of *Battlestar Galactica*. That would put it at least in the year 1983 assuming that the transmission seen in "The Hand of God" had *just* been transmitted when the *Galactica* identified it. Yet the series took place in *1980*, not 1983. The chronology does not work, and therefore the very title, the very premise of *Galactica: 1980*, does not work either.

There are other things that are hard to accept. Why does Boxey now go by the name Troy? Why is he suddenly 35 years old when he was six only 14 yahrens ago? Most damagingly, the new *Galactica: 1980* makes mincemeat of the Erich Von Däniken principle that was woven through so many episodes of *Battlestar Galactica*. Viewers of the original series longed to know how Apollo, Cain, Athena and other characters "jibed" with Earth's history. *Galactica: 1980* responds by simply saying there *is* no connection. Those names are just common names from two cultures. What a letdown!

About the only fun to be derived from watching *Galactica: 1980* comes from the large numbers of genre actors who guest star in the short-lived series. *Star Trek* alumni Marj Dusay ("Spock's Brain"), Arthur Batanides ("That Which Survives"), and Sharon Acker ("The Mark of Gideon") all appear in various stories, as do *Buck Rogers* guest stars John Quade ("Plot to Kill a City"), Judith Chapman ("Olympiad"), Ana Alicia ("Vegas in Space"), Richard Lynch ("Vegas in Space") and Pamela Susan Shoop ("Vegas in Space"). Other familiar faces from the 1960s, '70s and '80s include Peter Mark Richman (*Star Trek: The Next Generation*- "The Neutral Zone"), William Daniels (K.I.T.T. in *Knight Rider*) and Lara

Parker of *Dark Shadows* in "The Night the Cylons Landed." For many watchers, these guest stars may offer little of value, but to science fiction television aficionados some of them tend to make even the most dreadful episode of *Galactica: 1980* at least watchable.

The last rerun of *Galactica: 1980* aired August 17, 1980, and the cast and crew moved on to bigger and better things. Lorne Greene was back on Sunday nights at eight the following season in *Code Red*. This was the third series in three years to star Greene and to run on Sunday night on ABC. Greene again played the father figure in this short-lived show about a firefighting family. His sons were equally as good-looking and hunky as his children and grandchildren had been on *Battlestar Galactica*, but this time they were portrayed by Sam J. Jones (*Flash Gordon*) and Andrew Stevens (*The Fury*). *Code Red* folded after one season, and Greene retired from television. The world was saddened when the beloved actor passed away in 1987.

After the *Battlestar Galactica* sequel folded, Kent McCord, a TV veteran of *Adam 12* (1968–75), continued performing guest star roles, and he returned triumphantly to the science fiction genre after a decade for the big-screen horror/sci-fi adventure *Predator 2* (1990) opposite Danny Glover. Barry Van Dyke appeared in *Gun Shy* (1983), a short-lived TV Western based on the Walt Disney film *The Apple Dumpling Gang* (1975). He did not find TV series success until he teamed with his father, Dick Van Dyke, for the mystery program *Diagnosis: Murder* (1995–). Robyn Douglass and Patrick Stuart have remained relatively obscure since the failure of *Galactica: 1980*.

In 1981, following the cancellation of *Buck Rogers in the 25th Century*, Glen Larson left outer space behind for the time being. This was perhaps a wise move considering the hatred which *Battlestar Galactica* fans heaped on *Galactica: 1980*. He never completely abandoned science fiction, and he went on to produce marginal material such as *Manimal* (1984) starring Simon McCorkingdale and the popular *Knight Rider* (1982–85) with David Hasselhoff and Edward Mulhare ("Experiment in Terra").

After its cancellation, *Galactica: 1980* disappeared from television for over a decade. It was never rerun or syndicated until the Sci-Fi Channel purchased the production in 1996. *Galactica: 1980* aired briefly there on Saturday afternoons in 1996 before taking up a weekday afternoon time slot which it shared with fellow Glen Larson productions *Battlestar Galactica* and *Buck Rogers in the 25th Century*. For many, the Sci-Fi Channel's unveiling of *Galactica: 1980* could not have come at a worse time. Momentum had been gaining for at least a year to revive *Battlestar Galactica* (and thereby *forget* the events of *Galactica: 1980*). That plan experienced a bit of a hiccup as *Galactica: 1980* was given national exposure for the first time in 15 years, and fans could see again just how horrible it was.

Over the years, *Galactica: 1980* never disappeared all together, however. A compilation tape called *Conquest of the Earth*, which contains fragments of "*Galactica* Discovers Earth," "The Night the Cylons Landed" and "The Space Croppers," has been available from MCA/Universal since 1990. Before that, it was apparently syndicated with 12 other *Battlestar Galactica* "movies" (episode compilations). Unfortunately, *Conquest of the Earth* is a terrible production. It also intercuts moments from *Battlestar Galactica*'s "The Young Lords," and has voice-over dubs which explain what is happening in the so-called plot. Since there are two different actors playing Dr. Zee in *Conquest of the Earth*, Robbie Rist in "*Galactica* Discovers Earth" and Patrick Stuart in "The Night the Cylons Landed," Lorne Greene and other actors read voice-overs informing the audience that there are twin geniuses: Dr. Zee and Dr. Zen. (As if one of them was not bad enough by himself!) Another ludicrous addition to the edited-together episodes has Jamie Hamilton admitting her love for Dillon — again only in voice-over! This is a particularly vexing problem since actress Robyn Douglass apparently refused to lend her acting talents to this questionable purpose. So, in *Conquest of the Earth*, Jamie is voiced not only by Robyn Douglass, but by an unidentified actress with a terribly nasal, "New York"-style voice who sounds nothing like Douglass! It is another ignominious chapter for *Galactica: 1980*, but perhaps a fitting one for a show with as many problems as *Battlestar Galactica*'s best-forgotten spin-off.

Cast and Credits

CAST: Lorne Greene (Commander Adama); Kent McCord (Cpt. Troy); Barry Van Dyke (Lt. Dillon); Robyn Douglass (Jamie Hamilton); Herbert Jefferson, Jr. (Col. Boomer); Robbie Rist (Dr. Zee, Episode # 1); Patrick Stuart (Dr. Zee, Episodes #2–6); Alan Miller (Col. Sydell)

TECHNICAL CREDITS: *Created by:* Glen A. Larson. *Produced by:* Gary B. Winter, Jeff Freilich, Ben Kadish, Frank Lupo, David Zanetos.

Executive Producer: Glen A. Larson. *Supervising Producer:* David J. O'Connell. *Film Editors:* Jean-Jacques Berthelot, David Howe, John J. Dumas, Michael Berman, Bill Parker. *Directors of Photography:* Frank B. Beascoechea, Marco DiLeo, Ben Colman. *Unit Production Manager:* John Chulay. *Set Directors:* Morrie Hoffman, Jennifer Polito-Puma. *Based on Characters Created by* Glen A. Larson. *Adaptation:* Francesca Turner. *Story Editors:* Chris Bunch, Allan Cole, Robert Gilmer. *Sound:* James F. Rogers, Earl Crain, Jr. *Sound Effects Editor:* Sam Reynolds. *Music:* Stu Phillips. *"Galactica" Theme:* Glen Larson. *Music Editor:* Herbert Woods. *Casting:* Phillip Benjamin. *Costume Designer:* Jean-Pierre Dorleac. *Costume Supervisor:* Mark Peterson. *Special Optical Effects:* Universal Hartland. An MCA Universal Production

Episode Guide

1. "*Galactica* Discovers Earth"
(Parts I, II and III)
Airdates: January 27, 1980, February 3, 1980,
and February 10, 1980. Written by Glen A. Larson.
Directed by Sidney Hayers.

SYNOPSIS: After a journey of some 20 yahrens, the *Galactica* at last reaches the thirteenth colony, Earth. A bearded Adama still commands the battlestar, and an adult Boxey is the fleet's best warrior, Cpt. Troy. Also present is a young genius named Dr. Zee. On the evolutionary scale, this advisor to Adama is generations beyond the Colonials.

Dr. Zee summons Adama, Troy, Dillon and the fleet's greatest minds for a briefing about Earth. Zee has monitored Earth TV and deduced that Earthmen are too primitive to accept the Colonial convoy. Also, Cylons have pursued the *Galactica*, but remained outside scanner range to evade detection. Adama is thunderstruck: He has led the Cylons to the last refuge of man in the universe!

The *Galactica*'s new mission is to parlay with the greatest geniuses of Earth, including Professor Mortinson at the Pacific Institute of Technology, and bring the planet up to speed in a slow but productive manner. At least one Colonial council member, Xaviar, considers the mission a waste of valuable time. Using a Viper equipped with time warp capability, Xaviar disappears into Earth's history to introduce Colonial technology to Adolf Hitler and Nazi Germany. With the help of a reporter from UCB, Jamie Hamilton, Troy and Dillon attempt to prevent Xaviar's interference in Earth's history.

GUEST CAST: Fred Holliday (Mr. Brooks); Pamela Susan Shoop (Ms. Carlyle); Robert Reed (Professor Mortinson); Richard Lynch (Xaviar); Richard Eastham (Gen. Cushing); David Moses, Vernon Weddle, John Zenda (Policemen); Brion James, Mickey Jones (Bikers); Bruce Douglas, Duncan Mackenzie (F-15 Pilots); Eddie Firestone (Drunk Bum in Jail); Curt Lowens (Nazi Commandant); Eric Forst, Erik Holland, Tod Martin (Nazis); Sharon Acker (Mr. Brooks' Secretary)

COMMENTARY: Excited *Battlestar Galactica* fans tuned into the premiere of *Galactica: 1980* in late January 1980 only to discover that their favorite science fiction series had suffered a very unfortunate face lift — some might even say a lobotomy. In the eyes of the faithful, the new series already had one strike against it, since original series stars Dirk Benedict (Starbuck) and Richard Hatch (Apollo) had elected to bow out early when they concluded that *Galactica: 1980* was going to be a cheap ploy to re-use *Battlestar Galactica* special effects without exploring the interesting themes or family relationships of the original. Perhaps even more daunting to the audience than the absence of the two appealing lead actors was the fact that the new show seemed preoccupied totally with Earth — it was "grounded." The *Wagon Train* to the stars concept that served *Battlestar Galactica* well for 17 stories was missing in action, replaced by time travel clichés and "fish-out-of-water" humor. Gone too were the amazing space battles, the interesting aliens like Ovions and Borays, the sense of family and the quest concept. Despite these shortcomings, "*Galactica* Discovers Earth" is probably one of the two best-written episodes of *Galactica: 1980*, the other being "The Return of Starbuck." However, even that is not much of a compliment considering that even the best hour of *Galactica: 1980* is less satisfactory than the worst episode of *Battlestar Galactica*. It is simply that bad. Although this author always attempts to see good in a production that makes an effort, there are just too many negative features that bog down *Galactica: 1980*.

The special effects, for one thing, are terrible. Early in "*Galactica* Discovers Earth," Dr. Zee shows the warriors of the fleet a simulation of a Cylon attack on Los Angeles. People run through the streets, buildings collapse and Cylon raiders streak overhead. On the surface, it may all appear very impressive and very expensive. However, all of the incredible shots of the building collapses are lifted straight out of the 1976 Universal film *Earthquake* (which also starred Lorne Greene, ironically). In other words, the producers of *Galactica: 1980* have tried to make it appear as if they have spent a huge amount of money on this sequence, when in fact the special effects technicians have merely matted Cylon raiders over existing film footage! This sequence is disturbing not only because it attempts to fool viewers, but also because it sets a bad precedent. In the premiere episode of *V: The Series* in 1985, unmotivated special effects men pulled the same trick, this time matting Visitor spaceships over existing footage from the 1950s film *The War of the Worlds*!

Even more damningly, the Cylon mattes in the Los Angeles attack scene of "*Galactica* Discovers Earth" are atrocious. Black outlines (matte lines) are visible around the Cylon crafts at all times, scale fluctuates, and the black hooks used in the motion control process are clearly visible on the tails of the Cylon ships throughout the entire attack sequence. What little work the *Galactica: 1980* effects team did not steal from other, more impressive productions is lazy and poorly done. Adding insult to injury, the editing of the battle sequence is a disaster. At one point, a Cylon vessel swoops in on a large domed building (it resembles a big golf ball). There is an explosion and a huge hole is torn out of the dome. A few shots later, the dome is shown to be intact again, as if the audience cannot remember that the same building was just shown destroyed 30 seconds earlier! Also, when the battle cuts to interior shots of the Cylon ships, viewers can clearly see the blackness of space outside the cockpit window. Of course, this blackness does not fit the context of the miniature footage since the attack on Los Angeles is taking place during a bright, sunny afternoon! "*Galactica* Discovers Earth" seems to have been edited by people who had never watched a movie themselves.

Stock footage from *Battlestar Galactica* is also mercilessly reused in "*Galactica* Discovers Earth." When Troy and Dillon fly their Vipers into Earth's atmosphere for the first time, it is rerun footage from Starbuck and Boomer's suborbital approach in "Gun on Ice Planet Zero." This might not have been disturbing, since one cloud-filled sky looks much like any other cloud-filled sky, but the footage used in "*Galactica* Discovers Earth" includes the mountaintop Cylon base from "Gun on Ice Planet Zero." For a few seconds, the reflective glare of the Ravashol pulsar is clearly visible.

Since the United States has no such technology or mountaintop laser ranges, the inclusion of this particular stock footage is ridiculous. It reveals further sloppiness on the part of the editor. It is insulting to viewers that editors in both *Battlestar Galactica* and *Galactica: 1980* not only continually throw in repeat footage, they blend in contextually inappropriate repeat footage. They seemed to believe that the viewer's attention span is less than three seconds! This is a far cry from the much more careful use of special effects in *Star Trek* or *Space: 1999*, two of *Galactica: 1980*'s outer space predecessors.

When stock footage is not being used, the special effects of *Galactica: 1980* are just plain primitive. When Troy and Dillon fly away from the Los Angeles freeway on their motorcycles, fuzzy rear projection is utilized. In other words, Kent McCord and Barry Van Dyke were filmed in front of a screen, motionless, as the background footage (probably taken from a helicopter) mimics their flight. This might have been acceptable had the actors been buffeted by a "wind" effect, or had their motorcycles plotted slightly different trajectories. Instead, the two components of the scene (rear projection and live footage) do not mix at all. It is a botched, embarrassing effect immediately obvious to even the youngest *Galactica* fans.

The "*Galactica* Discovers Earth" teleplay was written in rather slapdash fashion as well. In his momentous opening journal entry, Adama declares that the space journey has taken many "years." Of course, the Colonials measure time *not* in years but in yahrens. This kind of mistake occurred frequently in the original series, but for it to occur in the first minute of the first episode of the new series is an indication that no one was really paying attention any more. The teleplay offers precious little in character development either. Dillon and Troy are, one supposes, likable enough, but they are carbon copies of Starbuck and Apollo, without any personal differentiation. Barry Van Dyke and Kent McCord are given nothing new, interesting or unique to work with. And the teleplay fails to answer viewer questions about the fates of Starbuck, Apollo, Tigh, Athena, Cassiopeia, Sheba, Muffey, Jolly, Baltar, Lucifer and the remainder of the original cast.

Time travel appears as a conceit for the first time in the world of *Battlestar Galactica* in "*Galactica* Discovers Earth." It is used in this story in a competent fashion, but the Nazi Germany section of the episode comes across as a *Voyagers'* episode or a *Time Tunnel* episode rather than something intrinsically important to the *Galactica* universe. "*Galactica* Discovers Earth" begs the question: If the *Galactica*ns have time travel and are willing to use it to alter Earth's history, why do they not instead employ the same technology to change their own history? Troy and Dillon could travel back to the time of the proposed armistice in "Saga of a Star World," and warn the fleet ahead of time of the Cylon deception. Even better, all of Blue Squadron could go back in time to the exact moment when the Cylon fighters massed near the old moon called Cimtar. They could blow away the attack force before it ever had a chance to attack the *Atlantia* or the fleet!

Significantly, time travel disappears completely from *Galactica: 1980* after this initial installment, as if the producers had not really intended to open up a whole can of worms with their time travel premise. It is probably just as well that it goes away because *Galactica: 1980* had enough trouble without resorting to time paradoxes every week. Still, the time travel incursions of extraterrestrial people or creatures called "Lucifer," "Cassiopeia," "Cain" or "Adama" would have gone a long way towards validating the Von Däniken presence of *Battlestar Galactica*. In fact, a great alternate premise for *Galactica: 1980* would have seen the Colonials, unable to settle on Earth of the present, send their people back through time — and thus the cast would actually become the legendary figures they share names with. Had Apollo survived, he could have fled to Ancient Greece with Athena only to be worshipped as a god there! Starbuck might have found himself later in man's history, as the first mate aboard a whaling ship, perhaps. Adama could have fled to the Dawn of Man with a female member of the Council of 12 named "Eve." It would have been the perfect "rounding out" of *Battlestar Galactica*'s continuing obsession with the heritage of man. Instead, *Galactica: 1980* dropped the "God is an astronaut" subtext completely, in favor of the "fish-out-of-water" humor so prevalent here.

That humor raises an interesting historical irony, however. As bad as *Galactica: 1980* is, it hit many of the same notes that *Star Trek IV: The Voyage Home* would later hit in 1986, albeit much less wittily or successfully. Still, one must give credit where credit is due. If one were to do a total accounting of similarities between "*Galactica* Discovers Earth" and *The Voyage Home*, one would find some intriguing, almost suspicious similarities. In both productions, advanced man arrives in the 20th century aboard a cloaked (invisible) vessel. In *Galactica: 1980* it is a Viper. In *The Voyage Home*, it is a captured Bird of Prey. In both productions, time travel is also involved (in *Galactica* to Nazi Germany, in *Star Trek* to 1986 San Francisco). In both productions, the "visitors" encounter and confound the military (in *Galactica* it is the Air-Force and their F-15 jets, in *Trek* it is the Navy and the aircraft carrier *Enterprise*). The further one delves into this line of investigation, the more interesting it becomes because there are so many similarities.

Consider also that in *Star Trek IV* and *Galactica: 1980*, the "alien" visitors befriend an assertive woman in the 20th century (Robyn Douglass in *Galactica: 1980*, Catherine Hicks in *The Voyage Home*). In both circumstances, that assertive woman is found to be enough of an asset that the "fish-out-of-water" visitors confide in her the true nature of their mission. And, in both circumstances, that woman is allowed to visit not only the futuristic spaceship, but to travel back to the alien civilization. In "*Galactica* Discovers Earth," Jamie Hamilton takes a Viper ride back to the *Galactica* and suits up in Colonial gear, while in *The Voyage Home*, Gillian Taylor returns to the future in the Bird of Prey, and suits up in the gear of a science ship she is assigned to!

In both productions, the futuristic main characters also misperceive how to operate 20th century technology. In *Galactica: 1980*, it is Cpt. Troy who begins speaking to a telephone ("How do you do?") without picking up a receiver. In *Star Trek IV*, Scotty picks up a computer mouse and uses it like a microphone ("Hello, computer!"). The two science fiction productions also share a "this is a primitive culture" mentality. In *Star Trek IV*, Cpt. Kirk asserts that Earth has a primitive and paranoid culture, and Dr. McCoy wonders how humanity ever survived this dark age. Six years earlier, Troy had asked Adama how the Earth could survive this dangerous time without an organization working for the common good! Furthermore, both *Star Trek IV* and "*Galactica* Discovers Earth" try to milk humor from our 20th century pollutants. In *Galactica: 1980*, Troy mistakes a smogbank over Los Angeles for an advanced force field, until Dr. Zee informs him it is just pollution. In *Star Trek IV*, Spock declares, "Judging by the pollution content of the atmosphere, I believe we have arrived in the latter half of the 20th century."

Lastly, the futuristic visitors of *Star Trek* and *Galactica: 1980* both make their presences known to the 20th century culture by providing advanced technology. In *Galactica: 1980*, Troy and Dillon provide a complex formula about nuclear degeneration to Professor Mortinson. In *The Voyage Home*, Scotty and Bones share the complicated formula for "transparent aluminum"! Frankly, just about every crucial plot detail of *Star Trek IV* mimics one found earlier in *Galactica: 1980*. Still, this is a prime example of "execution is everything." *Star Trek IV: The Voyage Home* is a charming, fun adventure filled with lively humor and interesting characters. *Galactica: 1980* is none of the above. The humor comes across as merely insipid when put in the hands and mouths of characters the audience has no real interest in. Maybe if Dirk Benedict and Richard Hatch had been allowed to play these scenes as Starbuck and Apollo, two characters the audience had become familiar with in the context of outer space, these scenes would have been greeted with outbursts of laughter. Without identifiable characters to sustain the cheeky humor, many *Galactica* fans were simply insulted that a grand story about the transgalactic exodus of man had been downplayed to the point where humor was a primary factor. Additionally, the show had so many motorcycle and car chase sequences that it came across like *CHiPs: 1999* or *Dukes of Hazzard: The Next Generation* rather than a legitimate heir to the outer space grandeur of the original *Battlestar Galactica*.

What explains the high humor quotient of *Galactica: 1980*? Robbie Rist (Dr. Zee) expressed his feelings about it with Karen E. Willson in a *Starlog* interview that ran in May 1980 (long after he had left the program):

> If you mix humor into science fiction, people feel more at ease. I don't think you could have a very good science-fiction show without mixing something that's light-hearted into it. That way the show becomes more human.[1]

While Rist was absolutely right in this appraisal, especially considering the importance of humor in *Star Trek*, the same style of humor did not play so well in the universe of *Galactica*, perhaps because the humor was generated by unfamiliar characters and actors, and as a whole was rather sophomoric ("The Super Scouts," "Spaceball").

"*Galactica* Discovers Earth" is a weak show from any sane critical standpoint, but besides its foreshadowing of the fourth *Star Trek* feature film, it does have a few nice touches. The best of these occur near the start of the show. As Adama dictates his notes into his journal, a photograph of Cpt. Apollo is seen briefly on his desk. Shortly thereafter, Dillon travels to meet with Boxey and passes several mechanical daggits, suggesting that Muffit was the prototype of a large number of daggit companions. Those are nice details that would have been even more welcome had the remainder of the show been as thoughtfully done.

If *Galactica: 1980* can be called prophetic for foreshadowing many of the riffs done in *Star Trek: IV*, it must also be acknowledged as a progenitor of the 1996 hit feature film *Independence Day*. In "*Galactica* Discovers

Earth," the Dr. Zee simulation details an extraterrestrial attack on the city of Los Angeles with disk-shaped alien fighters spitting twin laser blasts at everything that moves. *Independence Day* also features an extraterrestrial attack on Los Angeles with similarly disk-shaped alien vessels. The aliens in *Independence Day* also commit vicious strafing runs (but against Area 51 and another military base, not against pedestrians). Still, there is one moment in "*Galactica* Discovers Earth" that is truly evocative of *Independence Day*. In the sky, a group of small disk-like objects are seen in a swarm, high in the air. They move fluidly and independently, but they are so far away it is not easy to make out what they are. Of course, they are the Cylon raiders, coming down for the kill like a swarm of killer bees. There are several shots of the manta ray alien fighters in *Independence Day* that mirror this moment.

The first episode of *Galactica: 1980* is also significant for the number of genre actors and actresses it incorporates into one three-hour installment. Pamela Susan Shoop, Tangie in the "Vegas in Space" episode of *Buck Rogers* and a nurse in *Halloween II* (1981), shows up as Mortinson's secretary. Brion James, Leon the replicant of *Blade Runner* (1982), is a biker alongside Mickey Jones, a resistance fighter and friend to Ham Tyler in *V— The Final Battle* (1984). Sharon Acker, Odona in the *Star Trek* episode "Mark of Gideon," is also present as well. Even Robert Reed, father to the *Brady Bunch* and star of the grade-Z *Most Dangerous Game* riff *Bloodlust* (1961), joins the fun. Richard Lynch, who plays Xaviar, is familiar too. He appeared in the original *Battlestar Galactica* in "Gun on Ice Planet Zero," in "Vegas in Space" with Pamela Susan Shoop on *Buck Rogers*, in *Star Trek: The Next Generation* in "Gambit" and also as the evil cult leader in *Bad Dreams* (1987). Quite a motley crew, but every one of them has at least one interesting genre credit.

There is an interesting subtext to "*Galactica* Discovers Earth." A frustrated Xaviar travels back to Nazi Germany to share Colonial technology. His choice of cultures, a fascist one, is in keeping with *Battlestar Galactica*'s tone. Like the Colonial fleet, Nazi Germany is a military dictatorship under martial law. Xaviar has thus chosen the one culture in recent Earth history for which he apparently has an affinity. Also, he undoubtedly knows that a martial culture like Hitler's would make use of the advanced technology, rather than debate the morality of doing so. None of this text is voiced very eloquently in the story, but it is certainly implied.

It would be gratifying to report that the low quality of "*Galactica* Discovers Earth" was just an anomaly, but after this premiere it was all downhill.

2. "The Super Scouts"
(Parts I and II)
Airdates: March 16, 1980, and March 23, 1980.
Written by Glen A. Larson. Directed by: Vince Edwards.

SYNOPSIS: A Cylon attack bears down on the Gemonese freighter where the fleet's children are berthed. Troy and Dillon escape with the last of the Colonial youths just as the ship is destroyed. In the explosion, their shuttle is damaged and forced to land in Southern California. Pursued by Col. Sydell of the U.S. Air Force, Troy and Dillon disguise the children as terrestrial boy scouts. After drinking the water of a nearby lake, the children grow sick. Troy and Dillon confront John Stockton of Stockton Chemical Company, who has been dumping toxic chemicals nearby. Dr. Zee shows Stockton what will happen to California, and Stockton's family, should such pollution remain unchecked. Meanwhile, the children grow sicker and Sydell closes in.

GUEST CAST: Mick Brick, Jeff Cotler, Nicholas Davies, Ronnie Densford, Georgi Irene, David Larson, Eric Larson, Michelle Larson, Jerry Supirian, Eric Taslitz (Galactica Children/Super Scouts); George DeLoy (Dr. Spencer); Carlene Watkins (Nurse); John Quade (Sheriff); Michael Swan (Deputy); Michael Kellin (John Stockton)

COMMENTARY: The initial three-part broadcast of "*Galactica* Discovers Earth" was so successful in the ratings war that ABC immediately demanded the impossible of Glen Larson. They wanted *Galactica: 1980* on the air as a mid–season replacement by March — less than two months after the airing of the first episode! Perhaps Larson was crazy to say "yes" to this demand, or perhaps he just wanted to keep the *Battlestar Galactica* mythos alive. For whatever reason, he acquiesced and the rest, as they say, is history. Today *Galactica: 1980* is remembered by everybody associated with it, even Larson, as a frenzied mess shot at breakneck pace. To just about everyone, it represents a missed opportunity. "The Super Scouts," the first episode to air following "*Galactica* Discovers Earth," is indicative of the new series' faults. There is a typical TV subplot about pollution (as heavy-handed and preachy as anything one will find on an "ABC Afternoon Special") as well as a concentration on juvenile humor. And, rather than settling on interesting culture clash philosophies, the series opted instead to pursue the superhero paths of *The Six Million Dollar Man* and

The Gemini Man (1974) by endowing its main characters with superpowers (caused by the different gravity on Earth) and limited invisibility. What resulted in the case of "The Super Scouts," "Spaceball" and the rest was a distinctly childish show that any self-respecting ten-year-old would have been embarrassed to be caught watching.

Much time is wasted in "The Super Scouts" on the clichéd television character which this author calls "the hapless pursuer." This character probably originated on TV in the form of Barry Morse's (*Space: 1999, Tekwar*) Lt. Gerard in *The Fugitive* (1963–67), although that role may have been based on Javert in Victor Hugo's *Les Miserables*. Despite the literary origin, the hapless pursuer is perhaps the lamest and most useless of all TV characters. He is always the villain of the series, and therefore entitled only to a small piece of the action. Additionally, his success in catching the heroes would spell the end of the show, so the hapless pursuer inevitably fails to catch his prey. Thus he looks incompetent. The hapless pursuer has become, sadly, a common character in science fiction television. The hapless pursuer in *The Incredible Hulk* (1978–82) was reporter Jack McGee (Jack Colvin), a man determined to catch the Hulk at all costs. The pursuer in *The Immortal* (1970) was Fletcher (Don Knight), a man set on catching immortal Ben Richards at all costs. The pursuer in *The Phoenix* (1982) was Preminger (ironically Richard Lynch of *Galactica: 1980*) a man determined forever to capture Bennu of the Golden Light. Sadly, *Galactica: 1980*'s pursuer was the incompetent Col. Sydell, played by Alan Miller. Like all characters born of this desperate cliché, Sydell was always a day late and a dollar short when it came to catching those rascally Colonial Warriors. This ridiculous character is only one of the reasons why *Galactica: 1980* in general, and "The Super Scouts" in specific, fails.

The "message" about preserving the environment is delivered in "The Super Scouts" with all the subtlety of a sledgehammer blow. One of the things *Battlestar Galactica* never did was attempt to deliver touchy-feely moral messages to its audiences, but that policy was undone by the time of "The Super Scouts." Unbelievably, the villain of the piece here "turns" good when he sees the impact of the pollution on his family. It is a pat and unbelievable ending. If someone as rich and powerful as Stockton felt his family was threatened by their proximity to the pollutants, he might move his family away, and keep up the dirty practices. His change of heart is sickly-sweet and indigestible.

The "fish-out-of-water" humor that permeated "*Galactica* Discovers Earth" is back in the "Super Scouts" when cultural misunderstandings cause Dillon to rob a bank. It plays as stupid as it sounds, but evidently some people thought this material was funny, not insulting. Those were probably the same people who felt that a bunch of smart-mouth extraterrestrial kids (conveniently invisible) pelting dopey policemen with apples from treetops was also funny. There is no accounting for taste, but it is insulting that a series that had once been at least moderately adult (in the vein of *Little House on the Prairie* or *Star Trek*) had degenerated into camp humor and juvenile settings.

The superhero accoutrements do not help, either. Suddenly, the *Galacticans* and their offspring have superpowers due to the gravity on Earth. This means they are stronger than the average human, and able to leap tall buildings in a single bound. They can also, thanks to the technology engineered by Dr. Zee, become invisible for a limited amount of time. Essentially, these abilities and tricks make the Colonials invincible. There is never any feeling of tension in *Galactica: 1980* because the Earth forces, as represented by the incompetent Sydell and foolish police officers, are so outmatched. Even competent villains would have a difficult time with invisible, super-strong aliens, but the incompetent boobs trotted out by *Galactica: 1980* are hopelessly outclassed. Perhaps the feeling on the set of *Galactica: 1980* was that *The Six Million Dollar Man* had been a hit, so why not incorporate many of Steve Austin's abilities into the characters of Troy and Dillon? It was a mistake, however, because there is never any sense of danger or urgency in the plots. Troy and Dillon would have had to be lobotomized *not* to outmaneuver the Earthlings. One of the delights of *Battlestar Galactica* was that there was true tension in episodes such as "War of the Gods" and "The Hand of God." *Galactica: 1980* has none of that, and consequently plays as farce instead of drama or serious science fiction.

By "The Super Scouts," people on the *Galactica* set were all too aware of the problems. Ten years after *Galactica: 1980*'s cancellation, Kent McCord shared his feelings about the short-lived series in *Starlog* #162 with Marc Shapiro:

> ABC ... started demanding that we put kids in the show so that we could attract a young audience. I told anybody who would listen that we made *Adam 12* in a way that kids picked up on without having to do things to attract a kid audience. But the network wouldn't listen.... [B]y the time it got to the point where we saw alien kids playing baseball, that much of the show's original premise had been stolen from us.[2]

McCord's comments seem quite logical. The shift to a more juvenile approach is certainly what made *Galactica: 1980* seem so insipid at times. McCord, Lorne Greene, Robyn Douglass, Barry Van Dyke and even Patrick Stuart are competent performers giving their all for the show, but there was never any good material for them to work with. Adding to the sense of disappointment in "The Super Scouts" is the fact that the invisibility gimmick, used also for a jailbreak in "*Galactica* Discovers Earth," as well as the stolen police-car gimmick (also from the pilot), are both repeated here. The stock footage of the *Galactica* fleet and the space battle around the Gemonese freighter also add to the disappointing tenor of "The Super Scouts." Amazingly, this episode would not be the worst show in the series: The worst was yet to come.

3. "Spaceball"
Airdates: March 30, 1980.
Written by Jeff Freilich, Glen A. Larson
and Frank Lupo. Directed by Barry Crane.

SYNOPSIS: Troy and Dillon are called away on an assignment, so *Galactica*'s children on Earth are entrusted to Jamie Hamilton's care. She is sent to report on the baseball camp for underprivileged children run by Billy Ayres, a former professional pitcher now handicapped. Jamie takes the children to the camp, and admonishes them not to reveal their superpowers to the other children there. While Troy and Dillon attempt to repair their damaged Viper in outer space, Jamie must contend not only with Col. Sydell, but the villainous Xaviar, who has now taken the form of a Colonial Warrior called Nash.

GUEST CAST: Jeremy Brett (Xaviar/Lt. Nash); Paul Koslo (Billy Ayres); Bert Rosario (Hal); Fred Holliday (Brooks)

COMMENTARY: Just when viewers thought *Galactica: 1980* could not sink any further into the pit of lame plotting and poor story concepts, along comes "Spaceball"—a story that can only be accurately described as *Chariots of the Gods* meets *The Bad News Bears* (1976). Considering the weak premise (extraterrestrial kids win a baseball game and save a camp for underprivileged children from evil land developers), this is probably the very worst episode of *Galactica: 1980*. That is quite an achievement considering the general low quality of all ten hours of the short-lived production. Before "Spaceball," it would have been hard to imagine a more inconsequential, silly story than "The Super Scouts." Give the writers and producers credit: They not only conceived of a more inconsequential story, they executed it and foisted it on unsuspecting viewers! Like "The Super Scouts" before it, "Spaceball" is a wasted hour filled with preachy subplots, silly humor and bad special effects. Worst of all, the series again highlights the superpowered *Galactica* children as main characters instead of developing Troy, Dillon or Jamie Hamilton. "Spaceball" is an insult to the memory of the original *Battlestar Galactica*, a program that had its faults, no doubt, but at least a program that tried new things.

Little can be done with the hopeless premise of "Spaceball," so it is little wonder that the story fails. Much of the drama revolves around the children and their big game — a very minor issue considering the plight of the *Galactica* and her fleet in space! The remainder of the story is bogged down by another unwelcome appearance of the hapless pursuer, Col. Sydell, as well as the return of Xaviar. The only problem with this latter bit is that Richard Lynch opted (wisely) not to return in the part, causing Xaviar to miraculously change form!

The deathblow to "Spaceball" comes not in the ballpark, however, but in the realm where *Galactica: 1980* should have demonstrated at least some basic competence: outer space. One plot strand sees Troy and Dillon trapped in space in their sabotaged Viper. When all other repair attempts have failed, they leave their craft to fix the engine manually, but they do so *without* donning pressure suits. In nothing but regular warrior fatigues and fishbowl helmets, the men hightail it into the airless void. There is no explanation why their uniforms apparently double as pressure suits, and the series proves it knows less about outer space than the masochistic five-year-olds who were still watching the series.

Besides the pressure suit debacle, the special effects in "Spaceball" are badly done. When Troy and Dillon's Viper grinds to a halt in space, the editor does not cut to a shot of a Viper hovering believably in space. Instead, the editor freezes one frame of stock footage so that a shot of a Viper is literally "frozen" in space, as are all of the stars surrounding it. This "freezing" of the film is a cheap, obvious solution. Instead of filming a new special effects shot, the series opted again to be cheap and steal existing footage of a ship in flight from *Battlestar Galactica*. Then they froze the image and hoped no one in the audience would notice that the "special effect" was simply rerun footage on "pause" mode.

Despite these flaws, the real problem with "Spaceball" is its paucity of ideas. This is a series that can go anywhere in space and (thanks to

"*Galactica* Discovers Earth") anywhere in time as well. Instead of exploring the universe, or Earth history, or even the clash of two alien cultures on Earth, the series opts to rehash *The Bad News Bears* but with "bionic" kids! *Galactica: 1980*'s contempt for science fiction fans is so brazen and so overriding in "Spaceball" that it contaminates everything else in the show, even the sincere efforts of Greene, McCord, Van Dyke and Douglass to do something of quality. The cheapness of the whole affair is so astounding that it actually distracts from what little drama there is on the screen.

4. "The Night the Cylons Landed"
(Part I and II)
Airdates: April 13, 1980, and April 20, 1980.
Written by Glen A. Larson.
Directed by Sigmund Neufeld, Jr.

SYNOPSIS: A Cylon craft much larger than the ordinary raider carries a crew of five, including two humanoid androids. The Cylons have modified themselves once more, and can now mimic human form. When its lasers prove useless, Colonial Viper Probe Delta rams the ship, and the Cylon vessel careens into Earth's atmosphere. A centurion and an android, Andromus, survive the crash. They are soon stopped by Halloween partygoers, and invited to attend a costume party! At the party, Andromus enlists the help of a deejay named Wolfman Jack to take over a nearby radio station and send a homing beacon straight to the Cylon empire.

After facing many difficulties, including a hijacked airliner, a car chase, an appearance in an ABC stage revue, muggers and an out-of-control fire, Dillon and Troy confront the Cylons on the radio station rooftop. But have they arrived too late?

GUEST CAST: Roger Davis (Andromus); Rex Cutter (Century); William Daniels (Norman); Lara Parker (Shirley); Mark Richman (Col. Brigs); Marj Dusay (Mildred); Sheila DeWindt (Stewardess); Wolfman Jack (Himself); Val Bisoglio (Arnie); Paul Tuerpe (Fireman); Dan Ferrone (Policeman); Cosie Costa, Tony Miratti, Alexander Petala, Louis Sardo (Muggers); Jed Mills, Arthur Batanides (Cab Drivers)

COMMENTARY: "The Night the Cylons Landed" temporarily returns *Galactica: 1980* to moderately solid ground, even if it remains determinedly uninspired and unmemorable television. Though far below any episode of *Battlestar Galactica* in its quality, the episode nonetheless shines when compared with either "The Super Scouts" or "Spaceball," two of the worst hours of science fiction television in history.

"The Night the Cylons Landed" deserves at least some (minimal) praise because writer Glen Larson opted at least to examine some "larger" issues in the Colonial universe. The story wastes no time on the "babysitting" of superheroic children, and instead brings the Cylons back as a powerful enemy. For the first time since "*Galactica* Discovers Earth," there is new spaceship footage, and even a new miniature as well. The new Cylon craft is faithful to Cylon construction designs and precepts (it is a larger version of the disk-like Cylon raider but with sharper angles and a pulsating orange glow across the front section of its manta ray curves). Also, "The Night the Cylons Landed" reveals that the Cylons have developed humanoid androids such as Andromus — creatures indistinguishable from humans themselves. Some fans may questions why the Cylons, a race determined to destroy humans at all costs, would resort to mimicking humans, but within the universe of *Battlestar Galactica* it is a logical development. In "Saga of a Star World," Apollo told Boxey on Carillon that the Cylon centurions are humanoid in appearance because they found humans to be the most practical form of life in the solar system. Cylon androids who appear human are a logical extension of that philosophy. Since Cylons are first and foremost a technological race, they could improve and develop themselves in any way they see fit. The androids seen in "The Night the Cylons Landed" seem to mix the intelligence of the IL series Cylons (like Lucifer) with the physical adaptability of the Cylon centurions. Of course, it is a dramatic necessity that Andromus "blend" with humans in this story, since he will find himself amongst Earth humans throughout, but it is nonetheless refreshing that series creator Larson remembered *Battlestar Galactica* history and extended the limits of Cylon technology. After all, it has been over 14 yahrens since the events of *Battlestar Galactica*. It is logical that over time the Cylons would develop new vessels and new android designs. They have conquered most of the galaxy, and can therefore turn their attention to refining their technology. The Colonials, having lost the war, have turned all their attention inwards: towards survival, maintenance and the feeding of their people. The Cylons would thus develop more easily than the Colonials.

The return of the Cylons is a welcome plot development, as is Larson's return to the "mission" premise of *Battlestar Galactica* and *Galactica: 1980*.

141

"The Super Scouts" and "Spaceball" lost their way by obsessing over a small matter (*Galactica*n children). "The Night the Cylons Landed" is a return to the "big" picture, with a very important mission for Troy and Dillon. If they fail to stop the Cylons, the two evil creatures will make the Imperious Leader aware of Earth's location. The survival of the Earth and the fleet hang in the balance, and so the story has a measure of urgency that was missing from the last two ventures.

Still, these positive aspects in no way make "The Night the Cylons Landed" good television, good science fiction or even good *Galactica*. Once again, there is an unfortunate preoccupation with car chases. Troy and Dillon spend much of the two-hour running time evading police and again stealing police cars. The repetitive space battles of *Battlestar Galactica* have been supplanted by the repetitive car chases of *Galactica: 1980*. Since the human police are at a distinct disadvantage (no invisibility, no super powers), the chases are rather uninteresting and unimportant in the scheme of things. Humor is also highlighted, but it is the same kind of dopey "fish-out-of-water" humor that sunk "*Galactica* Discovers Earth." Here Troy and Dillon end up in tuxedos and on a stage with the likes of other ABC "stars" such as Scooby-Doo. It is an embarrassing interlude, and it undercuts the immediacy of the Cylon threat. Troy and Dillon also must do such mundane things as face down muggers, rescue an airplane from hijackers, swim across a lake, outsmart state troopers and put out a fire, again deflecting from the central threat of the story. At one hour, this episode could very well have been the best episode of *Galactica: 1980* (again, not much of a compliment), but at two hours it is hopelessly padded.

Larson's teleplay also relies uncomfortably on coincidence. There happens to be a "missing" Colonial Viper for a time, preventing the *Galactica*ns from reaching the Cylon threat when the AB craft is mistaken for the recon ship. This is silly. Wouldn't the *Galactica* constantly monitor Earth orbit for Cylon intrusions? Wouldn't they have some ships stationed relatively close by, in case a Cylon ship arrived? Furthermore, with the capability to jump to light drive, and the fleet well-hidden beyond Earth, why couldn't the *Galactica* swing around Earth orbit at close to light speed, identify the "mysterious" craft and then jump (again at light speed) away from the planet before being identified by our "primitive" sensing equipment? It is hard to believe that a non-functional Cylon craft could evade the advanced net of Colonial Vipers and sensors that must surely be in effect around Earth.

An even greater coincidence is that Andromus and "Century" the Centurion should survive a crash, wander onto a highway and get into a car which just happens to be driven by the owner of a radio station — the very object of the Cylon quest. Talk about good luck! With a huge length of road and hundreds of cars traversing it, it is a colossal stretch of the imagination that two aliens seeking a radio station should end up in the car of a radio station owner, and then be mistaken as "Halloweeners." It is also a wild coincidence that the Cylons should land in America on Halloween — the one night out of the year when they might be mistaken as something other than extraterrestrials. All of these coincidences are a result of bad writing and a dearth of imagination.

Like "*Galactica* Discovers Earth," "The Night the Cylons Landed" is notable mostly for the number of genre "names" it employs as guest stars. Lara Parker plays Shirley, the chick in the Elvira get-up who meets Andromus and Century. She is a graduate of the Dan Curtis series *Dark Shadows*, and she also appeared as Madelaine in "The Trevi Collection," a 1975 episode of *Kolchak: The Night Stalker*. A second familiar face is William Daniels, Shirley's husband in "The Night the Cylons Landed." He is famous not only for non-genre credits such as the film *The Graduate* (1967) and the TV series *St. Elsewhere* (1985–89) but also for supplying the voice of K.I.T.T. in the Glen Larson series *Knight Rider*. A cabbie is also seen briefly in this story, and he too is a familiar face. Arthur Batanides not only appeared in the Universal film *The Leech Woman* (1960) but also as Lt. D'Amato in the *Star Trek* episode "That Which Survives." Marj Dusay, the lead "eyemorg" in "Spock's Brain" and an android in *The Fantastic Journey* episode "Beyond the Mountain," also appears briefly.

Finally, Col. Sydell's replacement as "the pursuer" is played by Mark Richman, a 25-year veteran in the science fiction genre. He was the star of the 1961 series *Cain's Hundred*, as well as the secret agent in the James Bond knock-off *Agent for H.A.R.M.* (1965). Richman met the crew of the Enterprise-D as an irritating yuppie from the 21st century in the *Next Generation* first season finale "The Neutral Zone." He also met an uncomfortable death at the hands of Jason Voorhees in the 1989 feature *Friday the 13th Part VIII: Jason Takes Manhattan*. Rex Cutter, the man in the Cylon suit, would return to play "Cy" in "The Return of Starbuck." He has the honor of playing both of the Cylon Centurions in *Galactica: 1980* given nicknames by humans. In the non-genre category, guest star Wolfman Jack plays himself.

5. "The Space Croppers"
Airdate: April 27, 1980.
Written by Robert McCullough.
Directed by Daniel Haller.

SYNOPSIS: At the movies, Troy, Dillon and the children watch the sci-fi film *This Island Earth* until signalled by the fleet. It is under attack, and the relentless Cylons have destroyed the agroships. Facing a critical food shortage, Troy and Dillon set out to create a *Galactica*n agro colony at the farm of friendly Earthman Hector Alonzo and his family. When the Alonzos are persecuted by a racist land baron, John Steadman, Dillon and Troy must use every advantage they have to plant the crop that can save the fleet.

GUEST CAST: Ana Alicia (Gloria Alonzo); Ned Romero (Hector Alonzo); Anna Navarro (Louise Alonzo); Joaquim Gray (Chris Alonzo); Booth Colman (Rogers); Dana Elcar (John Steadman); Amy Jarrell (Maze); Philip Levine (Dante)

COMMENTARY: "The Space Croppers" is another *Galactica: 1980* story that is preoccupied with events on Earth and manages to neglect, for the most part, adventure in space. Although it is a battle in space and an encounter with the Imperious Leader (both represented by stock footage from *Battlestar Galactica*) which propels the events of this story, most of the drama concerns an immigrant family and its attempts to stave off the prejudice of another farmer. It is not science fiction, it is melodrama. "The Space Croppers" thus fits perfectly into a rule that this author has developed about science fiction television series: No sci-fi TV series can survive for more than a single season if it is only "part" science fiction and "part" something else.

Something Is Out There and *Alien Nation* were as much cop drama as science fiction, and they folded within one season. *V* was as much soap opera as it was science fiction, and it too died after a year. *Starman, Logan's Run, The Immortal* and *The Phoenix* were all chase shows inspired by *The Fugitive*, not serious science fiction, and they perished after their freshman outings as well. Why, one wonders, do producers insist on breeding science fiction with other TV forms and genres and creating such unholy hybrids? Perhaps producers believe that science fiction concepts will go over better with viewers if there is also a comfortable element of the show (cops, soaps, chases). Indeed, this attitude seems to mesh with Glen Larson's stated intent to make *Battlestar Galactica* a mainstream show with science fiction overtones. Nonetheless, *Galactica: 1980* was seen as a betrayal by most fans because from week to week it was more sitcom ("Spaceball"), chase show ("The Super Scouts") and police car chase drama ("*Galactica* Discovers Earth," "The Nights the Cylons Landed") than science fiction. The only episode of *Galactica: 1980* that is remembered today with any fondness is "The Return of Starbuck." Not coincidentally, that is also the only episode of the series to take place on a planet other than Earth, and thus in a pure "genre" setting. Science fiction fans want science fiction when they watch genre television — they do not want half-baked hybrids of other TV forms.

"The Space Croppers" is as unsatisfying as "The Super Scouts" or "Spaceball" because the same clichés and solutions are trotted out. The *Galactica*ns might be discovered by an evil land magnate and the cops? Oh, well, invisibility worked in "*Galactica* Discovers Earth" and "The Super Scouts," so it works again in "The Space Croppers." *Galactica*n "super" abilities saved the day in "Spaceball" and "The Night the Cylons Landed," so they do the same here (with Dillon conquering a mentally unstable horse, of all things). Therefore, the episode is incredibly predictable. Adding to the déjà vu, it is a disaster in space that precipitates the events of "The Space Croppers." Disasters in space (Cylon attacks or Cylon incursions) also precipitated "The Super Scouts" and "The Night the Cylons Landed." "The Space Croppers" is the fifth episode of *Galactica: 1980*, but it is a retread of the same tired, bad ideas already seen earlier in the young series.

Galactica: 1980 is a flawed series and "The Space Croppers" is certainly indicative of all of its flaws. The leads are as dull and square as can be, not to mention derivative of Apollo and Starbuck, and the villains are uninteresting because they are at a disadvantage. There is simply no fun in seeing Earth people constantly dumbfounded by the abilities of beings from another world. These men and women have faster-than-light drive, spaceships, laser guns, and advanced "computrons." On Earth, they have many of the same powers as Superman (increased strength and agility), not to mention invisibility. The series could never succeed because the Colonials had no worthy villains. There was never a real sense that this was a life-and-death assignment for Troy and Dillon.

As is the case in all episodes of *Galactica: 1980*, the most interesting element of "The Space Croppers" is the genre cast. Dana Elcar would later become Richard Dean Anderson's boss in *MacGyver*. Ana Alicia had already appeared in *Battlestar Galactica* as Starbuck's long-lost love Aurora in "Take the *Celestra*." She also played a kidnap victim in "Vegas in Space," a first season episode of *Buck Rogers*. The sheriff in "The Space Croppers" is none other than Kenneth Tobey, the star of the Howard Hawks/Christian Nyby classic film *The Thing from Another World* (1951).

There is one joke that works very well in "The Space Croppers." At the opening of the show, Troy and Dillon are in a movie theater with the "super children." They are watching the Universal picture *This Island Earth*. When one of the children sees the Metalunan mutant, he comments that it looks just like one of the "Gerkkons." It is a silly joke, but the pleasures of *Galactica: 1980* are so few and far between that this moment of mild wit seems like a revelation. "The Space Croppers" was not the last instance in which *This Island Earth* took some good-natured ribbing. It was also the source for humor in *Mystery Science Theater 3000: The Movie* (1996). In fact, *MST3K* has a bit of a link with the *Battlestar Galactica* universe. While watching the film *Laserblast* (1978), Mike and his bots added this riff when the hero of that film (Kim Milford) found a neat alien laser gun: "Wow! And to think, I was depressed when *Battlestar Galactica* was cancelled!" In 1997, Mike, Crow and Servo watched *Space Mutiny*, a forgettable space opera that used more than ten minutes of *Battlestar Galactica* space battle footage! How this theft got past Universal is a mystery.

"The Space Croppers" is not only an episode of *Galactica: 1980*. It shares that title with an episode of the insipid Irwin Allen series *Lost in Space*. *Space*'s version concerned Dr. Smith's marriage to a space cropper named Sybilla, who grows man-eating plants. As a whole, even that *Lost in Space* episode is more entertaining than this hour of *Galactica: 1980*.

6. "The Return of Starbuck"
Airdate: May 4, 1980.
Written by Glen A. Larson.
Directed by Ron Satloff.

SYNOPSIS: Dr. Zee recounts a strange dream to Commander Adama. It involves the last fight of a great Colonial Warrior named Starbuck, who was shot down from the stars and forced to endure isolation on a barren planet. Accompanied by a Cylon Centurion re-programmed to be amicable, Starbuck encountered a strange pregnant woman named Angela. While Starbuck toiled to construct a life-pod that could send the mother and child to the *Galactica*, the relentless Cylons closed in on Starbuck's makeshift family.

GUEST CAST: Dirk Benedict (Lt. Starbuck); Judith Chapman (Angela); Rex Cutter (Cy the Cylon); Gary Owens (Voice of Cy the Cylon); Ellen Lurkin (*Galactica* Bridge Officer)

COMMENTARY: Perhaps it is the presence of the delightful Dirk Benedict that makes "The Return of Starbuck" so enjoyable. Perhaps it is the return of the Cylons and the development of the centurion "Cy" that is responsible for the general feeling of euphoria. Or maybe it is the presentation of a story which takes place shortly after the end of the original *Battlestar Galactica* (and leaves behind the insipid Dillon and Troy) that gives one the impression that this episode of the series is light-years ahead of all other *Galactica: 1980* fare in terms of quality. Perhaps the story works because it continues the "angels" theme presented in stories such as "War of the Gods" and "Experiment in Terra." For whatever the reason, fans at last had cause to rejoice: "The Return of Starbuck" was a fun, thoughtful hour that recalls the "guilty pleasure" feelings and magic aura of Larson's first space epic.

It is somewhat amazing that "The Return of Starbuck" is as dense a story as it is. Thematic complexity is not one of *Galactica: 1980*'s strong suits, as "The Super Scouts," "Spaceball" and "The Space Croppers" reveal. Nevertheless, "The Return of Starbuck" is a beautifully done tribute to the original series. Firstly, the Boomer and Starbuck friendship is immediately re-established thanks to good dialogue and good acting between Benedict and Jefferson. Secondly, Adama is once more established as a commanding military figure (rather than the flunky of the irritating Dr. Zee). Lorne Greene, sans beard, gives one of his most moving and intense appearances as Adama. In his last scene, he declares that he love Starbuck like a son, and it is a powerful moment. The reason all of this works is that the characters of Starbuck, Boomer and Adama are so much more complex and interesting than Jamie, Troy, Dillon, Sydell, Xaviar or Dr. Zee. Viewers lived with these characters for an entire season, and through well-written adventures such as "The Living Legend" and "The Hand of God." The attachment was forged, and the viewer is reminded of that emotional attachment here. Other reminders, such as references to Cassiopeia and Athena, are also sprinkled throughout the teleplay. It is good, solid work that evokes the pleasant memory of a sentimental and sometimes powerful television series.

Best of all, character-wise, is the fact that Starbuck actually grows in this episode. He goes from being a cocky, self-assured hedonist to a lonely, isolated man. Then he experiences joy and love, and develops to the point where he is capable of self-sacrifice. There is a distinct character arc here, one that has been missing from *Galactica: 1980* all along. Damningly, Troy and Dillon never seem to change — they are as ignorant of Earth customs and as two-dimensional in "The Space Croppers" as they were in "*Galactica* Discovers Earth." Fortunately, Dirk Benedict is up to the challenge of playing Starbuck again, and he brings new layers of complexity to the part. In this story, Starbuck must not only face the possibility of fatherhood and permanent loneliness, but also the realization that he has lived a life of "meaningless" selfishness. By saving Angela and her child, Starbuck is redeemed. At one point, Angela even asks him, "Haven't you devoted enough of your life and resources to yourself?" It is a powerful moment, and as a story of redemption, "The Return of Starbuck" is unmatched in the *Galactica* canon.

Beyond the characterizations, "The Return of Starbuck" delves into new thematic terrain for *Battlestar Galactica* and *Galactica: 1980*. Neither the original series nor its offspring ever truly examined the Cylon nature. "The Return of Starbuck" reveals that Cylons are apparently able to adapt to new circumstances, as well as express sarcasm and pride. Though Lucifer expressed jealousy in "The Young Lords," it seemed out of his purview to express sympathy for humans, and he left Baltar to die at the conclusion of "The Lost Planet of the Gods." If "The Return of Starbuck" is a tale of redemption, then it is also the redemption of Cy the Cylon. In his last act, Cy sacrifices his life to save Starbuck and the *ad hoc* family he has grown to love. He is no longer a chrome tin can, but a feeling, emotional organism. This kind of depth in a Cylon is most unexpected. *Battlestar Galactica* usually treated centurions as faceless goons who existed only to be shot down by the heroes.

What is not so rewarding in "The Return of Starbuck" is that the Cy/Starbuck relationship is in some senses a regurgitation of the relationship delineated in *The Defiant Ones* (1958). It is a time-worn science fiction cliché to have two enemies crashland on a planet together, and then work out their differences and become friends. This story was the subject of the *U.F.O.* episode "Survival" in 1970. It was also the subject of director Wolfgang Peterson's 1985 film *Enemy Mine*. The plot of *Enemy Mine* was rehashed in thoroughly unimaginative fashion in the wildly overpraised yet completely uninventive *Star Trek: The Next Generation* third season story "The Enemy." It is an old story, but at least *Galactica: 1980* remembered with "The Return of Starbuck" that it could tell stories, even clichéd stories, about subjects other than prepubescent alien kids with super powers.

"The Return of Starbuck" features other interesting layers, beyond the completion of the Starbuck character arc and the development of the Cylons beyond two-dimensional villains. Angela is revealed to be a member of the angel race encountered in *Battlestar Galactica* episodes such as "War of the Gods" and "Experiment in Terra." Like Iblis, Angela is apparently a renegade. She is not an evil one, though. Beyond the fact that it is nice that *Galactica: 1980* remembers those old episodes of *Battlestar*, "The Return of Starbuck" finally gives a believable explanation for Dr. Zee. He is Angela's child and a member of that super race. After ten hours, background about an important *Galactica: 1980* character is finally divulged. If "The Return of Starbuck" had aired immediately after "*Galactica* Discovers Earth," the series would perhaps have looked very different. There would not have been so many unanswered questions, nor the perceived contempt for the regular *Battlestar Galactica* audience.

"The Return of Starbuck" is the best episode of *Galactica: 1980* because it has the daring to do something different. There are no car chases, no escapes from the police, no nosy reporters and no silly humor. The story breaks some new moral ground and recounts the fate of a beloved *Battlestar Galactica* character. Of course, the relatively high quality of "The Return of Starbuck" raises a number of difficult issues for fans of *Battlestar Galactica*. Most episodes of *Galactica: 1980* are so bad that it is a pleasure to dismiss them. Even Glen Larson has dismissed them. However, Dirk Benedict's performance in this episode is worth remembering. If fans trash all of *Galactica: 1980,* then they also trash this well-done story, and "negate" the power of Benedict's performance, as well as the character arc that takes Starbuck to new maturity. This is something of a dilemma. It is too bad that there is no way to fit the events of "The Return of Starbuck" into the context of the original series. It is too good a story to lose forever. Besides, it is dangerous when fans and producers begin to declare that one series is "canon" and another is "not." This has even happened in *Star Trek*. Before his death, Gene Roddenberry claimed that some characters and events in *Star Trek V: The Final Frontier* and

Star Trek VI: The Undiscovered Country were apocryphal. Thus some fans have negated the existence of these films. To this author that is unacceptable. Those films were produced, and they were put up on a screen for millions to see. They are as official as anything Roddenberry himself ever wrote. It is too convenient merely to wave a wand and insist that an unsuccessful story is "not" canon. In the case of *Battlestar Galactica*, however, the issue is a much more difficult one. Fans and Larson want to erase not just an episode or two, they want to erase the entire *Galactica: 1980* series, even though there are millions of people in this country who (reluctantly) remember it. How will a revival get around this sequel series? Did it exist in an alternate universe? Was it, as Larson insists, Starbuck's nightmare? It will be interesting to see how this issue of canon is finally settled in the *Galactica* universe.

Judith Chapman, who portrays Angela as a sort of ethereal otherworldly woman of incredible wisdom, was a regular on *General Hospital* during the 1980s. She is familiar to science fiction fans for her role as defector Lara in the "Olympiad" episode of *Buck Rogers in the 25th Century*.

With "The Return of Starbuck," *Galactica: 1980* ends on a relative high note. It is a strange conclusion to the series, however, since it does not feature series stars McCord, Van Dyke or Douglass. "The Return of Starbuck" proves that Larson was still capable of recapturing the magic, inexplicable spell of *Battlestar Galactica*, but one has to wonder why the other episodes of the series were so lacking. Even *Galactica: 1980*'s brother on the schedule, *Buck Rogers*, managed to produce some interesting stories in the science fiction arena without resorting to superpowered children and gimmicks such as invisibility and car chases. The question remains unanswered to this day: Why was *Galactica: 1980* such a disaster in conception and execution? It is tempting to blame the networks for rushing production of the series and scheduling it too early on Sunday evenings, but little can explain the series' dependence on comic book heroics, cardboard characters and stock footage. *Galactica: 1980* is perhaps the most vapid of all outer space series. It has nothing to say about space, no opinion about the universe and no philosophy of life. It is a good thing that it only survived six episodes. Had it lasted any longer, it might have actually further damaged *Battlestar Galactica*'s already questionable credibility with genre fanatics. As it stands now, *Battlestar Galactica* is remembered today for its first incarnation, not for its mutated, ill-conceived offspring.

PART IV

Morality and Mythology

Moses and the Military:
Morality in Battlestar Galactica

Since the early 1950s, science fiction TV has frequently espoused the most liberal ideals about the cosmos and life on Earth in general. This teleology, this unique approach to the universe, has for the most part been one of tolerance, acceptance and peace, perhaps because so many programs originated in a predominantly left-wing Hollywood. *Star Trek's Enterprise* was equipped with powerful offensive phaser banks, and gunboat diplomacy was a common story thread ("The Apple," "The Return of the Archons," "Spock's Brain"), but the starship also featured for the first time in television history a racially diverse crew. Even more significantly, it highlighted a humanist bent that exposed the evils of war ("A Taste of Armageddon"), racial bigotry ("Let That Be Your Last Battlefield") and traditional religious dogma ("The Mark of Gideon" was a debate about Catholicism and the restriction of birth control techniques). Interspecies tolerance was the order of the day, and quite popular was the *Star Trek* philosophy of IDIC: Infinite Diversity, Infinite Combinations.

Star Trek: The Next Generation was even more liberal in its approach to storytelling. Old enemies like the Klingons had been accepted into the Federation peaceably, and the handicapped or "physically challenged" had joined Starfleet in the form of the blind Geordi LaForge (Levar Burton). The philosophy was "We are the world" in space, not "We are the U.S." in space. "Nationalism" was derided as adolescent strutting nonsense in *The Next Generation* ("Encounter at Farpoint"); the enslavement of any being, even animals for food, was attacked ("Lonely Among Us"). *The Next Generation* basically posited a quasi-communist world in which there

151

was no such thing as money, and mankind was obsessed not with the accumulation of wealth but with bettering both himself and the species ("The Neutral Zone"). This delightfully subversive, far-left philosophy has been embraced by fans in the United States with surprising vigor. Apparently, political communism in a future of holodecks, replicators, universal health care coverage and warp drives sounds like a good thing to many Americans who equate 20th century big business not with humanity, but with the likes of the money-grubbing Ferengi, the ultimate space capitalists.

Outside of *Star Trek*, other space shows have been equally liberal. In *Space: 1999*, everyone on Moonbase Alpha lived in a kind of space commune with equal rights and equal respect. There was a commander only by necessity, a commander who stated in "Alpha Child" that "Ignorance is no reason to start shooting" and in "The Metamorph" that "We are all aliens until we get to know one another" — common liberal ideals of acceptance and tolerance. *Space: 1999* is also significant because it was the first show to have a "sexually" integrated cast. For the first time, women played roles as important as the men's. The chief medical officer (Helena Russell), the chief science officer (Maya) and the chief data analyst (Sandra Benes) of Moonbase Alpha were all competent women who even occasionally led missions ("The Last Sunset")! And since the Alphans were basically defenseless, they could not afford to take self-righteous moral stances about otherworldly societies. They just wanted to survive.

Blake's 7 and *V* both concerned left-wing revolutionaries attempting to end the reign of oppressive, fascist governments. *Doctor Who* was about an anti-establishment renegade who believed that all life forms have the right to self-determination, and *Alien Nation* and *Planet of the Apes* focused on the day-to-day reality of a social underclass in the United States. Each program supported the need for diversity and integration. Even *The Prisoner* was leftist in a way, as it was a diatribe against the overreaching, ever-watching eye of the political and military-industrial complex.

Amazingly, *Battlestar Galactica* does not at all follow the proud liberal traditions of science fiction television history. It is not concerned with tolerance, diversity, integration or cosmic friendship. It is a series about a WASP civilization (the Colonials) preserving its culture and its religion at all costs. It is no surprise then that many 1990s Republicans have flocked to the series. There is a site on the Internet called *Battlestar Republica*: a homepage devoted to all things GOP, and all things *Galactica*. In its hawkish "strength through superior firepower" philosophy, *Battlestar Galactica* most closely resembles Gerry and Sylvia Anderson's

U.F.O., which also set the universe very much into "us" versus "them" dimensions.

It is important to note that the Colonial civilization seen in *Battlestar Galactica* evolved from a mother race over a period of seven millennia, all before the beginning of the series. That mother race represents the religious foundation of the society. Throughout the series, comfort and wisdom come not from the honest expression and communication of emotions, beliefs and ideals to one another, but from the revered tenets of this age-old, traditional religion. The Colonials are thus an unrepentant spiritual, religious culture. Religion is *all* to these people. In fact, there is no separation of church and state in the *Battlestar Galactica* universe, even though such separation is the very principle upon which the United States (the culture reflected in *Battlestar Galactica*) is based.

Importantly, Commander Adama is not merely the military and familial leader of *Battlestar Galactica,* he is the spiritual leader as well. Instead of sound strategy or the advice of his underlings, he invariably uses his religious beliefs as a guide to important decision-making. This would be roughly like Jerry Falwell or Pat Robertson commanding the U.S.S. *Nimitz* in modern America. In his role as commander of the fleet, a seemingly secular post, Adama authorizes the fleet to enter a magnetic void in "The Lost Planet of the Gods." Why? Importantly, he makes this decision based not on desperation, strategy or advice but on cryptic clues presented in ancient religious scripture. Also, the very destination of the *Galactica,* the mythical planet Earth, is from the equivalent of the Colonial Bible called "The Book of the Word." Thus, it is not science that motivates *Battlestar Galactica,* nor the belief in humanity, but a strict interpretation of religious texts that fuels this cosmic journey. Obviously, religion is the ultimate wisdom in *Battlestar Galactica,* and it permeates every factor in Colonial life.

The importance of religion in *Battlestar Galactica* is a strong contrast to religion's role in the *Star Trek* universe. In *Star Trek: The Next Generation*, religion is frequently equated with superstition. Picard refuses to send the Mintakans of "Who Watches the Watchers" back to the dark ages of "superstition and religion" when they begin to worship him as a God figure. He would rather reveal the presence of extraterrestrials to the culture than allow it be negatively impacted by the religion-spurred hatreds (which Picard lines up quite nicely for viewers: crusades, holy wars, witch trials and inquisitions). To the men and women of Starfleet, religion is representative only of a weak, primitive and conflicted mind.

The same is also true in *Deep Space Nine*. In "In the Hands of the Prophets" and other stories, the Bajoran religion is considered quaint and charming, not believable, helpful or genuine. Its prophecies and tenets are seen by Bajorans as "religious," but given grounded scientific explanations by the non-spiritual humanists of Starfleet. In a way, then, science is *Star Trek*'s religion, and religion is *Battlestar Galactica*'s science.

Unfortunately, the importance of religion in *Battlestar Galactica* has some rather disturbing overtones. The only religious dissenters seen in the series, the Borellian Nomen, are segregated from the rest of the human population. The Nomen are forced to live on a freighter (a spacegoing ghetto?) and are persecuted by Colonial Warriors. In "The Man with Nine Lives," the Nomen are looked upon as pagan savages because they do not share the religious values of the military ruling class. They are even given the physical characteristics of neanderthals (bulbous, protruding foreheads) to cement their association with the "primitive." Importantly, the Nomen are feared because of their savage (non–Christian?) ways. Ironically, this persecution of the societal "other" is not considered wrong within the universe of *Galactica*. On the contrary, it is a positive thing. The savagery of Borellian Nomen culture represents a threat to the safety of the fleet. Better to repress these people and limit their freedom than to allow their strange ways to affect the "good," Christian-like people of the fleet.

Ironically, *Battlestar Galactica*'s belief that only one's own religion is a "good" thing is closely mirrored in 1990s America. At the 1992 Republican Convention, presidential candidate Pat Buchanan told a viewing audience of millions that it was time for the Christians of the United States to "take back our culture" (apparently from Jews, Buddhists and people of "alternate" lifestyles, all of whom are guaranteed the right to live in America unoppressed and unpersecuted). Of course, Buchanan's comment does not jibe with the fact that America was established to *prevent* religious persecution in the first place. The commonly held belief that the Founding Fathers of America are Christians is mistaken anyway: many were deists. Remarkably, *Battlestar Galactica* exemplifies the same kind of religious hypocrisy and rigidity as evidenced by the more conservative members of the GOP, in that the Colonial characters who follow the Book of the Word are considered noble and decent (Adama, Apollo, and Athena), but those who have altering religious views of life are viewed as savages (the Nomen of "The Man with Nine Lives"), devils (Count Iblis in "War of the Gods") or hedonists (Sire Uri in "Saga of a Star World").

There is no acceptance of atheists or religious dissenters in *Battlestar Galactica*. The Colonials of *Galactica* repress freedom of religion because they can: They control the military, the government and religious worship, so there is no possibility of alternate views. Apparently, the Colonials have never heard of the concept of "checks and balances."

The number of religious references in *Battlestar Galactica* is truly overwhelming. Each primary hero is viewed as noble because of his religious leanings, and each character even has his own stock reference to religion that is frequently repeated. Commander Adama is constantly exclaiming "By the Lords of Kobol!" while Apollo sanctimoniously refers to "God" in episodes such as "The Hand of God." Even the womanizing, down-to-earth Starbuck is associated with religion. In "The Long Patrol" and "Take the *Celestra*" (to name just two), he exclaims "For Sagan's sake!" a reference to a deity, named after the late Carl Sagan. Faith in a greater being is thus a primary factor for the characters of *Battlestar Galactica*. It motivates them in a way it does not motivate the futuristic humanists of other space series.

It is not just the prominent place of religion that makes *Battlestar Galactica* a unique series in philosophy and ideal. It is the conjunction of a state-sponsored religion with the glorification of the military. As a series, *Battlestar Galactica* seems to believe that the best way for humans to live is under the safe and nurturing care of a god-fearing military. Martial law is deemed the only "safe" form of government because the civilians presented throughout the series are seen as hedonistic, self-serving, blinded by peace, or just plain stupid. Only the military, religious upper class (Adama, Apollo and the rest of the Colonial Warriors) are seen as rational and capable.

The first non-military man seen in *Battlestar Galactica* is President Adar (Lew Ayres). He is a kindly old man garbed in impractical white robes who unknowingly leads mankind to destruction. He is also a man who does not believe in the Adama dictum of "preparedness." Like some modern conservative senators, Adama believes that his enemy, in this case the Cylons, represent an "Evil Empire." Only through constant bullying and brinkmanship can these baddies be held to a peace. Adama's (and *Galactica*'s view) is that the Cylons would never genuinely want peace unless the Colonials use their powerful arms and military might to *force* them to peace. Adar is different, however; he is a pacifist who believes in the ideal of peace, not preparedness. He is also a dupe. He shows no preparedness, no distrust, and no concern for his people. He blindly leaves the 12 Colonial home planets defenseless, and does not even mount a token defense of his fleet. He believes the advice of those around him (even the obviously duplicitous Baltar) and is willing to trust an enemy of over 1,000 years. The result of his idealistic foolishness is that nine-tenths of the human race is exterminated. Adama, the only warrior who is "prepared" during the Cylon attack, survives and becomes the new leader. Preparedness has thus replaced pacifism as the rule of law. According to *Battlestar Galactica*, pacifists may have noble intentions, but they are idealistic fools who will destroy our culture if put in a position of authority. It is the job of the military to "never again" (as Adama says) be conned into allowing ideals to impact policy.

In "Saga of a Star World," Sire Uri (Ray Milland) suggests a radical weapons reduction (as some liberals are prone to do in Congress). His proposal is not believable, however, within the dramatic context of *Battlestar Galactica*. Just days after the destruction of the Colonies at the hands of the Cylons, this official wants to destroy all arms! Why? What fool could propose such a notion? This is a hard-to-swallow stance because even the most pacifist person in the world would not want to throw away his only line of defense after an attack that destroyed nine-tenths of the human race. Sire Uri is thus revealed to be an exaggerated, comic figure not to be taken seriously. Hence his advocacy of arms reduction need not be taken seriously either. The message is clear: Civilian politicians cannot be trusted. When they suggest arms reductions, they are really suggesting that we surrender to the enemy! It is the paranoid view of an ultra-hawk, but it is also the view *Battlestar Galactica* consistently espouses.

Siress Belloby, a character seen in "The Magnificent Warriors," is the next prominent civilian seen in *Battlestar Galactica*. Like Sire Uri, Belloby is also selfish and misguided. She is interested only in what comforts she can enjoy, not in the safety of her people. The teleplay also treats her as a fool, since her actions cause her to be captured by the evil Boray. Of course, the fool must then be rescued by the military. That is the thing about civilians — they have high-flying notions about freedom and peace, but it is always the military who must come in and rescue them! Again, this is a very cynical look at civilian power-players. Like Uri, Belloby is also viewed as hedonistic. She is first seen in "The Magnificent Warriors" reclining on a plush, giant bed. It is also clear that she is interested in sex first with Adama, and then with Starbuck. Of course, that kind of desire makes her "bad." Through Adar, Uri and Belloby, *Battlestar Galactica* warns audiences that there are only two governmental options:

a nurturing yet oppressive police state replete with a state-run religion, or a foolish civilian government that is really concerned with hedonism rather than pacifism.

In "The Lost Warrior" and the aforementioned "The Magnificent Warriors," planets with civilian governments are menaced by exploitative locals (either LaCerta and Red Eye, or the Boray). The civilians are completely tyrannized until the Colonial Warriors arrive to save the day. Sire Bogan and LaCerta, the figureheads of each farming society, are duplicitous men interested in fulfilling their selfish needs rather than justice. Both civilians are also, significantly, cowards. Once LaCerta in "The Lost Warrior" has seen the military prowess of Apollo, he makes a quiet retreat. Once Bogan in "The Magnificent Warriors" has seen Boomer, Apollo, Starbuck and Adama in action, he suddenly treats them as gods, and says he is honored to be in the presence of such noble people. In other words, military might is equated with right and justice in *Battlestar Galactica*. Because Apollo and the rest manipulate hi-tech, powerful weaponry, they are honored as heroes, if not gods.

In "War of the Gods" and "Baltar's Escape," the civilians of the Colonial Fleet, as well as the Council of 12, are once more represented in the most unflattering light. In "War of the Gods," the civilians on the Gemonese freighter are self-interested sheep. They are ready to follow any leader, even the Devil personified as Count Iblis, who can put a few more scraps of food on their table and throw a good party. Only Adama, the spiritual, military man, can discern Iblis' deception. The point is again made abundantly clear: If not kept under rigid martial law, civilians will do stupid things. They cannot be trusted to govern themselves. If they do control the government, mankind will suffer. It will be, literally, "hell."

"Baltar's Escape" is much the same story. Adama and his warriors believe that the political prisoners of the Eastern Alliance should be debriefed and ruthlessly interrogated. The Council believes that the enforcers should be treated as guests, and that a diplomatic envoy should be sent to Terra. The Council speaks in the language of diplomacy, while the Military speaks in the language of war. When the Enforcers take over the prison barge and kidnap the Council, the military viewpoint is validated again: Enemies of the state will *always* be enemies of the state, and there is no possibility of growth or peace. The enemies must never be treated as friends, or potential allies, or they will destroy the traditional culture of the Colonials. In "Baltar's Escape," the Council of 12 is shown to be not only wrong-headed, but cowardly. As soon as the Council is kidnapped by the enforcers they hoped to befriend, its members become sniveling cowards screaming for Adama's help. They are so happy when the military pulls them out of the line of fire that they immediately re-establish martial law, and give Adama his authority back. Even *they* have learned that civilians are untrustworthy, and that the military (backed by religion) is their only savior.

The civilian Council government proves to be the bad guys again in "Greetings from Earth." A shuttle containing a family in suspended animation is brought aboard the *Galactica*. In this episode the roles are reversed, and it is the Council who wants to act to preserve the people. They want to open the cryogenic chambers and interrogate the family. The military wants to preserve the rights of the family and send them back into space unharmed. This is a weird *Battlestar Galactica* episode because it portrays the military mentality as more sensitive to individual liberties than the civilian government. Again the military is shown to be "right" and "good," even though the Council had the best intentions (saving the fleet and finding Earth!).

In "Experiment in Terra," the *Battlestar Galactica* manifesto is finally exposed as Apollo speaks to the Praesidium of Terra. The people of Terra are in danger of being tricked into destruction by the Eastern Alliance, just as the Colonies were by the Cylons. Apollo warns the people of Terra that they must give up their beliefs in pacifism and peace, because the result will be their enslavement. He tells them that "strength" and "strength alone" can guarantee freedom. In other words, only the political force with the biggest arsenal of deadly weapons can convince the enemies of freedom not to attack. Only the threat of mutual annihilation can keep the wolves at bay. Attempts at understanding, friendship, tolerance and compromise will not guarantee peace. Instead, *Battlestar Galactica* believes that only a strong deterrent will prevent an enemy from waging war. Peace through superior firepower has nowhere been more glorified than in *Battlestar Galactica*.

In "Take the *Celestra*," a rigid old disciplinarian called Kronus commands the civilian ship *Celestra*. He is a Colonial Warrior of great repute, and his methods have won him accolades across the fleet. Unknown to Adama and others, conditions on the *Celestra* are terrible. It is a police state. In keeping with *Galactica*'s support of the military, Kronus is not held accountable for this problem. On the contrary, it is his young upstart first officer Charka who is responsible. Of course, Charka is not a Colonial Warrior—he is a civilian. The military is thus taken off the hook for the conditions on the *Celestra* too. Kronus even saves the ship at the end of the episode, proving that he is not such a bad guy after all! Warriors might misstep, but they will always be there for the people in the end!

Even "The Living Legend," which features a military competition between Commander Adama of the *Galactica* and Commander Cain of the *Pegasus*, considers civilians a burden. Adama refers to the civilian population as if it is an albatross hanging around his neck when the more colorful Cain suggests a bold attack against the Cylons. The teleplay hints that Adama cannot be the same caliber of warrior as Cain because he is handicapped by the presence of civilians. If it were not for those pesky non-military people, the *Galactica* would be able to inflict serious hurting on those Cylons.

Taken as a whole, *Battlestar Galactica* is as fascistic a TV series as has ever been produced. Tom Shales noted this fact at the time of the show's original broadcast, and the observation seems as true today as it was 20 years ago. Every character in the show who is seen in a positive light is a member of the military. Why were no civilians featured as regulars? Why was the Council repeatedly seen to be stupid? Each story is a "stacked" deck in a sense, since the military is always presented as correct *a priori*, and the civilians are shown to be buffoons of the worst variety. The Colonial Warriors, who combine the might of the military with the righteousness of organized religion, are the ultimate extension of a police state. In their ornate, pristine uniforms, these physically beautiful men smilingly extend the policy of the police state.

In keeping with this fascist stance, the Cylons are always treated as two-dimensional villains. They are tin cans to be blown apart, not a galactic force that might have the right to exist itself. The Cylons are "evil" and the Colonials are "good." It is a black-and-white universe which reveals to audiences that military strength buttressed by a righteous, organized religion akin to Christianity is the only force in the galaxy that can keep mankind alive. Thus the great region of space, a region of mysteries and puzzles and enigmas, becomes a region instead of "enemies" and "danger." Mankind in *Battlestar Galactica* goes out into the galaxy not with good will and peace on his mind, but preparedness. *Battlestar Galactica* informs viewers that the cosmos is full of people waiting to kill man. If man attempts peace, he will be annihilated. If he even attempts a token civilian government, that attempt will lead to destruction. *Battlestar Galactica* is truly a fascist's dream.

Many actors and crew members associated with *Battlestar Galactica* over the years have rejected the notion that *Galactica* is fascist in design. They argue that if mankind is nearly annihilated and chased across the universe by evil robots, there will be little time for self-determination and liberty. Mankind, they assert, by needs and logic *will* resort to military rule. That is a valid argument, but the series never examined the dark underside or logical extensions of such a grim philosophy. How would mankind, weaned on seven centuries of self-determination and freedom, respond to being cooped up in spaceships for years on end with the military running things? The only episode which noted that the military might take advantage of this situation was "Murder on the *Rising Star*" and the "bad" warrior in that situation was seen as a bad seed, a misguided individual, not a man taking advantage of his privileged status in a police state. The real crux of the issue, that warriors wield authority indiscriminately over civilians and live in comparative luxury on the *Galactica* while the civilians lived in squalor, was never addressed.

Of course, *Battlestar Galactica* suffered a bit from weak writing, and as a result the fascist, right-wing elements of the series seemed alternately at times to be either completely considered (i.e., the speech in "Experiment in Terra") or the results of carelessness, or plot necessity. The goal in stories such as "Baltar's Escape" and "The War of the Gods" was to make it seem as if Adama's position of authority was truly threatened. This was done by giving him opposers within the Colonial universe: the Council of 12. The intent was not to make the Council a bunch of idealistic boobs, yet that was the cumulative effect of all the stories. The Council was wrong about Carillon in "Saga of a Star World." They were wrong about Count Iblis in "War of the Gods." They were wrong about the Eastern Alliance in "Baltar's Escape." And yet they never learned from their mistakes. They continued to challenge Adama and the military rule throughout the series.

Historical context is also important when considering the philosophical viewpoints that propelled *Battlestar Galactica*. The series premiered after *Star Wars*, and was undeniably influenced by it. *Star Wars* also featured hotshot pilots (Biggs, Luke, Wedge), a spiritual guru (Ben Kenobi) and a religious philosophy embodied by "The Force." But, importantly, *Star Wars* was a leftist fantasy in the vein of *Star Trek* or *Space: 1999*. It was about a group of freedom fighters (military and non-military) banding together to fight an oppressive, right-wing government. The "Force" was a religious icon relied on only by a few who remembered the ancient traditions. *Battlestar*

Galactica was very different. It was about a caravan of humans led to safety by military forces. In said caravan, the military controlled government and religion. The threat was "outside" Colonial considerations. In *Star Wars*, the rebels *fought against* the totalitarian government. In *Galactica*, the Colonials *represented* a totalitarian government imposed by an outside threat (the Cylons). The Colonials used the same tools as the Empire (state-sanctioned religion, warrior might, superior technology, the offer of protection).

Still, there is no doubt that, philosophically and politically, *Battlestar Galactica* was ahead of its time. Just two years after it was on the air, Ronald Reagan was elected President of the United States by a landslide, and his governing ideals echoed the conservative notions of *Battlestar Galactica*. He called the Soviet Union the "Evil Empire" and he defeated the "commies" not through peace talks, compromise, detente or even combat — but through Adama's old friend, preparedness. Quite simply, he outspent the Soviets on nuclear missiles. He was vigilant. He espoused the philosophy that strength, and strength alone, could make the world safe for democracy. *Battlestar Galactica*, by that time gone from the airwaves, was quite familiar with that stance. Of course, the Soviet Union did fall, and now we Americans can all rest easy at nights, and ponder how it was done. Maybe then, *Battlestar Galactica* was really on to something with its conservative Republican version of outer space. But then again, who wants to live in a society where there is no separation between church and state, no checks and balances between branches of government, and only martial law?

At the very least, the philosophy of "preparedness" and fascism makes *Battlestar Galactica* notably different from almost any other space series in the science fiction television pantheon. It is not good or bad *per se*, just unique. Although people may choose not to agree with its hawkish view of the universe, it is a change from the liberal edicts of the *Star Trek* universe. If a new *Battlestar Galactica* is produced, one wonders if it will continue to occupy the paranoid, fascist terrain of its originator, or tuck tail between its legs and offer a more optimistic, idealistic and (dare we use the word) "liberal" view of life in space.

Hit or Myth: Mythology, the Bible and Human History in Battlestar Galactica

Spiritualism in science fiction video and film epics is perhaps nothing new or particularly noteworthy. Immediately preceding *Battlestar*

Galactica in 1977, *Star Wars* popularized the notion that modern space operas should be crammed not just with darting and weaving snub-nosed spaceships but also with quasi-religious metaphors and popcorn philosophies such as "The Force." On television from 1975–1977, *Space: 1999* had been hit by a barrage of serious critical and fan brickbats because it consistently posited the notion of a cosmic intelligence looking out for man in episodes such as "Black Sun," "War Games," "Testament of Arkadia" and others. Interestingly, *Battlestar Galactica* features more religious and mythological references than either aforementioned production. While *Space: 1999* and *Star Wars* both suggested the existence of otherworldly and incomprehensible phenomena unrelated to Earth's religious dogma, *Battlestar Galactica*'s game was determinedly different.

After considering mysteries such as the statues of Easter Island and the Great Pyramids of Egypt, Glen Larson decided that his outer space adventure would focus squarely on the heritage of our human race. Larson's Von Däniken–like theory posited that mankind originated not on Earth, but far out in space with a mother-race that existed amongst the furthest stars. To cogently convey this point of view to the audience, the human race of *Battlestar Galactica* (the intrepid "Colonials") would have devices and names, and encounter planets and enemies that were named after various sources from Earth mythology, specifically of the ancient Greek and biblical variety. This sprinkling of familiar but mythological names would thus constantly remind viewers of the link between man on Earth and our brothers in space. The connection between mythical names and situations to the *Battlestar Galactica* universe could also suggest that the noble men and women in space, and the dangers they faced week-to-week on television, could be the actual originators of ancient myth and biblical writings, but that this fact has been forgotten or altered by Earthman after generations of retelling the ancient stories. Seen in this light, *Battlestar Galactica* could be the tale of mankind's dark prehistory.

This tapestry of mythology, this history joining all races of man in a common galactic heritage, was perhaps the most ambitious background context ever conceived for a modern science fiction television series. While *Star Trek* and *Space: 1999* both featured admirable consistency and unity in mood and philosophical drive, they had done so within a different context. Both earlier series examined the Earthman's place in the universe and made startlingly different conclusions about it. Not so of *Battlestar Galactica*: Its thrust was to relate the history, culture and myths of Earthman to a previous space society, in order that viewers might accept a fictional, common heritage. It was an interesting and unique conceit that sometimes worked well, and sometimes failed utterly. For the most part, the mythological and biblical aspects of *Battlestar Galactica* did not really affect the drama of a given episode, but merely added an element of recognition to characters or places within that drama.

Because the Bible and Greek mythology were joined, many felt that the "God is an astronaut" notion of *Battlestar Galactica* was a misconceived jumble, a philosophical hodgepodge concocted by unimaginative "TV thinkers" who had only a high school knowledge of science fiction, mythology and religion. In some instances, that argument may indeed seem accurate, but *Battlestar Galactica* had its moments of finesse too. From time to time the series intelligently and pointedly rehashed and reinterpreted biblical and Greek myth in unique fashion. Although some reinterpretations were not always solid, hence the "hit or myth" pun at the beginning of this essay, the mythological references did provide the series with a veneer of dramatic maturity, a context beyond the details of a given plot or adventure that made the series a thought-provoking one. The purpose of this essay is to tally the many mythological, biblical and even literary references made throughout the *Battlestar Galactica* series and determine not only where they were used with intelligence and wit, but also where the mythological context failed to inspire or inform the audience.

Before examining the specific storylines and episodes of *Battlestar Galactica* in relation to the mythology veneer, it is appropriate to first consider the central characters of the series and determine whether they have been named appropriately, considering the qualities of their mythological forebears. Since Commander Adama is the spiritual and military leader of the fleet and of *Battlestar Galactica* as a whole, let us study his name first. "Adama" is a moniker derived from the Old Testament name for the first man to inhabit the Earth, Adam. In Hebrew, "Adam" means "man," but "Adam" also comes from the word which means "Earth." Thus it is appropriate in *Battlestar Galactica* that the character Adama is the one who suggests the exodus to distant Earth, since his own name, his very identity, is inextricably linked with that destination. However, Adama does not fill the role of Adam completely. Although he may lack companionship and the comfort of a woman, *Battlestar Galactica*'s Adama is not an innocent, nor does he dwell in a perfect paradise. On the contrary, Adama is a battle-hardened soldier who defends himself and his people with fightercrafts called Vipers. That name is significant as well. Adama is not tempted by a serpent (a Viper), but he is protected by them instead. It is conceivable, one supposes, that the 12 Great Colonies could be considered a Garden of Eden–type paradise and that by leaving it, Adama is liberating his people from perfection and innocence, but that interpretation is undoubtedly stretching the matter. No, Adama indeed fulfills a biblical role but he is not related only to "Adam." He is also Moses.

Like Moses, who led his people, the Hebrews, out of Egypt circa 1250 B.C. in the great Exodus, Commander Adama too leads his people from dangerous territory — the domain of the Cylons. Again like Moses, whose lifespan is reported to have been over 120 years, Adama is a long-lived man (over 100 yahrens old if "War of the Gods" is accurate). Moses saved the Israelite Tribes (Asher, Dan, Ephraim, Gad, Issachar, Manasseh, Naphtali, Reuben, Simeon and Zebulun) by asking God to part the waves of the Red Sea and allowing the tribes to pass into safe territory. In *Battlestar Galactica*, Adama likewise saves his 12 tribes (named after the 12 signs of the Zodiac) by clearing the red-hued Nova of Madagon of space mines. Essentially, he too has "parted" a path for his people. After the Red Sea Incident, Moses delivered his people safely to their destination, the mountain called Sinai. In *Galactica: 1980*, Adama also completes the exodus, delivering his people to safety on Earth. In duty at least, Adama fulfills the role of Moses in the Book of Exodus more than he fulfills the role of Adam in the Book of Genesis. The parallels to Moses and the Book of Exodus are so clear that *Battlestar Galactica* was often referred to by journalists in 1978 as *Battlestar Moses*.

Adama plays another critical role as well. In addition to being part Adam and part Moses, the commander of the *Galactica* is also one part Zeus, the king of the ancient Greek gods, for he is father to the children Apollo and Athena. Although Adama does not have Zeus' womanizing qualities (those were reserved for Starbuck), he is nonetheless an imposing authority figure and the head of a regal family. His son in *Battlestar Galactica* is appropriately named Apollo.

Apollo was the personification of youth, athleticism and physical beauty to the ancient Greeks. He was also the god of light and the god of knowledge. Importantly, he is remembered for having piloted his chariot across the skies of Earth to Mount Olympus. In essence, all of those characteristics are a perfect description of Richard Hatch's Cpt. Apollo. He is physically handsome, even beautiful with his high cheekbones and long hair. He is also athletic, a professional Triad Player on the *Rising Star*, in fact. Significantly, Cpt. Apollo streaks across the stars in a technological chariot: the Colonial Viper. Apollo represents one case in *Battlestar Galactica* where mythology and television character merge perfectly. It is not hard to envision the noble and kind Apollo of Richard Hatch as the mythological god revered by the ancient Romans and Greeks.

Athena was the Greek goddess of war in ancient myth. She was a daughter of Zeus, and thus a sister of Apollo as *Galactica*'s Athena is the sibling of Richard Hatch's Apollo. The goddess Athena emphasized the importance of justice and skill in battle. She represented wisdom and was widely known as Zeus' favorite child. Like Cpt. Apollo, Athena in *Battlestar Galactica* almost perfectly mirrors the fine qualities of her namesake. Maren Jensen's Athena is a competent bridge officer of high rank aboard a battleship, a position requiring skill above all else. She is also wise and just, as evidenced by her fair treatment of Cassiopeia, a rival in love, in "The Long Patrol." A case could also be made that it is Athena who is Commander Adama's favorite child. When she weeps on the *Galactica* bridge at the destruction of Caprica, Adama consoles her in a loving fashion, very different from the more macho and hearty affection he demonstrates with Apollo. Additionally, it is Athena who constantly worries about her father's well-being in "Saga of a Star World" when he seems devastated by their situation. She is both a confidante and a daughter, arguably Adama's favorite child, as Athena was of Zeus.

Starbuck is another *Battlestar Galactica* character who embodies the qualities of earlier figures. Surprisingly, those figures in this case come not from biblical or ancient Greek sources, but from 19th and 20th century literature and pop culture. First and foremost, "Starbuck" is also the name of an outer space comic book hero (Cody Starbuck) devised by artist Howard Chaykin. Secondly, it is also possible that the Starbuck of *Battlestar Galactica* is a sly reference to another, more popular space-going "Buck": Buck Rogers. *The Official Battlestar Galactica Scrapbook* offers two alternative origins for the name Starbuck. After noting that his name means literally "bucking the stars," author James Neyland suggests Starbuck comes from Herman Melville's classic novel *Moby Dick* and the N. Richard Nash play *The Rainmaker*. Neyland quotes from *Moby Dick* and *The Rainmaker* to paint a portrait of a courageous character "who lived by his charm and his wits, daring the impossible, and depending upon luck to fulfill his dare."[1] That is as apt a description of Dirk Benedict's creation as is likely to be written, but the source material is nonetheless bothersome. Why in this case has Glen Larson chosen from a different literary era and tradition than ancient mythology? Is the flip, happy-go-lucky character of Starbuck designed not to carry the same psychic "weight" as Adama, Apollo or Athena? By Larson's very choice of a name, the audience is being informed that Starbuck is not a serious man in comparison with his cohorts.

"Starbuck" is not the only non-mythological name in *Battlestar Galactica*. There is also the name "Boomer," a tag which evokes images of explosions and chaos, appropriate pictures for a Colonial Warrior. Other non-mythological names include "Greenbean," a name for a tall thin man, and "Jolly," a name for a fat Colonial Viper pilot, which evokes images of jolly St. Nick, another overweight man.

The remaining central characters of *Battlestar Galactica* do not seem nearly so well thought-out in their references to legends. Cassiopeia, for instance, is a socialator (prostitute) turned medical officer in *Battlestar Galactica*. In Greek myth, Cassiopeia was the vain, egotistical Queen of Ethiopia and mother of Andromeda. Those character qualities of vanity and ego do not seem at all appropriate to the healing, gentle love of Laurette Spang's Cassiopeia. She is so sweet and forgiving of Starbuck in episodes such as "Take the *Celestra*" that one wishes she had a little more of the ego of her mythological counterpart. "Sheba" is another name in *Battlestar Galactica* that does not seem to translate well from myth to character. In *Galactica*, Sheba is a Colonial Warrior of uncommon bravery. The word "Sheba" refers to a territory in modern Yemen, and one Biblical story tells of the Queen of Sheba's visit to the kingdom of the wise King Solomon. Sheba makes no such pilgrimage in *Battlestar Galactica*, unless one considers her service under Apollo's command a visit to a figure of wisdom and knowledge. Again, like Cassiopeia, the connection between myth and main character is not forged successfully by the writers.

The villains of *Battlestar Galactica* also share characteristics with ancient figures described in classical mythology and the Bible. The one-eyed Cylon warriors are undoubtedly named after the creatures known in legends as "cyclops." Like a Cylon, a Cyclops sports but a single eye, and would aptly be described as a hulking giant. Lucifer, the robot given mellifluous voice by Jonathan Harris, is even more significant. This robot, of course, is named after the fallen angel who prefers to rule in Hell than serve in Heaven. The root of the name "Lucifer" is the Latin word "lux," meaning light, and Lucifer the Cylon boasts a transparent skull alive with pulsating orbs of light. From a physical standpoint at least Lucifer is perfectly named — a creature of light.

At first glance, Lucifer on *Battlestar Galactica* hardly seems to be a figure of pure evil, like the Lucifer of Milton or the Devil of modern Christianity. On closer inspection, though, perhaps the robot does meet some characteristics of Satan. Like the Prince of Darkness, this robot is a consummate liar. In "Lost Planet of the Gods," he agrees to follow Baltar's orders. Yet when Baltar leaves the baseship, Lucifer launches a devastating strike on the planet Kobol, the Colonists and Baltar himself. He is a deceitful being, a creature of lies. Like Satan, a master manipulator by all accounts, Lucifer also plays on the fears of those he wishes to corrupt. He plays on Baltar's insecurities ("War of the Gods," "The Living Legend"), twists Baltar's orders ("Lost Planet of the Gods") and displays negative emotions such as jealousy ("The Young Lords"). Although the robotic Lucifer may not be the embodiment of pure evil in the strictest sense of the word, the character is worthy of his name.

Spectre, the name of another IL Cylon seen in "The Young Lords," comes from the word meaning apparition or ghost. Though not strictly mythological in origin, this tag is appropriately evil and fear-provoking. And what of Baltar? Where does his name come from? That is not so easy to determine, although the *Official Battlestar Galactica Scrapbook* reports that his name is most likely derived from that of an ancient Canaanite god of darkness and shadows who was considered a false god.[2] This would certainly seem appropriate, since Baltar is first worshipped by the Colonials of *Battlestar Galactica* as a bringer of peace, and then reviled as an agent of total destruction.

Many of the situations encountered in the 17 episodes of *Battlestar Galactica* have tantalizing mythical implications and connections. "Saga of a Star World" has already been discussed at some length for its parallels to the Book of Exodus, which details the Israelite journey from Egypt to Sinai. But there are other mythological notes of interest. The millennium-long war between the Cylons and the Colonials is ended in *Battlestar Galactica* by a Cylon deception, much as the ten-year-long Trojan War was ended by a deception: the Trojan Horse gambit. Seen in the context of the Trojan War, Commander Adama may represent a kind of futuristic Aeneas, leading his people from a site of ruin to found a new "Rome" on distant Earth. Perhaps coincidentally, Adama's grandson is renamed "Troy" upon reaching Earth in *Galactica: 1980*, another reference to the ancient war of Achilles, Odysseus and Agamemnon. If the mythological aspects were fulfilled on *Battlestar Galactica*, one might rightly expect the Colonials to build a great empire on Earth, and defeat the Cylons (the Greeks?). Of course, that did not happen. But then again, *Battlestar Galactica* was cancelled after one season, and if *Galactica: 1980* is ignored, a new human empire spanning the galaxy could ultimately be the conclusion of the series.

"Saga of a Star World" has other biblical flourishes. President Adar carries a name of distinction. "Adar" is a Hebrew word associated with the twelfth month of the Jewish ecclesiastic year. Interestingly, the month of "Adar" corresponds roughly to March in our current calendar. March is the historically favored month for betrayals. Julius Caesar was betrayed by his own men and was murdered during the Ides of March, just as a character named Adar, after March, is assassinated through the treachery of a robed fellow space senator. *Et tu,* Baltar?

President Adar has frequently been considered by many writers, including those writing for *Time* magazine, to be a surrogate for Jesus Christ because he espouses peace, love and brotherhood. Cementing the parallel, Adar is surrounded by the Council of 12 — not unlike Christ's Twelve Apostles. Ironically, an apostle is a servant of Christ who is to accompany him on his "ministry." In *Battlestar Galactica,* the Council of 12 accompany Adar on his final ministry: death. Lending even further credence to this reading of Adar as Christ, the treacherous Baltar plays the role of Judas, betrayer of Christ, when he sells out Adar to the Cylons. The Christ analogy can only be taken this far, however, as Adar, at least during the *Battlestar Galactica* series, is not admired as a messiah figure (Adama's role!) but rather as a peace-loving fool who sent humanity spiralling towards total destruction. And importantly, Adar is never resurrected (except in reruns).

Another critical issue in "Saga of a Star World" is the distribution of food, a tangential reference, perhaps, to the "fishes and loaves" parable of the Bible. Christ was speaking before a large audience when he noted that many of his listeners appeared hungry. He caused a miracle, and their food multiplied. In *Battlestar Galactica,* Adama preaches to his audience about Earth, and in the follow-up scenes his son learns of a food shortage. The problem is solved when Apollo redistributes the miraculously found wealth of food to the starving people.

"Lost Planet of the Gods" and "The Lost Warrior" demonstrate that Cpt. Apollo is indeed a variation on his ancient Greek namesake. Apollo was a God who was consistently cursed with short-lived, tragic, love relationships. His attraction to the nymph Daphne was cut short when her father transformed the beautiful girl into a laurel tree. Similarly, "Serina," the name of Apollo's ill-fated wife, probably hails from the word Cyrene. Like Daphne, Cyrene was an innocent spring nymph in myth. More importantly, the city of Cyrene, a home of philosophers and medicine men, was widely known in antiquity as a sanctuary for the god Apollo. Thus the love of Serina for Apollo in *Battlestar Galactica* could be considered a brief sanctuary for the captain before he, like his mythological forebear, faces tragedy. Serina is lost to Apollo forever in "The Lost Planet of the Gods" when she is killed by Cylons. He then loses Bella, another woman he has grown to love, when he must return to the "heavens" in "The Lost Warrior."

Much of the action of the episode "The Long Patrol" takes place on a penal asteroid called "Proteus." In Greek myth, Proteus was a sea deity who was able to transform into various forms and shapes. The man who could capture him while he slept could also make him foretell the future. Menelaus in Homer's *The Odyssey*, for instance, caught the napping god. In *Battlestar Galactica*, the Proteus Society has for all intents and purposes been "asleep" for hundreds of generations, unaware of the destruction of the Colonies or the end of the Great Cylon War. When the *Galactica* crew happens upon Proteus in this "sleeping" state, they are able to derive from it the secrets of their future when Starbuck infiltrates the culture and discovers an exact schematic of Earth's solar system carved on a prison cell. Had the culture not been caught napping in an age past, it is very likely that Starbuck would not have been captured, and therefore the diagram would never have been found. Only by encountering Proteus Prison in its antiquated state was the *Galactica* able to find this crucial information. In the case of "The Long Patrol," an ancient myth has been translated to television in an interesting, if oblique, fashion. Since the elements of the myth also fit the *Battlestar Galactica* adventure, "The Long Patrol" resonates with viewers in a way that space Westerns such as "The Magnificent Warriors," do not.

"The Young Lords" features another example of a name from antiquity helping to define the nature of a *Battlestar Galactica* story. In this adventure, Starbuck crashes on a planet named Attila, a planet no doubt named after the ancient historical figure Attila the Hun. Attila was not strictly a mythical character, but rather a ruler of the Huns circa A.D. 453. Nevertheless, his name no doubt inspired fear and many legends among the ancient Romans. He was so powerful a figure that he launched deadly raids against the Roman army, and was frequently victorious. He was such a threat that Theodosius II was forced to make a pact with him: payment in gold for Attila if he stopped the attacks. Attila stuck to the pact for a time (six years) and then resumed the fighting with fervor. In "The Young Lords," the same strategic dynamic is played out on the distant world Attila. The young family led by Kyle constantly stages successful blitzkrieg raids against the all-powerful Cylon garrison stationed there. The attacks are so successful that the Cylon ruler Spectre is forced for a time to consider a truce and prisoner exchange with the human forces. For a short duration, Kyle conforms to the specifics of Spectre's plan, but then with Starbuck's help launches an attack that sends Spectre scurrying from the planet. In all senses, this situation is a perfect parallel to that of Attila the Hun and Theodosius. Again, an ancient story, this time historical, is worked into a *Battlestar Galactica* with surprising validity.

The name Ariadne also pops up in "The Young Lords." In ancient myth, Ariadne was the daughter of Minos, the tyrant who sent helpless Athenians to their deaths in the labyrinth built by Daedalus. The character in "The Young Lords," however, shares no traits with the mythical daughter of Minos and brief lover of Theseus. She is a child of minimal importance to the plot of the *Galactica* adventure, so this is one occasion where the mythical name adds no value to the story.

"The Living Legend" is another *Battlestar Galactica* story rife with mythological overtones and names. It is the story of a rogue named "Cain" who commands a ship called *Pegasus*. In Genesis 4, Cain, son of Adam, slays his brother Abel. For this crime, Cain is cursed by God to wander the Earth forever alone. Similarly, Cain in *Battlestar Galactica* is seen to be a sort of younger contemporary of Adama, not quite a son, who betrays Adama for his own self-aggrandizement and glory. As punishment for his egotism, at the close of the story Cain disappears for good, presumably to wander space in the *Pegasus*. The name of his ship is also significant. Tamed by Bellerophon with the help of Athena and created by a droplet of Medusa's blood, Pegasus was a winged horse of intense beauty. Bellerophon attempted to ride Pegasus to Heaven, but was thrown from his steed along the way. Pegasus then rode off to Heaven alone, just as the Battlestar *Pegasus* flies off alone into the void at the conclusion of "The Living Legend."

Cain, "a wanderer," and the *Pegasus*, a ship journeying the heavens alone, both suggest images of loneliness, of wandering alone in a new realm. *Battlestar Galactica* never solved the mystery of where exactly Cain and the *Pegasus* disappeared to at the conclusion of "The Living Legend," so it is easy to read this story as a direct reference to characters from the Bible and Greek antiquity.

"War of the Gods" found the *Galactica* and its fleet in the grip of a deadly creature called Iblis, a creature who, it seemed, was Satan himself. Although the name Iblis does not seem indicative of ancient myth or biblical parable, it is revealed in the course of "War of the Gods" that Iblis is known by other names, specifically "The Prince of Darkness" and "Mephistopheles," two time-honored aliases for Satan himself. Like Satan, Iblis is an outcast from an angelic society. He is a rebel who delights in death and the seduction of innocent souls, namely Sheba. More importantly, he reveals that he is involved in the ongoing war between good and evil, just as Satan has a stake in winning all of our souls from goodness. When Starbuck fires his weapon at Iblis, the "real" Iblis is seen for an instant. He is a horned, monstrous thing, part-animal and part-human. He is not far from the horned, tailed, goat-like imaginings of Satan that have appeared in Western art and religion for the last two millennia.

Interestingly, "War of the Gods" features an encounter not only with a devil-creature, but also with the society of angels. The blue spaceship which captures Apollo, Starbuck and Sheba at the close of the tale is bathed in a heavenly white glow, and the beings within are beautiful apparitions of serenity and purity. Thus *Battlestar Galactica* defines a new order to the galaxy. Far in advance of man, it posits, there exists a race of super-evolved beings in a war between good and evil. The good are called "angels" and the bad are led by the Prince of Darkness. A curious television watcher keeping up with these details is thus led to believe that our own Earthly legends of Heaven, Hell, God, angels and the Devil actually originate from visitations by these advanced beings. Like *Star Trek: The Next Generation*, *Battlestar Galactica* accepts the tenet that any being sufficiently advanced would seem a god to men and women of primitive cultures.

"The Man with Nine Lives" does not tell a story derived from myth or the Bible, but does provide one character who has an interesting name derivation. Starbuck's father is called "Chameleon." Of course, a chameleon is a lizard able to change color in response to various environmental stimuli. It is an appropriate description of the character essayed by Fred Astaire, a man who can be Cpt. Dmitri, a Fleet Network Executive, and Starbuck's father in a span of a few minutes. With perfect ease, Chameleon changes his colors according to what is required of him in a given situation. Chameleon is not a biblical, mythological or historical term, but it is a name like "Viper" that nonetheless carries a dramatic resonance. It is not hard to imagine that Colonial surveyors discovering life on Earth for the first time would name a peculiar color-shifting lizard after a con-man of notable ability.

"Take the *Celestra*" offers another intriguing reference to mythology. The industrial ship *Celestra* is commanded by a hard old man called Kronus. Kronus is derived from the name "Cronos." Cronos was the king of the gods and the father of Zeus. Eventually he was undone by his own child, and exiled. In the *Battlestar Galactica* story, Kronus is betrayed by his second-in-command Charka. Both the mythical Cronos and the television "Kronus" are characterized as extremely harsh individuals. In the *Battlestar Galactica* mythos, the character redeems himself by saving the *Celestra*. The cost for this is his life.

"Aurora" is the name of Starbuck's long-lost lover in "Take the *Celestra*." She is a bold woman who fights for the freedom of the workers on the industry ship. She is appropriately named because Aurora was the Roman goddess of the dawn, and her *Galactica* namesake brings a metaphorical "new dawn" to the downtrodden aboard the *Celestra*. Not so well-named is the *Celestra*'s navigator, Hermes. In Greek myth, Hermes was a playful god who was the protector of thieves and travelers. He was also the son of Zeus, and renowned for conducting the shades of death to Hades. The character Hermes in "Take the *Celestra*" does literally (as navigator) lead the ship into the darkness of space, but otherwise there is no connection between myth and the Colonial man. Like Ariadne in "The Young Lords," the name Hermes does not carry any special weight because of the audience's knowledge of myth.

As the previous details and descriptions make abundantly clear, mythology, biblical stories and even human history was applied rather unevenly to *Battlestar Galactica* as a whole. Although many of the references are enlightening and do illuminate viewers about the characteristics of the *Galactica dramatis personae*, namely Apollo, Lucifer, Pegasus, and Athena, other allusions do not connect nearly so well, such as Sheba, Ariadne in "The Young Lords" and Hermes in "Take the *Celestra*." The flight through the Red Sea in space has a nice resonance in "Saga of a Star World" as do the planet names "Proteus" in "The Long Patrol" and "Attila" in "The Young Lords," but other references seem merely muddled. For instance, is Adama supposed to be Jesus, Zeus, Moses, Adam, Aeneas, a Cartwright or all of the above? Perhaps it does not matter at all. The characters, planets and plots of *Battlestar Galactica* are reminiscent enough of our oldest myths to remind modern TV viewers that humanity is universal, despite specific planet of origin. The characters in *Battlestar Galactica* recall characters in myth, may be intended as the origin of those myths, or perhaps even suggest that they are the inheritors of our ancient myths. Whatever the answer, *Battlestar Galactica* dramatically suggests through the use of so many allusions that man has sprung from a common root, shared common stories, and developed from a common beginning. It is a nice, positive message that goes mostly unrecognized by critics who slam the series as nothing but a *Star Wars* rip-off.

It is tempting for analysts to suggest that too much has been read into the use of the Bible and mythology in *Battlestar Galactica*, but one must remember that Glen Larson was brought up as a Mormon, and had a very heavy religious indoctrination. He has been fascinated with the heritage of man all his life, and thus he has used myth, legend, prophecy, the Old Testament, the New Testament and even ancient history to define a larger heritage: that of man as a transgalactic species descended from a mother race. How can one not read importance into names such as "Adar" or "Apollo" or "Cain"? Those are names at the root of our human culture. The designers of *Battlestar Galactica*'s Cylons, Joe Johnson and Andy Probert, knew the agenda and acted accordingly:

> We understood the Colonial Warriors were to have an Egyptian motif; and Joe and I were suddenly taken with the idea of making the Cylons Centurions look more like ancient warriors. He went in the direction of Genghis Khan, with heavy chain mail, and I went toward Greek or Roman warriors.... To complete the feeling of a Greek warrior, I added a waist skirt and a sword.[3]

From the designs and character names to story, *Battlestar Galactica* was always meant to be a combination of ancient history and the far future. This blending of time periods distinguishes it from *Star Wars* and other TV sci-fi productions.

If or when *Battlestar Galactica* is revived, it must not forsake its mythic heritage. The biblical and mythical angles should be played up in a consistent, thought-provoking fashion. The new series could feature plots based on the story of Pandora, the Book of Job, Helen of Troy, Odin and Thor and even the Prodigal Son. Mythology and science fiction, hand-in-hand, could continue to make *Battlestar Galactica* a unique addition to the Valhalla of televised science fiction.

<h1>PART V</h1>

The *Galactica* Universe Today: Converts, Computers, and Collectibles

Battlestar Galactica *Fans*

Since the rebirth of *Star Trek* in syndication, virtually every science fiction television series transmitted in the United States has inspired a dedicated fandom. Even obscure, short-lived programs from the 1970s such as *The Fantastic Journey* (1977) and *Logan's Run* (1977) for a brief time sported sizeable followings. Sometimes the candle of fan appreciation burns bright for a few years, and then fades away; sometimes it is an ongoing fire that burns for generations. *Beauty and the Beast* (1988–90), for instance, was the hub of a large, fanatical fandom in the late eighties and early nineties, but appreciation for that show dimmed significantly within a decade. The same is true for Don Bellisario's *Quantum Leap* and Glen Larson's *Buck Rogers in the 25th Century*, two other programs that were popular while on the air but do not look either interesting or well done in retrospect. Of course, even their standing may change when eighties nostalgia comes back into vogue in the next few years. With the rerelease of *Dirty Dancing* (1987) on theater screens across the United States in August of 1997, eighties nostalgia may already be here.

Unlike the aforementioned programs, however, *Battlestar Galactica*, like *Star Trek* or *Space: 1999*, has enjoyed nonstop fan appreciation for twenty years. For whatever reason, these three "outer space" productions have never experienced a total cessation of fandom, although there have been serious dips and valleys. *Battlestar Galactica* and *Space: 1999* cults both suffered serious discontent in the early '80s during a '70s backlash, only to burst back at full strength in the face of derivative *Star Trek* sequels in the late 1980s and mid–1990s. Now their fandoms seem to expand each year.

By contrast, *Star Trek* is experiencing its first real fandom "dip" in more than 30 years. Many longtime fans have grown tired of the much-traveled *Trek* universe and of the nationwide *Star Trek* media oversaturation. In a July 1997 *TV Guide* poll, *Space: 1999* unexpectedly finished well ahead of all generations of *Star Trek* in fan devotion! *Battlestar Galactica* performed at a level roughly equivalent to *Star Trek: Voyager* and the original *Star Trek*; not at all a bad result for a series that disappeared from first run two decades ago, after only 17 episodes! It is even more impressive a feat when one considers that *Battlestar Galactica*, with its slim roster of episodes, was not seen far and wide in syndication like *Star Trek*, which listed 79 episodes.

It is no wonder then that a large network of *Battlestar Galactica* fans are more devoted to the series today than they have been since the cancellation of the original series in 1979. In some senses, modern *Galactica* fans must feel as if all their years of patient waiting have paid off. In the long run, and seen within the context of a possible late–1990s or 21st century revival, they have supported a winning team. Glen Larson's often-maligned space series has experienced a most unexpected renaissance of new comic books, toys, model re-releases and novels since 1995. This merchandising blitz, an unparalleled one since the days of Mego's mid–1970s *Star Trek* toys, has undoubtedly turned around normal dissipation and entropy in *Galactica* fan circles. As chances for a television revival increase, so too will the breadth and population of *Battlestar Galactica* fandom.

Who are *Battlestar Galactica* fans? Interestingly, they are a slightly different bunch than the Trekkers or the *1999* fans. For the most part, contemporary *Battlestar Galactica* fans are young adults of Generation X who vividly remember watching the series on the air in 1978–79. Most of them were between the ages of five and ten when *Star Wars* came out in 1977. Importantly, that blockbuster film is considered a turning point in their lives, like the discovery of religion. Many die-hard *Battlestar Galactica* fans likely viewed *Star Wars* at least four times on the big screen during its initial release. To them it was fresh, it was different and it was more exciting than any other film they had seen before, much more so than the other contemporary genre hits such as the Dino DeLaurentiis *King*

Kong (1976) or MGM's *Logan's Run* (1976). When *Battlestar Galactica* arrived on TV in 1978, it was like a tasty dessert for these children after the feast of *Star Wars.* It featured more space battles, more neat robots and flashy lasers galore. *Battlestar Galactica* was thus a cause to celebrate for these children, because now they no longer had to wait till 1980, an "endless" three years, for a new *Star Wars* film. In the age before VCRs and cable television, *Battlestar Galactica was* the next *Star Wars* film for many starving adolescents. It fulfilled their interest in swooping space-ships, swashbuckling heroes and evil robotic villains. For many fans, *Star Wars* and *Battlestar Galactica* are forever linked together because of their historical proximity. They are remnants of a joyous childhood, and hours of fun on school playgrounds or in a neighbor's basement. It is no accident that *Battlestar Galactica* fever has heated up at the same time (1997) as *Star Wars* fandom reignited for the "special edition" of George Lucas' saga. They are both part of the 1977–79 outer space "battle" craze. When young adults think of one production, they inevitably remember the other.

Twenty-somethings today tend to recall the glory days of *Battlestar Galactica* with a sincere fondness, with the feeling that they watched something that was "special," if not necessarily of high quality. The message boards on the Internet and America Online are filled with admissions from *Galactica* fans about the show's many shortcomings. They hated Muffitt, Troy or Boxey. They despised the fact that science was such a stumbling block. They nitpick the terminology, and recall in detail every incident in which an actor said "year" instead of "yahren." Nevertheless, they still love the show with an almost childlike glee. It is, and may always be, a guilty pleasure that recalls the glow of youth, the advent of *Star Wars* and the beginning of modern space opera.

Not surprisingly, *Battlestar Galactica* fans can be found around the world; there are fans from Adelaide, South Australia, to Wokingham, England. All remember and glorify the program. They see it not as a rip-off of *Star Wars,* but almost as an extension of the magic spell woven by *Star Wars,* as well as a reminder of the freewheeling, experimental 1970s.

Over the years, there have been many *Battlestar Galactica* fan clubs to unite distant fans of the series. "The Caprica Society," a club headquartered in Brooklyn, New York, is a prominent example. It offers members a starting package of two gold cubits, a Colonial Warrior patch, a Colonial insignia, a membership card, and six issues of the fan club magazine (*The Book of the Word*). Other fan clubs include "The Thirteenth Tribe" and "*Galactica* One: Australian Fan Club." Many *Battlestar Galactica* fan clubs are dedicated specifically to the personable stars of the series. Richard Hatch (Apollo) is probably the most popular cast member, in large part because he is working so vigilantly to revive *Battlestar Galactica*. "Streets and Stars" is just one fan club devoted to Hatch and his career. It covers not only his work on *Battlestar Galactica*, but also his short stint opposite Karl Malden on *The Streets of San Francisco*. "The Richard Hatch Fan Club" is another such organization.

The background universe of *Battlestar Galactica* has also proven interesting enough to inspire detailed speculations on the part of many enterprising fans. *The Pegasus Chronicles* is a fan magazine authored by Sharon Monroe and dedicated to the continuing adventures of Commander Cain (Lloyd Bridges) and his legendary rogue battlestar (story elements that appeared in only "The Living Legend" episode of *Battlestar Galactica*). Another fanzine, *KOBOL*, endeavors to recount the history of the ancient mother world and the development of the Colonies prior to the Cylon attack and the great galactic exodus.

Crossover stories (stories blending the characters and situations of *Battlestar Galactica* with characters and situations of other science fiction movies and television programs) are also very popular with many *Battlestar Galactica* fans. "Survive the Alliance" is a story by Sharon Monroe and J. D. Rich that involves the *Galactica*'s arrival at Earth. In this unique tale, the Colonials discover to their surprise and horror that the humans on the planet have already been conquered by the reptilian visitors of *V*! "Battlestar Red" is the unlikely blending of the somber, sentimental *Battlestar Galactica* and satirical *Red Dwarf* universes. "Dark Dawn" and "Dark Dawn II" concern the *Galactica*'s encounter with the Enterprise-D of *Star Trek: The Next Generation*. There is even a *Galactica: 1980/A-Team* crossover story by Michele Martin! All of these crossover ventures prove that *Battlestar Galactica* fans tend to enjoy other sci-fi experiences in conjunction with *Galactica*. Perhaps that is not surprising since many were *Space: 1999* or *Star Trek* fans who fell in love with *Battlestar Galactica* when their favorite shows were cancelled. On a less positive note, *Battlestar Galactica* crossovers may be so numerous because of its propensity for space Westerns and its lack of curiosity about the universe. The shallowness of the drama may account for its pairing with another, more powerful show to make it seem more palatable, or more interesting.

Outside of the many crossover ventures, there is also much "straight" *Battlestar Galactica* fan fiction. "Birth of a Battlestar" by Paul Scheltz,

"*Galactica:* 2000" by Michael Gibrall, "Into the Great Wide Open" by Sarah Lubin and "Red Squadron" by Tice Leonard are just a few of the interesting titles that explore the background and themes of Glen Larson's universe. Even tender poetry has a place in *Galactica* fandom. Tina Vivian wrote the sensitive "Hidden Hunger" about the Cassiopeia-Starbuck relationship, and Cynthia Howe penned "The Lore of Adama." All of these works reveal a genuine love of *Battlestar Galactica*. Fan fiction of the traditional variety comes from all over the world: "Anomaly" from Richmond, Virginia, "Blue Squadron Reserve" from Michigan, "*Rising Star*" from Australia and "Legend of the *Rising Star*" from California.

Besides writing crossover stories, straight fiction and poetry, *Battlestar Galactica* fan clubs also indulge in role-playing. The currently in-vogue scenario offers various players the chance to man battlestars *Galactica, Atlantia, Pacifica* and *Rycon* in the yahren prior to the destruction of the Colonies.

Battlestar Galactica fans are also collectors. Fortunately for them, there is much memorabilia to collect. There are old toys which are frequently found at collectible shows — but usually for outrageous prices. There are also new toys from Trendmasters, videos from MCA, comic books (Marvel and Maximum Press) and new novels such as Richard Hatch's *Armageddon*. Beyond collecting, *Battlestar Galactica* fans enjoy the two staples of all TV sci-fi fandom: reminiscing and griping.

Reminiscing is a pleasurable pastime, and fan reminiscences about *Battlestar Galactica* run the gamut of human experience. People recount in detail the first time they saw each show, and they remember what was going on elsewhere in the world and on television while *Battlestar Galactica* was on. Three Mile Island, the ABC-TV premiere of *Jaws* and Sensurround are just a few of the topics that account for fan time. Other subjects for reminiscences include the actors ("They look so young!") and adolescent crushes on Maren Jensen or Dirk Benedict. The griping segment of fan time is perhaps less fun. It usually comes from fans unhappy with *Battlestar Galactica*'s many scientific blunders (fires in space, no light speed drive) or disillusioned by the low quality of *Galactica: 1980*. In fairness, griping is common in all fandoms, not just *Galactica*'s. In fact, *Battlestar Galactica* fans are probably more optimistic about the failings of their particular show than fans of other programs. They accept these glitches and defects, and still declare that they love the show. One of their primary arguments for a revival of *Battlestar Galactica* is what one message board participant called "The *Seinfeld* Defense." Simply stated, "The

Seinfeld Defense" states that *Seinfeld* was not very good during its first season on NBC, but that it improved dramatically each year until it was the top-rated show on television. *Battlestar Galactica* fans believe that *Galactica* could also have grown into a high-quality show if ABC had not cut it off in its prime.

What exactly is so appealing about *Battlestar Galactica* to long-time fans? Beyond the all-important nostalgia factor, series fans tend to derive enjoyment from the character relationships. One is tempted to state flat-out that *Battlestar Galactica* fans are less intellectual or philosophical than *Star Trek* or *Space: 1999* fans since their favorite sci-fi is conspicuously short on the "sci" and weak philosophically on the "fi," but that assertion is not necessarily true. Besides enjoying the adventure, mythology and special effects (the same things, incidentally, which draw fans to *Star Wars*), series fans pontificate at length about the significance of the Erich Von Däniken aspects of *Galactica*. They debate the nature of the crashed ship in "War of the Gods," and worry about Cain's fate following "Living Legend." They are just as curious about the implication of their favorite shows as *Star Trek*, *Star Wars* and *Space: 1999* fans are, even if their series of choice seems at times far more derivative and flawed than the aforementioned productions.

Star Trek fans tend to idolize Gene Roddenberry as "The Great Bird of the Galaxy." *Babylon 5* fans revere J. Michael Straczyinski, and *Star Wars* fans treat George Lucas as if he were a god. Interestingly, *Battlestar Galactica* fans, for the most part, do not worship Glen Larson with the same kind of intensity. Perhaps this is because fans have already seen him bastardize his creation with the dreadful *Galactica: 1980*, or because they have watched him churn out low-quality dreck like *Knight Rider* and *Manimal* with alarming regularity. Instead, fan devotion centers around Richard Hatch. Fans have undeniably pinned their hopes on him. If a revival is filmed, fans expect they will have Hatch to thank for it. He is a constant presence on the Internet with his home page, and he just penned the first original *Galactica* novel in years, *Armageddon*. He is the one carrying the torch. He is the one meeting with executives at Universal, the Sci-Fi Channel and Fox Television. He is the one rallying fans and pushing hard for *Battlestar Galactica* to be recognized as a pop culture phenomenon. Fans have responded and taken him into their hearts, going so far as to invite him to play their role-playing scenario with them.

Battlestar Galactica fans may be the first science fiction television fans since the Trekkers to be rewarded for their long years of diligence and devotion. No other genre series fans have experienced a television revival complete with the original actors, a second chance to grab national attention and even win over a new generation to the tenets of an "old" adventure. Of course, the promise of a revival has its own inherent dangers for fans. What if a new *Battlestar Galactica* does not improve on the original? Even worse, what if it is as bad as *Galactica: 1980*? If the latter becomes reality, *Galactica* fandom will face a grave crisis, one it may not be able to survive even in the face of fan fiction, new toys and model re-releases.

Battlestar Galactica *on the Internet*

In the mid-to-late 1990s, it has practically become *de rigueur* for science fiction television productions from *Alf* to *The X-Files* to have multiple fan sites on the Internet. In fact, the Internet has become perhaps the ideal place to buy and trade memorabilia, listen to series sound effects, appreciate seldom-printed series photographs and read thoughtful fan fiction and background speculation. For many intrepid fans, the information superhighway of the Internet is like an ongoing, online convention. Gerry and Sylvia Anderson's *Space: 1999* boasts sites such as "The Cyber Library" and "The Cybrary," and many interesting *Star Trek* sites are available for perusing on Bill Gate's Microsoft Network (MSN). Like these other popular genre TV programs, *Battlestar Galactica* has a burgeoning cyberlife on the World Wide Web.

Perhaps the best place to begin a survey of *Battlestar Galactica* online is with the America Online (AOL) service. In the "Vintage Science Fiction TV Series" section of its sci-fi bulletin board, America Online currently sports two message boards devoted totally to the universe of the lost colonists. One is called simply *"Battlestar Galactica,"* while the second goes under the moniker *"Battlestar Galactica* Revival." The same kind of discussion occurs in both. Fans of all ages discuss the series in detail, sometimes recalling interesting plots, sometimes remembering incidents related to the series such as the Mattel toy recall. Recent topics include whether *Galactica: 1980* is actually a "bad dream" from which Apollo or Starbuck will awaken, the disappearance of *Battlestar Galactica* from the Sci-Fi Channel's afternoon schedule (it was replaced by *The Incredible Hulk*) and brief reviews of Richard Hatch's book *Armageddon*. Every scrap of revival news is ritually discussed on the message boards in minute detail, from crazy rumors (Wil Wheaton will star as Boxey and Gary Coleman will be playing Boomer's son in the big screen remake of *Battlestar Galactica*!) to verifiable facts (The Sci-Fi Channel expressed interest in a revival to Richard Hatch). The quality of recent MCA video releases of "Lost Planet of the Gods" and "Gun on Ice Planet Zero" is also discussed on both message boards; toys, action figures, books and other collectibles are often traded for relatively fair prices.

Unlike some science fiction message boards, discussions do not tend to become ugly in either *Battlestar Galactica* boards unless a non-fan shows up and posts his unflattering opinion of the series in an obnoxious manner (all caps, with lots of exclamation points). These relatively innocuous message boards are a good place to visit periodically if a fan is interested in new trading card releases from Dart Flipcards, information on current roles of *Galactica* stars or advertisements for upcoming convention. For the more zealous, combative and Internet-experienced series devotee, there is another offering on the Internet: the *Battlestar Galactica* mailing list administrated by Kriss Tessin at Maiser@lib01.Ferris.Edu. Discussion is more heated and passionate at this location, and the topics range from those related to hard science fact to interesting *Battlestar Galactica* character studies.

To his credit, Richard Hatch has made the Internet a serious arena for the revival of *Galactica* in the last two years. At his personal website, The Richard Hatch Website at Richard Hatch Enterprises, the actor has provided a questionnaire for series fans to fill out and e-mail back to him. It asks questions about which characters and stories aficionados liked best and least on the 1978 series, as well as what elements they would like to see most in a new video revival of *Battlestar Galactica*. Ostensibly, Hatch utilizes this fan data and information as leverage in his ongoing meetings with various studio brass and network executives.

Hatch's website is worthwhile and amusing for other reasons as well. It features such unique comical items as "Favorite Movies of the Fleet" and "Starbuck's Top 10 Pick-Up Lines," as well as informational pages like "How to Support the Revival." The Richard Hatch Home Page also features a preview of his book with Golden, *Armageddon*, and a personal note of welcome from the actor himself. Hatch has effectively employed the capabilities of the Internet to make fans aware of his ongoing activities and convention appearances, as well as of toy, book and model releases related to *Battlestar Galactica*. The Internet, it seems, will be the primary tool of the revival revolution, and Hatch manipulates the medium expertly. He may be the first actor in history to take full advantage of the medium.

For fans who are looking for other *Galactica*n fun, there is much to choose from on the roadways of the Internet. The Official John "Baltar" Colicos Fan Club, the Star Galaxy Noah "Boxey" Hathaway Home Page and Michael Worrell's Lt. Starbuck Home Page all offer fans the opportunity to remember favorite *Galactica* characters and actors. Universal Studios has also offered fascinating online "chats" with *Battlestar Galactica* actors and behind-the-scenes personnel. A chat was held with Dirk Benedict on May 4, 1997, and with Richard Hatch on June 12, 1997. Donald Bellisario (5/27/97) and Christian Nyby, Jr. (6/04/97) also had the opportunity to share with fans their first-hand accounts of working on the series. All of these discussions centered around *Battlestar Galactica*, but other roles and jobs were mentioned as well.

Moving on to other *Battlestar Galactica* Internet joys, Robert Hanczyk's Archive of Fan Fiction offers original *Galactica* fan stories by various authors, and John P. LaRocque's Brief History of *Battlestar Galactica* displays a series timeline from preproduction to the revival news and new merchandise releases of the 1990s.

Also of great value to the online explorer is the *Battlestar Galactica* site administrated by Chris Pappas. Pappas is a die-hard *Galactica* fan and a serious collector of costumes, props and artwork from the series. He has thoughtfully scanned much of his impressive collection, and offered a sort of "online museum" so fans can examine Colonial Warrior fatigues, Egyptian-style space helmets and the like. Thoughtfully, Pappas' site goes beyond the limits of his collection. There is a database section which includes the original series *Writer's Guide* from 1978. Also conveniently accessed is a complete photo gallery and a link to photographs of fan-built models and miniatures. One of the most interesting and amusing of the fan models on display there is John Karpisak's four-foot-long rendering of the *Galactica*. Karpisak's battlestar appears to be extremely accurate, but it is made out of cardboard! At another model-builder's Internet site, one can examine John J. Fleming's Lego Viper and Raider models.

Perhaps the most unique site on the Internet is Battlestar Republica, an index of all things *Galactica*n and Republican. This site is dedicated not only to the survival of humanity in space, but also to the survival of Newt Gingrich and the GOP in Washington! More fun and less political is Battlestar MUSH (a role-playing game site) and Adam Stacey's WWW Page which offers a favorite episode poll as determined by fans.

Stacey's list places "Living Legend," "The Hand of God," "Saga of a Star World" and "War of the Gods" near the top of the roster, and "Take the *Celestra*" near the bottom.

If all of this *Battlestar Galactica*–related material is not enough to inspire a fan, he or she can also take a gander at Andrew Probert's early series design for the Cylons, or head straight to "Realm of Darkness" by Andre Jacques, an examination of Cylon history. Also available on a variety of sites are *Battlestar Galactica* and *Galactica: 1980* episode guides which feature complete cast and credits, airdate information and capsule summaries. Personal webpages belonging to fans Troy Vigil and Mark Heiman are also packed with interesting series information and are well worth a look. For those fans looking for more laughs than inspiration or information, they can go to sites featuring *Battlestar Galactica* drinking games, or pages which feature the complex rules of Pyramid, Lt. Starbuck's favorite card game.

From fan fiction to revival news, from sound clips to photographs and 3-D graphics, from message boards to archived reviews of *Battlestar Galactica* by *Izvestia*, Tom Shales or even *Time* magazine, the Internet is the perfect forum for fans to investigate the ever-expanding universe of *Battlestar Galactica* and its fandom.

A Survey of Battlestar Galactica *Memorabilia and Collectibles*

In some respects, the 1970s shine as a golden age for the science fiction toy collector. The Mego *Star Trek* and *Planet of the Apes* action figure craze dominated the first half of the decade, and the Kenner *Star Wars* merchandise empire closed it with a bang. Amidst this glut of sci-fi collectibles stand the various and sundry treasures of *Battlestar Galactica*.

Twenty years after its cancellation, *Battlestar Galactica* memorabilia is hotter than the Nova of Madagon, and raking in the gold cubits like there is no tomorrow. Interestingly, the Lords of Kobol are not the deities responsible for this unexpected resurrection. Instead, Richard Hatch can be thanked for all the renewed interest. He has spearheaded a well-organized, national campaign to revive the program as a new weekly syndicated series like *Hercules: The Legendary Journeys* or *Star Trek: Deep Space Nine*, and although no new *Battlestar Galactica* production has yet commenced, Hatch's cunning battle strategy has instigated a tidal wave surge of new interest in this two-decade-old teleseries. New comic books, model kits, trading cards and the re-release of the series on videotape are all recent additions to the collectible craze. All of this is surely good news for that patient collector of original *Battlestar Galactica* memorabilia who has been hording his collection for many a yahren and waiting for just the right centon to display it, revisit it or even sell it.

Action Figures and Spaceship Toys

Like *Space: 1999*, *Battlestar Galactica* was a big-bang publicity event and merchandising bonanza before the first episode even aired on ABC. A variety of toys and models were available on the shelves of Toys "R" Us and hundreds of hobby shops before the first review of the series was even written. Weeks before children even knew who or what a "Cylon" was, they were begging their beleaguered parents to buy them one. *Star Wars* had broken box office records just a year earlier, and enthusiastic toy-makers were eager to repeat Kenner's incredible success with sci-fi toy-lines of their own. Mattel, which had foolishly passed on the rights to *Star Wars* merchandise, introduced a group of 3.75-inch figures that bore a strong likeness to the *Galactica*'s leading men. This initial figure release included the dashing Lt. Starbuck, regal Commander Adama and the tan daggit, Muffit. Both Starbuck and Adama sported fancy cloth capes that could be removed, as well as molded black boots and warrior fatigues. They also came equipped with black pistols called "Colonial blasters" though their stiff, relatively immobile hands had a difficult time grasping them.

Representing evil in the universe were four additional action figures. The chrome Cylon Centurion was an accurate reproduction of the gargantuan robot seen in the series, right down to his black bayonet/laser rifle. Strangely, the Cylon figure's lower half was totally immobile: he could swivel 360 degrees at his hips, but his legs did not move. The Centurion's superior, the lavender-robed Imperious Leader, was also available from Mattel in 1978. Interestingly, this action figure revealed the Leader's reptilian facial features far better than the actual production ever did. During the series, the character was usually kept cloaked in shadows and filmed from a distance — a money-saving gimmick that enabled the Leader to speak without his prosthetic mouth ever moving. Then, the same footage could be used over and over again, and new dialogue could be recorded in post-production by actor Patrick Macnee. Mattel's toy

Top: Mattel's smaller line of figures included (*left to right*) Baltar, Lt. Starbuck, Muffit, Commander Adama and the Cylon Imperious Leader. *Bottom:* More bad villains from Mattel's line of small action figures: Ovions (*outer left and right*), Cylons and Lucifer (*center*).

revealed the Imperious Leader to be a rather dopey-looking lizard with a pink afro. He wore a lavender robe, and under his robe was an undetailed pink body that resembled Gumby's!

From "Saga of a Star World," the three-hour series premiere of *Battlestar Galactica,* came the six-armed insectoid drone called an Ovion.

Molded by Mattel in forest green, this action figure was garbed in a removable yellow, sleeveless shawl. He is worth substantially more money if this filigree drapery is still intact. The last villain of this *Battlestar Galactica* pack was the pig-like marauder seen in the episode "The Magnificent Warriors." Sculpted with an orange alien face, this Boray is among the rarest and most sought-after of all *Battlestar Galactica* action figures. It is not unusual to see a mint Boray selling for $50–$75 at antique shows.

After the success of its initial figure line, Mattel struck back with further additions. Not surprisingly, they were all fascinating bad guys. Dapper in a black suit and white collar, the human turncoat Baltar today fetches a high price. He was designed with a good resemblance to his alter ego, John Colicos, but the character's outfit on the show was green, not black. The Cylon IL–series droid, Lucifer and a recast of the Cylon Centurion (this time in gold) were also offered. Amazingly, no Cpt. Apollo action figure was made available by Mattel, despite the fact that he was the primary series lead of *Battlestar Galactica*. Young children probably would have preferred to play with an Apollo doll rather than an Adama doll. Also significant is the fact that Mattel never produced any figures based on the female characters. Kenner's *Star Wars* figure line included Princess Leia in 1977, and other lines such as Mego's *Star Trek*, *The Black Hole* and *Buck Rogers* toys all featured females such as Lt. Ilia, Kate McCrae, Wilma Deering and Princess Ardala.

Mint condition, still on their blue cardboard backings, the *Battlestar Galactica* action figure line from Mattel can often fetch $30 apiece in 1998. Intrepid collectible scouts may find them "loose" at flea markets for as little as $3 apiece, but most often sans weaponry and accoutrements such as capes, cloaks or shawls. However, *caveat emptor*. After 20 years of wear and tear, the detailing on the faces of the humans (Starbuck, Adama, Baltar) has an alarming tendency to disintegrate or crack.

Also in 1978–79, Mattel marketed two impressive, 12-inch figures from *Battlestar Galactica*. The Cylon Warrior was especially well done. With a flashing red eye that could dart back and forth in the Centurion's head like a ping pong ball, and a glowing crimson "heart," this robot creation was quite menacing. Matching his onscreen person, the large Cylon figure modelled a reflective chrome head and a chrome, removable chest-plate. He came equipped with a variety of laser gun attachments which also lit up.

The second large figure, called simply "Colonial Warrior," resembled neither Starbuck nor Apollo, and looked suspiciously as if he had pointed, Vulcan ears. He also had stark-white hair, jet black eyebrows and a tan cloth

Left: In addition to a line of smaller action figures, Mattel also released two large-scale replicas of *Battlestar Galactica* characters. Along with a Colonial Warrior (who came complete with a cloth jacket and white-blond hair), there was this menacing Cylon Warrior. When a panel on his back was pressed, his red eye and chest plate lit up. *Top right:* The Colonial Scarab was also released by Mattel. This combination Viper-landram was a vehicle never actually seen on *Battlestar Galactica.* *Bottom:* Mattel's toy Vipers were designed to spit missiles from the nose section. When the missiles turned out to be a choking hazard, the toy was re-released with the missiles glued in place.

warrior's vest. Like the Cylon, he came with various "light up" laser attachments. Today, these large-scale toys are more prized than a plate of fresh Mushies or a well-aged bottle of Amgrosia. They go for as high as $75–120 apiece at antique/collectible shows.

Unlike the Kenner *Star Wars* line, no vehicles or spacecrafts were produced to scale with either the 3.75- or 12-inch *Battlestar Galactica* figure sets. Instead, Mattel released a separate line of smaller plastic crafts. The Colonial Viper and the Cylon Raider were accurate depictions of the John Dykstra miniatures. The Colonial Stellar Probe and the Colonial Scarab, however, were original Mattel designs that were never featured on the weekly program. In 1978, all of these spaceships were designed to shoot small red missiles.

After a lawsuit concerning a child who had swallowed a projectile and choked to death, Mattel re-released the toys with the projectiles glued to the turrets of the ships. These toys, especially those that fire the red missiles, are extremely hard to find in the '90s. One should expect to shell out $30–$50 at collectible shows, even for ones in less than mint condition.

Also from Mattel came a rendering of the *Galactica*'s massive launching bay. From the Viper Launch Station, two plastic Colonial Vipers could be launched out into space to knock down cardboard stand-ups of Cylon attack crafts. The Viper Launch Station in mint condition sometimes sells for as high as $200 at sci-fi specialty stores. For Christmas of 1979, Mattel planned a two-foot-long Electronic *Battlestar Galactica* Command Ship complete with a dorsal laser cannon and pop-open landing bays with small Viper replicas inside. Because *Battlestar Galactica* was cancelled by Christmas 1979, the toy was never mass-produced or released on the market. *Starlog* #24 (July 1979) reported its existence, and even offered a photo of the toy alongside such memorabilia as the *Star Trek: The Motion Picture* Electronic *Enterprise*, Milton Bradley's "Star Birds" and Parker Brothers' "Rom the Space Knight."

In 1997, a new line of *Battlestar Galactica* toys and action figures were released from Trendmasters, the same company which produced the action figures and ships for the highly successful feature film *Independence Day* in 1996. The *Battlestar Galactica* Trendmasters' releases were based not on the designs of the original 1978 series, but on the revisionist drawings of the 1995 Maximum Press comic book series. Trendmasters already showed an unfortunate tendency towards idealizing the action figures they produced (the Jeff Goldblum action figure from *ID4* looked like a steroid-pumping Arnold Schwarzenneger clone with glasses). The same style was applied to the Trendmasters' *Battlestar Galactica* figures, and the Starbuck action character looked more like an angry superhero from Todd McFarlane's *Spawn* than a recognizable human being. The Trendmasters' Starbuck arrived on the scene with two gigantic black laser cannons that could fire missiles, an Egyptian-style Viper helmet faithful to the concepts of the series, and a see-through red "Viper battle blade," something never seen on *Battlestar Galactica*. Additionally, Starbuck was the only hero of the first and so far *only* toy release.

Representing the villains were the Cylon Centurion and the Cylon Commander, each with double-pulse laser missile blasters, LED "light up" eyes and "piercing battle blades." These two Cylon soldiers were essentially the same figure, but the Centurion was chrome/silver and the Commander was gold. Most questionable of all, however, was the final figure

Battlestar Galactica **figures mirrored the revisionist designs of the Maximum Press comic series.**

of the Trendmasters' set: The Cylon Imperious Leader. This toy did not at all resemble the creature shown on the series (a cloaked, sedentary being with a sparkling purple afro), but was instead depicted as a hunched-over, winged, lizard creature with claws for feet. He came with a "double-blast" staff of power, poseable wings and a removable "mask of pain."

The Trendmasters' toy ships, like the Mattel spaceships of 20 years earlier, did not accommodate the full-sized action figures. Instead, they carried tiny replicas of Colonial Warriors and Cylon Centurions. The Raider and the Viper, like the Trendmasters' figures, were based on the revisionist blueprints of the modern Maximum Press comic book rather than the designs of the '70s TV series. Each ship came with engine lights, wing mounted turbo lasers and ejecting missiles.

Model Kits

The massive Battlestar *Galactica* itself was released as a model kit by Monogram in 1978. It was an incredibly detailed and accurate recreation of the spectacular warship down to the most minute turret and hull out-cropping. Molded in metallic gray, this cosmic battleship is surely the high-light of any serious *Battlestar Galactica* collection. The *Galactica* also came complete with a decal sheet offering modelers the option to build *Galactica Atlantia* or even Cain's ship, *Pegasus.*

Other model kits in the Monogram series included the Cylon base-star, which resembled two flying saucers jointed at the hip, the boom-erang-shaped Cylon raider and the outer space jet fighter the Colonial Viper. In 1978, these Monogram kits sold for $5 (fighters) and $13 (base-ships) respectively. As with any model kits, the *Battlestar Galactica* kits are worth substantially more today if they are unassembled and in their original packaging. As unbelievable as it may sound, the *Galactica* and Cylon basestar kits sold recently (1995–1996) in mail-order model catalogs for as high as $250 apiece! Those prices quickly proved unsustainable when the *Battlestar Galactica* re-issue kits arrived in early 1997.

On January 18, 1997, Revell-Monogram sponsored the *Battlestar Galactica* model reissue in stores around the United States, offering the same four spaceship kits as those listed above, but with new box artwork (as well as new misspellings: on the new Viper instructions, "Boomer" is spelled as "Bommer"). The reissued model kits also feature higher price

The great Battlestar itself! An assembled, highly detailed model of the *Galactica* was produced by Monogram and reissued in 1997.

tags, reflecting 20 years of inflation. The two fighters have been selling for $12–15 apiece, and the *Galactica* and Cylon baseship have been selling for $22.50–$25 apiece. Perhaps this is not too much to ask considering the hefty $250 price tag of 1995–1996.

More Toys

Other original *Battlestar Galactica* memorabilia from Mattel includes a soft tan stuffed daggit who emits a screeching mechanical yelp when its string is pulled. Mattel also introduced the world to the *Battlestar Galactica* lasermatic pistol and rifle, two supposedly "Colonial" weapons which did not all resemble the guns seen on the weekly series. The daggit and the guns are rare and today sell for $50–75. Inevitably, there were also commonplace 1970s toys such as the Parkers Brothers *Battlestar Galactica* Board Game. This game put the player into the role of Colonial Viper pilot. The specified mission was to capture a Cylon Raider after space

The box of Monogram's Cylon Raider 1978 model kit affords a closer look at these deadly manta ray shaped war machines.

Top left: A Colonial Warrior's best friend: a stuffed animal, plush Muffit. Notice the cord under his mouth. When pulled, it created authentic "mechanical daggit" barks. *Right:* The *Battlestar Galactica* thermos shows original series artwork by artist Ralph McQuarrie. *Bottom:* For Christmas 1978, Parker Brothers marketed a *Battlestar Galactica* game that saw intrepid game players fighting Cylon fighters.

combat. During the dogfight, evasive action, force field attack and black holes all played a significant part. Also released by Parker Brothers in 1978 were three jigsaw puzzles (Starbuck on Carillon, a dogfight in space, the *Galactica*'s ragtag fleet). Inevitably, there were also *Battlestar Galactica* Colorforms, a lunchbox and thermos from Aladdin, a space combat game for Colonial Warriors from FASA, a Vertibird flying set with a spinning Viper and even a bubble machine in the shape of a Cylon warrior. In 1978–1979, there was no toy shortage for kids looking to have hours of fun in the universe of *Battlestar Galactica*.

Battlestar Galactica *Books*

In 1977, George Lucas' novelization of *Star Wars* started a trend. Directors of popular films and TV shows began to write adaptations of their work. *Close Encounters of the Third Kind* was allegedly written by Steven Spielberg, although the work was actually ghost-written by a more experienced writer, and Gene Roddenberry penned the novelization of *Star Trek: The Motion Picture* in 1979. Glen Larson joined this group. Together with authors Robert Thurston and Michael Resnick, Larson was the scribe for many *Battlestar Galactica* episode adaptations for Berkley Books' Science Fiction publishing division. *Battlestar Galactica* was an adaptation of "Saga of a Star World." It was a very good read, and filled with information about the Cylons and even Adama's history. It was more thoughtful and informative than most episodes of the TV series.

The Cylon Death Machine, a novelization of "The Gun on Ice Planet Zero," was the second book in the series. It was followed by *The Tombs of Kobol*, an adaptation of "Lost Planet of the Gods;" *The Young Warriors*, an adaptation of "The Young Lords;" *Galactica Discovers Earth*, a novelization of the first episode of *Galactica: 1980*; *Die Chameleon!*, a write-up of "The Man with Nine Lives" and *Surrender the Galactica*, based on "Baltar's Escape." Other books in the *Battlestar Galactica* literary series were named after the episodes they adapted. These books included *The Living Legend*, *War of the Gods*, *Experiment in Terra*, *The Long Patrol* and *Greetings from Earth*. *Apollo's War*, the last *Battlestar Galactica* book until 1997, was an original adventure.

Perhaps none of the adaptations or stories listed above are as significant as the hardback *Armageddon* written by Richard Hatch and Chris Golden and released July 7, 1997. This fine work begins 18 yahrens after the end of *Battlestar Galactica*. Boxey has grown up and become Cpt. Troy, but there is no other reference to *Galactica: 1980*. Commander Adama has recently passed away, and Apollo and Athena are the Council of 12's top two candidates to replace him. Lt. Starbuck is missing in action, and the Cylons have a deadly new weapon. Even more strangely, Baltar is apparently being manipulated by an evil influence (Count Iblis?). *Armageddon* is a well-written yarn and a legitimate, believable sequel to *Battlestar Galactica*. It also thoughtfully provides a lexicon of the Colonial language in an appendix.

Besides novelizations and continuations, there have been many other *Battlestar Galactica* books on the market during the last 20 years. *Encyclopedia Galactica* offers full color pho-

Glen A. Larson and Michael Resnick penned the Berkley Books adaptation of "*Galactica Discovers Earth*," the first episode of *Galactica: 1980*.

tographs of cast members, spaceships and planets. It also provides details on places and people such as Cyranus, Equellis, Lucifer and Iblis (spelled "Ibley" for some reason). *The Official Battlestar Galactica Scrapbook* from Grosset and Dunlap is a text dedicated to the making of the short-lived series. Written by James Neyland, this 1978 book is filled with great black-and-white photographs and preproduction sketches from the series. Brief biographies are given for *Galactica*'s creators, crew and cast members, but the book reads mostly as propaganda. The series is hyped as incredibly popular, and it is even called "a major step in our popular culture."[1] It also predicts that the series will run for many years on ABC. Not surprisingly, Universal's name is all over this particular book, suggesting much of the authorial hyperbole was written at the studio's bidding.

A more interesting work is *The Official Battlestar Galactica Blueprints*,

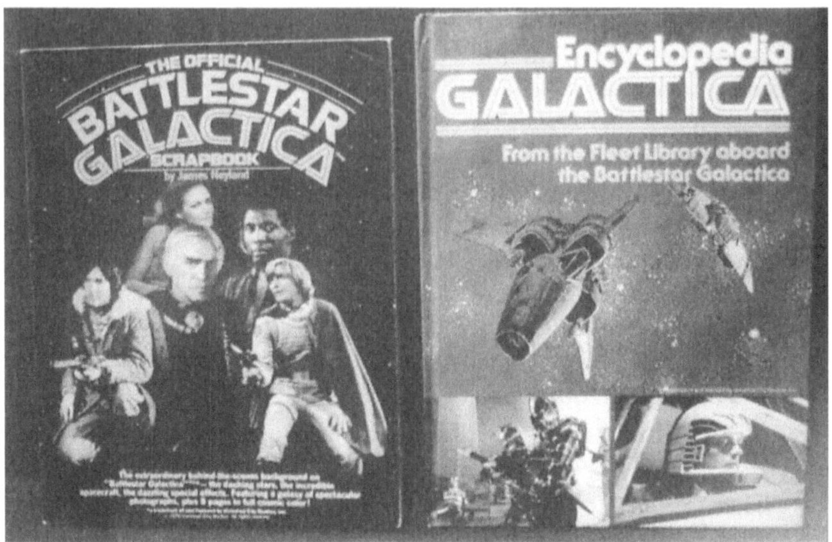

Two official *Battlestar Galactica* releases: *The Official Battlestar Galactica Scrapbook* by James Neyland and the *Encyclopedia Galactica: From the Fleet Library Aboard the Battlestar Galactica.*

which sold in the U.S. at the time of the series for a cheap $7.95. From Today Press, this impressive set of highly detailed plans came with ten blueprints of series vehicles and locales. There were blueprints for the following: interior Cylon fighter cockpit, interior small shuttlecraft, the landram, Imperious Leader's Chambers, Interior Laser Station (apparently from "Gun on Ice Planet Zero"). Catapult Launch Deck section, Viper landing gear, Section of Viper, Command Deck, *Galactica* Bridge (rotating platform) and General Overview *Galactica* Bridge. The blueprints came in a small brown folder emblazoned with the *Battlestar Galactica* logo.

For younger audiences, Scholastic Book Services published *The Battlestar Galactica Storybook*, a simplistic work by Charles Mercer that reinterpreted the Glen Larson script for "Saga of a Star World." With over 100 full-color photographs, this book is a visual treat for *Galactica* fans, if not an intellectual one. An auditory feast was provided courtesy of MCA Platinum Plus, the company which released the *Battlestar Galactica Original Soundtrack* with musical selections from "Saga of a Star World" performed by the Los Angeles Philharmonic Orchestra and conducted by Stu Phillips. Interestingly, one selection on side two is called "Boxey's Problem, Serena's Illness," relating to the deleted Jane Seymour space "cancer" subplot. Another composition is called "Dash to the Elevator," although the word "elevator" is not part of Colonial nomenclature.

A unique kind of *Battlestar Galactica* publication was also released by Windmill Books/E.P. Dutton in 1975. For $4.95, fans could purchase the official *Battlestar Galactica Iron-On Transfer Book*. This book noted that colors "come alive when ironed on," and provided careful instructions for ironing many *Battlestar Galactica* transfers onto T-shirts. Among the photos that could be ironed on were a medium shot of Apollo aboard the *Galactica*, a scene of two Cylon Centurions attacking the casino on Carillon, a close-up of the double-mouthed alien singer in the casino, a shot of Starbuck in the underground tunnels of the Ovions, another shot of

Stu Phillips' memorable music was captured on vinyl for the *Battlestar Galactica* soundtrack album.

Although iron-on transfer books have fallen out of fashion in the 1990s, in the 1970s *Galactica* fans could emblazon their shirts with scenes straight out of the cosmic adventure.

two Cylon Centurions on Carillon, a close-up of the Cylon Raider, a full-body shot of Boomer kneeling and aiming his laser blaster, a side-view of an Ovion playing his harp, a red-lit snapshot of Adama pointing to his starchart, a close-up of Muffit and special effects shots of Vipers and a Cylon basestar. Although iron-on transfer books have fallen out of vogue in the 1990s, they were a hot item in the 1970s and well worth collecting if one is a *Battlestar Galactica* fan.

Comic Books

Since the late 1960s, it has been inevitable that every time a new science fiction epic is released on the big screen or on television, a comic book series soon follows it onto newsstands. Marvel Comics hit it big by producing an ongoing *Planet of the Apes* comic book and magazine series in the early 1970s. They attempted to repeat that success with four-color adaptations of *2001: A Space Odyssey*, *Logan's Run* and, of course, *Star Wars*. Charlton Comics played the TV/movies game as well, offering continuing comic book adventures of *The Six Million Dollar Man* and *Space: 1999*. It is no surprise then, that *Battlestar Galactica* was a prime candidate to be converted into comic book form in 1978.

A sampling of magazines featuring *Battlestar Galactica* on their covers.

Marvel Comics, which was already producing a monthly *Star Wars* comic, was the lucky company to win the rights to the *Galactica* property. Presented in full "Marvelcolor" by editor-in-chief Jim Shooter, and penned by Roger McKenzie with art and coloring by Ernie Colon, the first *Battlestar Galactica* comic was an oversized Marvel Super Special. This special collector's edition sold for $1.50 and featured a cover painting of the *Galactica* by Rick Bryant. It recounted the story of "Saga of a Star World" with some strange alterations. Baltar, for one, was a bald homunculus who was decapitated on page 41 in full, gory color. Sire Uri was depicted as an obese, round man, and Serina was called "Lyra," a name from an early draft of the teleplay. The ending of this adaptation is especially confusing since Lyra begs Apollo to take care of Boxey "no matter what happens!", indicating that she is dying from the space cancer that was originally part of Serina's character arc.

The "superspecial" adaptation of "the television sensation" of *Battlestar Galactica* also featured a Steve Swires interview with John Dykstra entitled "The Wizard of Hollywood's Dream Factory." Other nonfiction pieces about the universe of *Battlestar Galactica*, including "Life in the Future," "Battle Tactics," "Spaceships and Such: Hardware of the Future" and "Aliens and Robots," were written by Tom Rogers. There were also two poster-sized illustrations in this special: one of Adama and one of Muffit.

When the regular Marvel comic began, it started with the same art and text of the superspecial, but the story was split into three regular-sized monthly editions. The first segment of the story debuted in March 1979. It was called "Annihilation" and the cover depicted a Cylon raider strafing the people of Caprica. That was followed in April 1979 by "Exodus." The cover of part two featured a view from the bridge of the *Galactica* with a blond in Apollo's arm, and Adama, Boxey and Muffit all standing around. The final part of the trilogy, released in May 1979, was called "Deathtrap." The cover depicted a hulking Cylon gargantuan pointing his weapon at Boxey and Muffit as an Ovion looked on from the background.

Issues #4 and #5 of the Marvel *Battlestar Galactica* series featured an adaptation of "Lost Planet of the Gods." This story was adapted in part to account for the death of Serina/Serena/Lyra. With #6, Marvel began telling original stories. The first continuing adventure featured Commander Adama entering a strange device called the "Memory Machine." This invention would allow one to experience all sorts of repressed memories, and it was Adama's hope that he would be able to remember from his youth the exact location of the mysterious planet Earth. The villain

Marvel Publications' oversized adaptation of "Saga of a Star World" featured not only the bloody beheading of a bald Baltar and a Serina renamed "Lyra," but also several pages of information about the special effects, robots and ships of the series.

in this series of stories was not the Cylons, but Sire Uri. After one adventure in September 1979, Adama became trapped in the Memory Machine for a time, and forced to relive early adventures with Col. Tigh against old model Cylons. In #8, Adama also remembered his youthful hatred of and competition with Baltar (who now resembled the character seen on TV instead of the bald Nosferatu-style character of the superspecial).

After the Memory Machine subplot, Apollo faced off against a deadly living planet in issue #10 and Starbuck became involved with the alluring Queen Eurayle of ScavengeWorld. The Marvel series continued unabated with stories such as "Shuttle Diplomacy," "Space Mimic" and "Berserker" carrying on the drama. One particularly interesting new character in the Marvel series was the fleet engineer Shadrach, who provided all the ships in the fleet with light speed — a welcome addition. Unfortunately, by the end of its first year *Battlestar Galactica* the comic book had outlived *Battlestar Galactica* the TV series, and interest in the title began to wane. The last issue, #23, was published in January 1981, a year after *Galactica: 1980* had premiered, and six months after it was cancelled. When the Marvel title folded, it was the end of *Battlestar Galactica* in comic form for more than a decade.

In July 1995, *Battlestar Galactica* burst back on the comic scene with

Marvel's *Battlestar Galactica* comic series ran until 1981. The cover of this issue, alongside official series blueprints, highlights the actions of "Berserker."

a vengeance. Marvel Comics was out of the picture and the up-and-coming Maximum Press successfully published a hip, exciting comic series that was ostensibly based on the tenets and situations of *Battlestar Galactica*, but it featured revisionist designs of costumes, characters and spacecrafts. The *Galactica* became a much more baroque-looking spacecraft (complete with a dorsal spine to make it look more like an outer space alligator). The Colonial Viper was adjusted to be sleeker in appearance and to feature turbo laser cannons on the lower tip of the bottom wings instead of at the upper point of the wing-triangle. The top wing was revised to have a forward hook, and the engine blocks were made to look more elliptical. The Cylon manta ray crafts also received an unnecessary face-lift. They became more sleek and advanced-looking, as if the designs of 1978 had become outmoded. Of course, this was a strange conceit. After all, what comic book artist would dare to redesign the U.S.S. *Enterprise* or the spaceships seen in *Star Wars*?

"War of Eden" was the first Maximum Press comic story to be published in Summer 1995, and it was followed by "The Enemy Within," "Starbuck" and "Apollo's Journey," a multipart story written by Richard Hatch and published from April 1996 to June 1996. That story was followed by "Journey's End" and others. The Maximum Press series offered an alternate vision of *Battlestar Galactica*, not the world seen on TV. For the faithful fans, the new comic was strangely vexing. It was great to read new adventures and understand that the series was receiving new attention, but at the same time many of the designs that made the series so memorable had been abandoned. Perhaps that is why the novel *Armageddon* was received with such enthusiasm by the *Battlestar Galactica* faithful: It did not attempt to go back and revise what had been established on the series. Instead, it legitimately continued the adventure with characters, ships and creatures similar to the TV show.

If *Battlestar Galactica* is revived as a new series, it will have to contend with the Maximum Press situation. Should new miniatures of the *Galactica*, Vipers and Cylon Raiders be faithful to John Dykstra's designs, or to Maximum Press conceits? This author favors a return to the original designs so that footage from the old show can be cut (as "flashbacks") into new adventures. A shift in the look of Colonial technology would preclude that possibility (and thus preclude any scenes in which Apollo recalls the words of his father, the late Adama). Anyway, if *Battlestar Galactica* is revived on television, one fact is certain: There will be more *Battlestar Galactica* comic books on the horizon.

Epilogue: A Shining Quest

Battlestar Galactica is not dead. New toys, new MCA video releases, new models from Revell-Monogram and new books by Richard Hatch insure that the series will survive well past the year 2000. Richard Hatch has focused fan attention with his resurrection efforts, and he currently dispenses news updates and wisdom on his Internet page. But what of a *Battlestar Galactica* series revival? Is it possible? Will anything come from the hush-hush negotiations between Hatch and Fox TV? Or between Hatch and the Sci-Fi Channel? And what about Glen Larson's plans to revive the series with new actors and characters? What of the rumors of an animated series (according to Internet scuttlebutt, John Colicos has reportedly already signed up to voice Baltar)? These are the questions that burn like a space fire in the minds of *Battlestar Galactica* fans as of this writing.

More significant to the science fiction genre as a whole is this question: Should *Battlestar Galactica* be revived at all, considering its spotty history, its frequently bad writing and the loud accusations of "rip-off" that have plagued it for so long? Does *Battlestar Galactica* merit a second chance?

If the series is revived, fans must be prepared for the acerbic commentary of critics who will undoubtedly see a revival as a hopelessly bad idea. Frankly, they are wrong. A new *Battlestar Galactica* could fix a lot of the problems that inhibited serious enjoyment of the first series 20 years ago. First of all, taking *Deep Space Nine* or *Voyager* as an example, a revised *Galactica* could visit new alien worlds, and no longer be tied to the Western back lot at Universal (if it even exists any more!). There is just no way that space Westerns like "The Lost Warrior" and "The Magnificent Warriors" would pass muster today, and Larson and Hatch are undoubtedly aware of that. Secondly, the scientific inaccuracies displayed in "Gun on Ice Planet Zero" and "Fire in Space" could be addressed successfully today. After all, how hard would it be to equip the fleet with light speed? It need not even be a major plot point. In his first journal as Commander of the *Galactica*, Apollo could comment on the fact that Colonial Engineers have just finished a 20-yahren project to retrofit the fleet with new light speed generators. As for the space combat? Leave it alone. *Star Wars* also features space combat with "winged" spaceships, and this convention has become accepted now. When *Space: Above and Beyond* aired in 1995-96, it featured winged spaceships too. The look of *Battlestar Galactica* can still compete today.

Most importantly, a reunion of the original characters would give the series a whole new context of stories. What has Tigh been doing for 20 yahren? Or Boomer? Did Starbuck marry Cassiopeia? What became of Baltar? Excellent stories could hinge on these characters. Additionally, viewers would come to the show with a sense of familiarity and nostalgia. They would not have to adjust themselves to new characters (as they did with the casts of *Voyager*, *Deep Space Nine* and *Star Trek: The Next Generation*). On the contrary, a new *Battlestar Galactica* series with the original cast would have the nostalgic feeling of the *Star Trek* feature films. Apollo and Starbuck would be older, but not too old to command the upper deck of a battlestar.

Why else should *Battlestar Galactica* return? It is different enough from today's science fiction television epics to stand tall. It is not hopelessly insular, as is *Babylon 5*, nor as familiar as *Deep Space Nine* and *Voyager*, which are still telling recycled *Star Trek: The Next Generation* stories (which are in turn recycled *Star Trek* stories). A new *Battlestar Galactica* as outer space war drama could put the action-adventure back into science fiction television. Since *Battlestar Galactica* never focused on either moral quandaries (like *Star Trek*) or duplicitous wheeling-dealings among various alien republics (like *Babylon 5*), it could concentrate instead on exploring the hearts and minds of its travelers. What has it been like for the people of the fleet to be cooped up for two decades? Is martial law still in effect? How will the people respond to the death of Adama, the man who delivered them from certain death? Will Apollo ever be able to follow his father's footsteps? What of Starbuck? Does he have what it takes to develop from cocky young buck to seasoned, conservative professional? How has he coped with aging, and the fading of his good looks? There is a whole universe of character issues to explore. Beyond those possibilities, there is the return of the Cylons or Count Iblis to contemplate, as well as new foes. A new *Battlestar Galactica* series, if it addresses these concepts and corrects the flaws of its first incarnation, could be the best science fiction drama of the early 21st century, despite its origins as a '70s space Western and exploitation of *Star Wars*.

Today, many people who play in the science fiction television field would prefer to see *Battlestar Galactica* as a one-year anomaly, a bloated turkey that waddled onto the stage and then was heard no more. That interpretation could not be more incorrect. In 1995, the Fox Network ran *Space: Above and Beyond*, a one-season series about a group of space fighter pilots battling an intractable enemy. The young hotshots flew ships with wings, and the series began with a treacherous surprise attack. Much of the action even took place aboard a deep space "aircraft" carrier much like the *Galactica*. In conception and design, it was *Battlestar Galactica* redux. Another interesting coincidence was that *Space: Above and Beyond* aired on Sunday nights, like its spiritual predecessor. *TV Guide* even compared it to Glen Larson's 1970s series, wondering if it would survive to enjoy a lucrative *Star Trek* fandom or be remembered only as a *Battlestar Galactica* fade-out."[1] That line was more prophetic than *TV Guide* writer Michael Logan realized. Costing a hefty $2 million per episode (twice the cost of the average *Battlestar Galactica* episode in 1978-79), *Space: Above and Beyond* disappeared after its maiden season. And *Battlestar Galactica*, for having been such a "fade-out," is showing remarkable strength today. Twenty years after its premiere, there are new books, new merchandise and intense fan devotion. Will *Space: Above and Beyond* be able to boast the same kind of demographics in 2016?

On other fronts, *Battlestar Galactica* has also been highly influential. Borellian Nomen, as the details of this text have (I hope) demonstrated, are very likely the basis for the revisionist Klingons seen in *The Next Generation*, *Deep Space Nine*, and the popular *Star Trek* feature film series. Even on a more simplistic level, the special effects of *Battlestar Galactica* are important because they were recycled heavily in later series such as *Buck Rogers in the 25th Century*. The *Battlestar Galactica* theme song also showed up as the main overture of *Airplane 2: The Sequel* (1982)! Even the miserable *Galactica: 1980* has had an impact. Its "fish-out-of-water" scenario was mimicked in surprising detail by *Star Trek IV: The Voyage Home* in 1986, and its alien invasion of Los Angeles was reprised by the runaway hit *Independence Day* (1996). That is not a small impact considering the series ran only ten weeks in 1980.

Even though *Battlestar Galactica* is by no means sterling science fiction, it is nonetheless enjoyable television. It is a "guilty pleasure," but a pleasure all the same. If it is being watched, remembered and loved in 1997 and 1998, chances are it will also survive into the 21st century. Though that possibility may be none-too-appealing to fans of *Star Wars* and *Star Trek*, or to hard-line genre critics, it is positive proof that *Battlestar Galactica* had *something*. Call that *something* magic, call it chemistry, or just call it good luck. For whatever reason, the series has survived into the late 1990s, after just one season on the air in 1978. That is no small feat considering that other science fiction TV and film epics of perhaps approximate quality, including *Buck Rogers in the 25th Century*, *Planet of the Apes* and *Beauty and the Beast*, have all disappeared (at least for the time being) from the national consciousness. Let everyone hope that *Battlestar Galactica* treads a bold new path if and when it returns. It has supplanted *Star Trek* as the science fiction show that will not die, and so now has an obligation to speak to its loyal fans and to the future in provocative new ways. If history is repeated and a new version of *Battlestar Galactica* offers only the same silly clichés, *Star Wars* riffs and space Westerns, then *Battlestar Galactica*'s future will tarnish faster than the chrome armor of the Cylons.

Perhaps unjustly, worthy TV visions such as *Space: 1999*, *The Prisoner*, *Kolchak* and *U.F.O.* have never been granted a second chance to woo science fiction fanatics around the world. When these series died, they died hard. *Battlestar Galactica* looks as if it could be granted an opportunity these shows were denied. It must not squander its second chance, lest it be remembered not as the show that would not die, but as the show that could not learn.

Planets Visited by the *Galactica*

Battlestar Galactica ran only 17 episodes. However, it seems a revival may occur soon, perhaps before the 21st century. Already, dedicated *Galactica* fans have made inroads with new comic books (1995), new toys (early 1997) and even new novels such as *Armageddon* (1997). For the avid *Galactica* scholar looking to pick up continuity plot threads and references in these inevitable new products (and possibly in a new TV series), the author has accumulated a planet-by-planet guide to the *Galactica*'s TV journey in chronological order from the Great Colonies to cancellation. *Galactica: 1980* has not been included here because in all likelihood it will be ignored in any future *Galactica* productions.

Planet Name	Description	Inhabitants
1. Carillon	Desert/rich in Tylium	Ovions
2. Kobol	Mother world of the Great Colonies	None
3. Equellis	A farming community	Humans
4. Proteus	Penal asteroid of the Colonies. First planet encountered outside Cyranus	Humans
5. "Zero"	Ice planet	Cylon, Theta Clones
6. Sectar	A farming community	Humans, the Boray
7. Attila	Swamp world	A human family
8. Gamorray	Fuel Base, outer capital of Cylon Empire	Cylons
9. Iblis	A red-hued planet where *Galactica* first ran into Count Iblis	?
10. Paradeen	A farming community	Terrans
11. Terra	A technological planet on the verge of a nuclear holocaust	Terrans: Eastern Alliance Western Bloc

Battlestar Galactica in *Buck Rogers in the 25th Century*

Glen A. Larson debuted *Buck Rogers in the 25th Century* the season after *Battlestar Galactica* was cancelled. In an effort to make *Buck Rogers* look more impressive and expensive than it really was, a whole catalogue of *Battlestar Galactica* effects, miniatures, stock footage and even costumes and makeup were constantly reused in the 1979–81 Gil Gerard series. Indeed, part of the fun of watching *Buck Rogers in the 25th Century* today is spotting all of the material culled from *Battlestar Galactica*. Below is a list of events, ships and effects that were made for one Larson series, but were appropriated by the other.

Seen in **Buck Rogers** Episode:	SPFX/Prop/Locale	Originally Seen in *Galactica* Episode:
"Awakening"	Buck's *Ranger III* shuttlecraft	"Greetings from Earth" as Terran family shuttle
"Awakening"	"Location" shots of New Chicago	"Greetings from Earth" as city on Paradeen
"Planet of the Slave Girls"	The planet Vistula	"Saga of a Star World" as the planet Carillon
"Planet of the Slave Girls"	Vistula's hangar bay (miniature)	"Lost Planet of the Gods" as Cylon base
"Return of the Fighting 69th"	Astro sled dorsal turret chair	"The Hand of God" as the Celestial Chamber chair
"Unchained Woman"	Background alien	"The Magnificent Warriors" as a Boray

Seen in ***Buck Rogers*** **Episode:**	**SPFX/Prop/Locale**	**Originally Seen in** ***Galactica* Episode:**
"Unchained Woman"	Buck's tunic	"The Lost Warrior" as Apollo's Equellis tunic
"Unchained Woman" "Time of the Hawk"	The Zetan village The Throm village	"The Lost Warrior" as Equellis
"Planet of the Amazon Women"	The Ruathan space cruiser	"Baltar's Escape" as the Prison Barge
"Space Vampire"	The derelict spacecraft	"Saga of a Star World" as the Gemonese freighter
"Space Vampire"	Vorvon crucifix	"Lost Planet of the Gods" as Adama's command emblem
"Ardala Returns"	Buck's personal ship	"Man with Nine Lives" as shuttle Canaris
"Journey to Oasis" "Time of the Hawk"	Searcher shuttle	*Battlestar Galactica* Colonial Shuttle
"Journey to Oasis"	Planetary landscape	"The Return of Starbuck" as landscape of the planet Starbuck
"The Crystal" "The Satyr"	Searcher shuttle	"Greetings from Earth" as Terran family shuttle
Buck Rogers second season	Second year premise: Buck and Searcher look for "the lost tribes" of Earth	*Battlestar Galactica* redux

A Catalogue of Science Fiction Television Clichés in *Battlestar Galactica*

Despite the assertions of many critics, *Battlestar Galactica* is not the worst offender in the Valhalla for reusing sci-fi TV clichés. However, various episodes do fall uncomfortably into that category. Below is a listing of *Battlestar Galactica* and *Galactica: 1980* stories that ended up repeating tried-and-true TV formulas, usually with little success. Please consider that *Battlestar Galactica* is not the latest series to use the hackneyed premises listed below. On the contrary, series as recent as *Voyager* and *Deep Space Nine* have trotted out the same clichés avid TV viewers have been familiar with now for well over 30 years. At least *Galactica* never featured any evil twins (the bane of *Star Trek*) or space "vampires" (*Babylon 5*, *Buck Rogers*).

Episode: "The Lost Warrior"
Sci-fi cliché: *The Single Woman in Jeopardy:* a main character befriends a lonely widow or a single mother and her child.
Also seen in: *Buck Rogers* as "The Satyr," *V* as "The Wildcats," *Galactica: 1980* as "The Return of Starbuck"

Episode: "Murder on the *Rising Star*"
Sci-fi cliché: *The Court Martial:* a main character of sterling reputation is accused of murder, but his friends investigate and discover he has been framed.

Also seen in: *Star Trek* as "Court Martial," *Star Trek* as "Wolf in the Fold," *U.F.O.* as "Court Martial," *Buck Rogers* as "Testimony of a Traitor," *The Next Generation* as "A Matter of Perspective," *Deep Space Nine* as "Dax," *Deep Space Nine* as "Rules of Engagement," *Voyager* as "Ex Post Facto"

Episode: "The Magnificent Warriors"
Sci-fi cliché: *The Universe is a Western Movie:* a sci-fi show recounts a story straight out of the American west, often involving a shoot-out.
Also seen in: *Star Trek* as "Spectre of the Gun," *Battlestar Galactica* as "The Lost Warrior," *The Next Generation* as "A Fistful of Datas," *Moon Zero Two* (1969, film), *Battle Beyond the Stars* (1980, film), *Outland* (1981, film)

Episode: "Fire in Space"
Sci-fi cliché: *The Disaster Movie:* There is a disaster aboard a ship or station and several crew people are trapped and cut off in various areas of the ship (usually recreational) until the disaster is ended.
Also seen in: *The Next Generation* as "Disaster," *Deep Space Nine* as "Civil Disorder," *Voyager* as "Twisted," *U.F.O.* as "Sub Smash"

Episode: "The Super Scouts"
Sci-fi cliché: *The Hapless Pursuer:* A dedicated man, usually in the military, attempts to track down the heroes every week. Since the series would end if the pursuer ever caught his prey, the hapless pursuer always loses. In *Galactica,* the pursuer is played by Alan Miller.
Also seen in: *The Phoenix* — Richard Lynch, *Logan's Run* — Randy Powell, *The Incredible Hulk* — Jack Colvin, *Starman* — Richard Jaeger, *Otherworld* — Jonathan Banks, *Planet of the Apes* — Mark Lenard

Episode: "The Return of Starbuck"
Sci-fi cliché: *The Defiant Ones:* Two enemies meet on an inhospitable planet and learn to overcome barriers (communication, culture) in order to survive.
Also seen in: *U.F.O.* as "Survival," *The Next Generation* as "The Enemy," *The Next Generation* as "Darmok," *Buck Rogers* as "Time of the Hawk," *Enemy Mine* (1985, film)

Ten Recommendations for Improving *Battlestar Galactica* Should It Be Revived

If the *Battlestar Galactica* revival takes flight, it is important that the new series walk a fine line between maintaining the continuity of the first series while simultaneously "fixing" some of the problems that plagued the 1978-1979 original. Below is a list of ten "improvement" recommendations for the producers of the new *Battlestar Galactica*, if it ever gets off the ground:

1. Beef up the female characters. Hire Maren Jensen back as Athena and promote her to colonel, first officer or commander of the *Galactica*. Since 20 "yahrens" have passed and she could have completed medical school, it would be appropriate also to promote Cassiopeia to *Galactica* CMO. Sheba should also play a prominent role as a fighter pilot. This way, the new *Galactica* could deflect cries of "sexism."

2. Make prominent mention of the fact that the *Galactica* and her fleet are equipped with faster-than-light drive. This is a necessary adjustment to make the "interstellar" migration believable.

3. Do not, under any circumstances, modify the look of the series to match that of the Maximum Press comic book. Since Lorne Greene has passed away, if Adama is to be a presence at all in the new series it will be through flashbacks to the *first* series. If the new show does not resemble the old show at least marginally, then such flashbacks will be impossible. The look of *Battlestar Galactica* has always been solid and believable. It is unnecessary to jazz it up. "Looks" were never the show's problem.

215

4. Employ realistic fighter tactics in the space combat scenarios. Fighters should not just launch from the *Galactica* and hot-dog it all over the spaceways. There should be believable, well-orchestrated strategy at work. If the new show is to be a war or military drama, this improvement is a must.

5. Have a C.O.R.A.-style computer (from "The Long Patrol") in each Colonial Viper, to make the functioning of the ship more believable. C.O.R.A. can serve as an autopilot when necessary, or verbally convey scientific or military data about planets, ships, etc.

6. Concentrate on the plight of the people in the fleet. They have been stuck in tin cans for 20 yahrens now. Remember that there was internal unrest as far back as "Take the *Celestra*," and imagine how more time in space would affect people. What would the new generation of humans, born in space, look like? How would they feel? What are the politics of the fleet? Is it still under martial law? Will there be elections for new commanders or members of the Council of 12? These are the background details that will give *Battlestar Galactica* a "mature" veneer.

7. Encounter planets that are neither Colonial nor Cylon, but instead relate somehow to ancient myths, religion or biblical stories, thus furthering the Von Däniken Theorem of the original. What about strange stories based on the legend of Medusa? Or Theseus and the labyrinth? Or Sodom and Gomorrah? Again, this would give the series an admirable air of consistency, and contribute to the notion that the journey of the *Galactica* represents Earth's ancient myths.

8. Upgrade the Cylons and Baltar to be more menacing. They should not be jokes, but believable, serious threats. The Cylons should be capable pilots and marksmen, and they should have improved response times. Their look is fine, but they need to be more imposing in their villainy. And bring back Lucifer and Jonathan Harris.

9. Do not rely on space Westerns ("The Magnificent Warriors," "The Lost Warrior"), plots based on popular films ("Gun on Ice Planet Zero," "Fire in Space"), crash-landings ("The Return of Starbuck," "The Lost Warrior," "The Young Lords") or TV clichés ("Murder on the *Rising Star*").

10. Completely ignore the events and characters of *Galactica: 1980*.

Notes

Part I. The History

1. T.N. Tumbusch, *Space Adventure Collectibles* (Radnor PA: Wallace-Homestead, 1990), page 77.

2. Kerry O'Quinn, "Journal of the Con Wars," *Starlog* #127, February 1988, page 54.

3. David Hutchison, "The Magical Techniques of Movie & TV SFX, Part XII: Explosions for Miniatures," *Starlog* #17, October 1978, page 60.

4. *Ibid.*, 59.

5. Roger Ebert, *Roger Ebert's Home Movie Home Companion 1993 Edition* (Kansas City: Andrews and McMeel, 1993), page 762.

6. Karen E. Willson, "Production Science Fiction for TV, an Interview with Glen Larson," *Starlog* #36, July 1980, page 30.

7. James Delson, "*Battlestar Galactica:* Two Views — Glen Larson," *Fantastic Films* 1, no. 6, February 1979, page 9.

8. *Ibid.*, 18.

9. Harry Waters, "Blast Off!" *Newsweek*, 11 September 1978, page 63.

10. Dale Pollack, *Skywalking: The Life and Films of George Lucas* (New York: Harmony Books, 1983), page 198.

11. David Houston, "ABC's Multi-Million Dollar SF Gamble: *Battlestar Galactica*," *Future* #6, November 1978.

12. Dale Pollack, *Skywalking: The Life and Films of George Lucas*, page 142.

13. Roger Ebert, *Roger Ebert's Home Movie Home Companion 1993 Edition*, page 762.

14. David Houston, "Buck Rogers Is Back," *Starlog* #19, July 1980, page 25.

15. Harry and Michael Medved, *The Golden Turkey Awards, Nominees and Winner — The Worst Achievements in Hollywood History* (New York: Putnam, 1980), page 109.

16. Kyle Counts, "Laser Gun in Hand, Richard Hatch Recalls Life in Space as Captain Apollo," *Starlog* #196, November 1993.

17. James Delson, "An Outspoken Interview with John Dykstra," *Fantastic Films* 1, no. 5, December 1978, page 62.

18. "Space Explodes as Cylons Battles Capricans in *Battlestar Galactica*," *Famous Monsters* #150, January 1979, page 15.

19. James Delson, "An Outspoken Interview with John Dykstra," page 13.

20. Howard Zimmerman, "Lastword," *Starlog* #19, February 1979, page 78.

21. James Delson, "*Battlestar Galactica*: Two Views — Glen Larson," page 9.

22. Williams Adams, "What Killed *Battlestar Galactica*?" *Fantastic Films* 1, no. 29, June 1982.

23. "*Battlestar Galactica:* You Can't Quite Call it a 'Wrap,'" *Starlog* #27, October 1979, page 35.

24. "The *Battlestar Galactica* Movies," *Starlog* #39, October 1980, pages 46–47.

25. "*Battlestar Galactica:* You Can't Quite Call it a 'Wrap'," page 35.

26. "Cylons for the Tourists," *Starlog* #26, September 1979, page 13.

27. Alan Brender, "The Battle of *Galactica* at Universal Studios," *Starlog* #28, November 1979, page 28.

28. "Three Cheers for *Galactica*," *Starlog* #31, February 1980, page 9.

29. David Bassom, "Richard Hatch," *TV Zone: The Magazine of Cult Television*, Special 17, 1995, page 55.

30. "*Galactica* Wins the War," *Starlog* #41, December 1980, page 10.

Part II. Battlestar Galactica

1. Harry Waters, "Blast Off!" *Newsweek*, 11 September 1978, page 63.

2. Alan Brender, "Jane Seymour," *Starlog* #40, November 1980, page 26.

3. Gene Roddenberry and Stephen E. Whitfield, *The Making of Star Trek* (New York: Ballantine Books, 1968), page 257.

4. Larry Nemecek, *The "Star Trek: The Next Generation" Companion* (New York: Pocket Books, 1992), page 4.

5. Peter Bloch-Hansen, "John Colicos — the Quintessential Klingon," *Starlog* #138, January 1989, page 19.

Part III. Galactica: 1980

1. Karen E. Willson, "The New Faces of *Galactica: 1980*— Robbie Rist," *Starlog* #34, May 1980, page 19.

2. Marc Shapiro, "Police Record," *Starlog* #162, January 1991, page 44.

Part IV. Morality and Mythology

1. James Neyland, *The Official Battlestar Galactica Scrapbook* (New York: Grosset and Dunlap, 1978), page 48.

2. *Ibid.*, 90.

3. David Houston, "The Secrets of the Cylons," *Fangoria* #5, April 1980, pages 29–30.

Part V. The Galactica Universe Today

1. James Neyland, *The Official Battlestar Galactica Scrapbook* (New York: Grosset and Dunlap, 1978), page 98.

Part VI. Epilogue: A Shining Quest

1. Michael Logan, "Space Odyssey," *TV Guide* 44, no.3, issue 2234, 20 January 1996, page 14.

Bibliography

Anchors, William E., Jr. *"Battlestar Galactica." Epilog* 33 (August 1993.)

Brooks, Tim, and Marsh, Earle. *The Complete Directory to Prime Time Network TV Shows 1946–Present.* New York: Ballantine, 1985.

Ebert, Roger. *Roger Ebert's Home Movie Home Companion 1993 Edition.* Kansas City: Andrews and McMeel, 1993.

Javna, John. *The Best of Science Fiction TV.* New York: Harmony, 1987.

Larson, Glen A., and Thurston, Robert. *Battlestar Galactica.* Universal City CA: Berkley, 1978.

_____, and Resnick, Michael. *Battlestar Galactica 5: Galactica Discovers Earth.* Universal City CA: Berkley, 1980.

Maloni, Kelly; Greenman, Ben; Miller, Kristin; and Hearn, Jeff. *Net Trek: Your Guide to Trek Life in Cyberspace.* New York: Random House Electronic Publishing, 1995.

Menville, Douglas, and Reginald, R. *Futurevisions: The New Golden Age of the Science Fiction Film.* North Hollywood CA: Newcastle, 1985.

Meyers, Richard. *From Rollerball to Return of the Jedi: The Great Science Fiction Films.* Secaucus NJ: Citadel, 1984.

Muir, John. *Exploring Space: 1999 An Episode Guide and Complete History.* Jefferson NC: McFarland, 1997.

Nemecek, Larry. *The "Star Trek: The Next Generation" Companion.* New York: Pocket, 1992.

Neyland, James. *The Official Battlestar Galactica Scrapbook.* New York: Grosset & Dunlap, 1978.

Stanley, John. *Creature Features Movie Guide Strikes Again, Fourth Revised Version.* Pacifica CA: Creatures at Large Press, 1994.

Tumbusch, T.N. *Space Adventure Collectibles.* Radnor PA: Wallace-Homestead, 1990.

Index

The A-Team (TV series)
34, 43, 50, 68, 178
Abatemarco, Frank 28
"The AB Chrysalis" (*Space:
1999* episode) 45
ABC 2, 4, 9, 17, 18, 27,
29, 30–33, 37, 44, 91,
125, 135, 137, 140, 142,
143, 185, 195
Acker, Sharon 124, 128,
134
Adam 12 (TV series) 125
Adam's Ark (unproduced
TV series) 15
Adventures of Superman
(TV series) 51
Agent for H.A.R.M. (film)
143
Airforce One (film) 34
Airplane 2: The Sequel
(film) 207
Aladdin 194
Alf (TV series) 181
Alien Nation (TV series)
144, 152
Aliens (film) 97
Allen, Irwin 2, 51, 79,
146
Allen, Jerry 53
Allen, Nora 53
Alias Smith and Jones (TV
series) 4, 14
Alicia, Ana 50, 111, 112,
124, 144, 146
Alien Resurrection (film)
36
"All Good Things" (*Star
Trek: The Next Genera-
tion* episode) 107

All My Children (daytime
soap opera) 17
"Alpha Child" (*Space:
1999* episode) 152
Altman, Mark A. 37
Alyn, Kirk 50, 90
Amazing Stories (TV
series) 2
America Online 177, 181
American Graffiti (film) 14
"Amok Time" (*Star Trek*
episode) 71
Anchors, William 38, 120
Anderson, Gerry 1, 4, 10,
12, 22, 61, 72, 152, 181
Anderson, Melody 107,
110
Anderson, Peter 53
Anderson, Richard Dean
146
Anderson, Sylvia 1, 4, 10,
12, 22, 61, 72, 152, 181
The Andromeda Strain
(film) 43, 72
Angress, Percy 53
"Another Time, Another
Place" (*Space: 1999*
episode) 45
"Apollo's Journey" (*Bat-
tlestar Galactica* Maxi-
mum Press comic) 203
Apollo's War (*Battlestar
Galactica* novel) 194
"The Apple" (*Star Trek*
episode) 108, 151
The Apple Dumpling Gang
(film) 125
"Ardala Returns" (*Buck
Rogers* episode) 212

Armageddon (*Battlestar
Galactica* novel) 36,
179–182, 194, 195, 203,
209
Ashmore, Frank 50, 99,
101
Asimov, Isaac 2, 23, 25,
28, 132, 137, 139
Astaire, Fred 43, 50, 94,
95, 98
Automan (TV series) 2
Avalanche (film) 73
The Avengers (TV series)
92
"Awakening" (*Buck Rogers*
episode) 41, 103, 123
Ayres, Lew 54, 55, 59,
155

B.J. and the Bear (TV
series) 14, 34
Babylon 5 (TV series) 1,
5, 52, 116, 180, 206
Bad Dreams (film) 134
The Bad News Bears (film)
138, 140
Bailey, Bos 53
Bain, Barbara 62
Baker, Colin 70
Balin, Ina 105
"Baltar's Escape" (*Bat-
tlestar Galactica*
episode) 29, 35, 41,
49, 51, 68, 86, 104,
105–108, 113, 157, 160
Banacek (TV series) 72
Banks, Jonathan 214
Barney Miller (TV series)
64

Barr, Doug 34
Barr, Roseanne 35
Barton, Dan 94
Bassom, David 33
Batanides, Arthur 124, 140, 143
Battle Beyond the Stars (film) 43, 78, 214
"Battle of Galactica" (Universal Studios Tour Attraction) 30, 34
Battle Star Galactica (unused title for *Battlestar Galactica*) 17
Battlestar Galactica (novel) 194; *see also* "Saga of a Star World"
Battlestar Galactica Iron-on Transfer Book (memorabilia) 197, 198, 199
Battlestar Galactica Original Soundtrack 196
Battlestar Galactica Storybook (book) 196
"Battlestar Red" (*Battlestar Galactica* fan fiction) 178
Battlestar Republica 152, 183
Baywatch (TV series) 14
Beascoechea, Frank 127
Beauty and the Beast (TV series) 175, 208
Begley, Ed, Jr. 35, 53
Belford, Christine 72
"The Bellero Shield" (*Outer Limits* episode) 107
Bellisario, Donald 35, 41, 42, 53, 61, 64, 68, 71, 94, 98, 105, 175
Benedict, Dirk 3, 17, 20, 31, 32, 34, 36, 47, 50, 52, 68, 70, 78, 98, 100, 110, 114, 117, 128, 133, 147–150, 179, 183
Benjamin, Philip 127
Bennett, Richard 53
Berkley Books 194
Berkos, Peter 53
Berman, Michael 127

Berman, Rick 1
Berryman, Michael 34
"Berserker" (*Battlestar Galactica* Marvel comic) 202
Berthelot, Jean-Jacques 127
"The Best of Both Worlds" (*Star Trek: The Next Generation* episode) 64
"Beyond the Mountain" (*The Fantastic Journey* episode) 143
Bill & Ted's Bogus Journey (film) 110
Bills, Phillip 53
Binney, Geoffrey 54
"Birth of a Battlestar" (*Battlestar Galactica* fan fiction) 178
Bishop, Ed 49
Bisoglio, Val 140
B.J. and the Bear (TV series) 14, 34
The Black Hole (film) 187
"Black Orchid" (*Doctor Who* serial) 77
"Black Sun" (*Space: 1999* episode) 109, 162
Blade Runner (film) 134
Blake's 7 (TV series) 1, 152
Bloch, Robert 41, 42
Bloodlust (film) 134
Bloom, Charles 79
The Blue Lagoon (film) 80
"Blue Squadron Reserve" (*Battlestar Galactica* fan fiction) 179
Bochner, Lloyd 102, 104, 105
Bolger, Paul 53
Bolger, Ray 50, 102, 104
Bonanza (TV series) 17, 37, 48, 76
Borgnine, Ernest 34
Boxleitner, Bruce 14
The Brady Bunch (TV series) 122, 134

"Bread and Circuses" (*Star Trek* episode) 77
"Breakaway" (*Space: 1999* episode) 10
Brender, Alan 63
Brennan, George 53
Brett, Jeremy 138
Brick, Mike 135
Brier, William 53
"Brian the Brain" (*Space: 1999* episode) 46
Bridges, Lloyd 51, 81, 83, 84, 178
Bring 'Em Back Alive (TV series) 14
Broccoli, Albert "Cubby" 78
Bryant, Rick 200
Bryant, William 85
Buck Rogers (1939 film) 21
Buck Rogers in the 25th Century (TV series) 4, 5, 10, 28, 29, 31, 34, 35, 41, 42, 43, 52, 64, 66, 72, 76, 83, 99, 103, 107, 112, 123–125, 134, 146, 150, 175, 187, 207, 208, 211, 214
Buechler, John Carl 83
Bunch, Chris 127
Burroughs, Edgar Rice 22
Burton, James 53
Burton, Levar 151
Butch Cassidy and the Sundance Kid (film) 14
Byrne, Johnny 41

"The Cage" (*Star Trek* pilot) 50, 107, 112
Cain's Hundred (TV series) 143
Cannon, Kathy 65
"The Caprica Society" (*Battlestar Galactica* fanzine) 177
Carlson, Jim 84, 85, 98, 110
Carter, Terry 53, 85, 98, 110
Casey, Shaun 53
Casino Royale 78

Cassidy, Shaun 14
Cassutt, Michael 120
Catania, Jim 53
CBS 4, 28
The Changeling (film) 35
Chapman, Judith 124, 150
Chariots of the Gods (book) 15, 138
Charlie Chan and the Dragon Queen (film) 84
Charlton Comics 199
Chaykin, Howard 165
Chilberg, John E, II 17, 53
The China Syndrome (film) 63
CHiPS (TV series) 14
Chopper One (TV series) 17
Chulay, John 127
City on the Edge of Forever (book) 14
"Civil Disorder" (*Deep Space Nine* episode) 86, 214
Clooney, George 19
Close Encounters of the Third Kind (film) 17, 93, 194
Code Red (TV series) 35, 125
Cole, Allan 127
Coleman, Booth 144
Coleman, Gary 182
Colicos, John 4, 18, 19, 34, 36, 53, 79, 84, 106, 115, 187, 203
Colla, Richard 20, 41, 54, 58
Collins, Stephen 14
"Collision Course" (*Space: 1999* episode) 50
Colman, Ben 53
Colon, Ernie 200
"Colony in Space" (*Doctor Who* serial) 43
Columbia House 36
Columbo (TV series) 18
Colvin, Jack 136, 214

"Confetti Check, A–OK" (*U.F.O.* episode) 49
Connery, Sean 43, 78
Conquest of the Earth (*Galactica: 1980* compilation film) 29, 126; *see also* "*Galactica* Discovers Earth"; "The Night the Cylons Landed"; "The Super Scouts"
Coogan's Bluff (film) 14
Coon, Gene 15
Corman, Roger 78
Costa, Cosie 140
Coufos, Paul 54, 90
Counts, Kyle 22
"Court Martial" (*Star Trek* episode) 99, 213
"Court Martial" (*U.F.O.* episode) 99, 213
Cowles, Charles 53
Crabbe, Buster 21
Crain, Earl 127
Crane, Barry 124, 138
Craven, Wes 34
Credel, Curtis 72
Crichton, Charles 73
Crisps, Millicent 62
Crist, Paula 54
"Cruise Ship to the Stars" (*Buck Rogers* episode) 123
"The Crystals" (*Buck Rogers* episode) 103
Curse of the Cylons (*Battlestar Galactica* compilation film) 20; *see also* "Fire in Space"; "The Magnificent Warriors"
Curtis, Dan 1, 143
Curtis, Jamie Lee 43, 76
Curtis, Janet Lynn 62
Cutler, Jeff 135
Cutter, Rex 65, 140
Cylon Death Machine (*Battlestar Galactica* novel) 194; *see also* "Gun on Ice Planet Zero"

"The Daleks" (*Doctor Who* serial) 77

Daniels, William 124, 140, 143
Danning, Sybil 78
"Dark Dawn" (*Battlestar Galactica* fan fiction) 178
"Dark Dawn II" (*Battlestar Galactica* fan fiction) 178
Dark Shadows (TV series) 125, 143
Dark Skies (TV series) 14
"Darmok" (*Star Trek: The Next Generation* episode) 214
Dart Flipcards 182
Davies, Nicholas 135
Davis, Roger 140
Davis, Walt 72
"Dax" (*Deep Space Nine* episode) 99, 213
The Day the Earth Stood Still (film) 121
Deadly Blessing (film) 34
"Death's Other Dominion" (*Space: 1999* episode) 73
DeCarl, Nancy 68
The Defiant Ones (film) 148
DeLancie, John 50, 107, 110
DeLaurentiis, Dino 23, 110, 176
DeLongis, Anthony 50, 94, 96, 105
DeLoy, George 135
Delson, James 16, 25
Denby, David 11
Densford, Rome 135
Dern, Bruce 21
"The Devil in the Dark" (*Star Trek* episode) 45, 74, 104
DeWindt, Sheila 62, 140
Diagnosis: Murder (TV series) 100, 125
Diamonds Are Forever (film) 80
Diamos, Angela 53
Die Chameleon! (*Battlestar*

Galactica novel) 194;
see also "The Man with Nine Lives"

DiLeo, Marco 127

Dimension X (radio show) 15

Dirty Dancing (film) 175

The Dirty Dozen (film) 75

"Disaster" (*Star Trek: The Next Generation* episode) 86, 214

Doctor Quinn: Medicine Woman (TV series) 63

Doctor Who (TV series) 43, 60, 70, 77, 97, 152

Donny & Marie (TV series) 27

Donohue, Jay 65

Dorleac, Jean-Pierre 17, 25, 53, 55, 121, 127

Douglas, Bruce 128

Douglass, Robyn 122, 123, 126, 132, 137, 138, 150

"A Dream of Jennifer" (*Buck Rogers* episode) 83

Dullaghan, John 53

Dumas, John 127

Dune (novel) 13, 20, 21

Dusay, Marj 124, 143

Dykstra, John 5, 18, 22, 23, 24, 33, 45, 188, 200

Earth—Final Conflict (TV series) 36

Earthquake (film) 121, 129

Eastham, Richard 128

Eastwood, Clint 14

Ebert, Roger 20, 21

Edwards, Vince 41, 135

Ekland, Britt 50, 72, 73, 80

Elam, Ray 53

Elcar, Dana 144–146

Ellen (TV series) 14

Ellison, Harlan 2, 11, 14, 41, 42

Emergency (TV series) 41, 50, 104

"The Emissary" (*Star Trek: The Next Generation* episode) 68

Empire (TV series) 72

The Empire Strikes Back (film) 26, 60, 73

"Encounter at Farpoint" (*Star Trek: The Next Generation* episode) 151

Encyclopedia Galactica (book) 195, 196

"The Enemy" (*Star Trek: The Next Generation* episode) 149

Enemy Mine (film) 149, 214

"The Enemy Within" (*Battlestar Galactica* Maximum Press comic) 203

Epperson, Sherry 53

ER (TV series) 19

"Errand of Mercy" (*Star Trek* episode) 18, 104

Every Which Way but Loose (film) 14

Evie the Chimp 53

"Ex Post Facto" (*Star Trek: Voyager* episode) 99, 213

"Experiment in Terra" (*Battlestar Galactica* episode) 29, 41, 45, 47, 58, 74, 103, 104, 107–110, 147, 149, 160, 158, 160

The Fall Guy (TV series) 41, 123

Fame (TV series) 50

Famous Monsters (magazine) 24

Fantastic Films (magazine) 16, 25

The Fantastic Journey (TV series) 5, 9, 41, 143, 175

Farrell, Mike 58

FASA 194

Feero, Robert 95, 105

Ferrone, Dan 140

Fimple, Dennis 75

"Fire in Space" (*Battlestar Galactica* episode) 2, 29, 41, 46, 51, 70, 84–89, 109, 114, 205, 214, 216

Firestone, Eddie 128

"A Fistful of Datas" (*Star Trek: The Next Generation* episode) 214

Fitzgerald, Wayne 53

Fix, Paul 50, 111, 112

Flash Gordon (comic) 20, 21

Flash Gordon (1980 film) 110, 125

Fleming, John J. 183

Fonda, Jane 62

Fontana, D.C. 11, 42

"Force of Life" (*Space: 1999* episode) 41

Forst, Erik 128

The Four Preps (singing group) 13

Foxworth, Robert 58

Frederkc, Vance 53

Freilich, Jeff 138

Friday the 13th VIII: Jason Takes Manhattan (film) 143

Friends (TV series) 14

From Here to Eternity (film) 84

The Fugitive (TV series) 136, 144

Funke, Alex 53

The Fury (film) 125

Future (magazine) 19

"Future's End" (*Voyager* episode) 35

"*Galactica* Discovers Earth" (*Galactica: 1980* episode) 29, 33, 77, 119, 121, 123, 126–135, 138, 145, 149, 194

Galactica Discovers Earth (*Galactica: 1980* novelization) 194

Galactica: 1980 (TV series) 4, 6, 30, 31–35, 67, 68, 77, 112, 115, 116, 119–150, 179, 181, 194, 200, 216

Galactica One (fan club) 177

Galactica: Star Worlds (unused title for *Battlestar Galactica*) 17

"*Galactica:* 2000" (*Battlestar Galactica* fan fiction) 179

Gallagher, Joseph 20

"Gambit" (*Star Trek: The Next Generation* episode) 72, 134

Garber, David 53

Gastaldo, Mike 53

Gehring, Ted 68

Gemini Man (TV series) 136

General Hospital (TV series) 150

Gerard, Bryson 53

Gerard, Gil 29, 72, 112

Gerrold, David 25, 37, 40, 42

Get Smart (TV series) 30

The Ghost and Mrs. Muir (TV series) 50, 110

Gibbons-Fly, Peter 53

Gibrall, Michael 179

Gilmer, Robert 127

Glover, Bruce 79, 80

Glover, Danny 125

Gods from Outer Space (book) 15

Gold of the Gods (book) 15

Golden, Chris 36, 182, 194; see also *Armageddon*

Gooze, Dan 53

The Graduate (film) 143

Gray, Erin 29, 72

Gray, Joaquim 144

Grease (film) 27

Greenan, David 53

Greene, Lorne 3, 17, 24, 31, 32, 35, 37, 48, 52, 55, 65, 70, 76, 83, 84,

101–105, 107, 117, 119, 123, 125, 126, 129, 138, 147

"Greetings from Earth" (*Battlestar Galactica* episode) 29, 41, 45, 47, 67, 123, 158

Grosset & Dunlap 195

"Guardian of Piri" (*Space: 1999* episode) 45

Guerdat, Andy 28

"Gun on Ice Planet Zero" (*Battlestar Galactica* episode) 19, 29, 41, 42, 44, 45, 51, 57, 61, 67, 71–75, 77, 78, 80, 114, 121, 129, 134, 194, 196, 205, 216

Gun Shy (TV series) 125

The Guns of Navarone (film) 51, 75

Gunsmoke (TV series) 76

Haase, Rod 81

Hall, Robert 53

Haller, Daniel 41, 89, 110, 144

Halloween II (film) 134

Hamaguchi, Ted 111

Hamill, Mark 67

Hancock, Prentis 49

Hanczyk, Robert 183

"The Hand of God" (*Battlestar Galactica* episode) 2, 25, 27, 29, 41, 45, 46, 48, 52, 74, 83, 114–117, 124, 127, 137, 147, 155

Happy Days (TV series) 4, 14

The Hardy Boys/Nancy Drew Mysteries (TV series) 14, 17

Harmon, Kelly 102

Harris, Johnathan 18, 53, 84, 166, 215

Harrison, Gregory 9

Hasselhoff, David 14, 125

Hatch, Richard 3, 18, 22, 32–36, 48, 49, 52, 70, 92, 109, 116, 117, 133,

177, 178, 179, 181, 182, 194, 195, 203, 215, 216; authorship of *Armageddon* 181, 182, 194, 195; authorship of Maximum Press comic series 203; *Battlestar Galactica* revival effort 116, 181, 182, 194, 195, 203, 215, 216

Hathaway, Noah 18, 34, 49, 183

Hawks, Howard 146

Hayers, Sidney 127

"Heart of Glory" (*Star Trek: The Next Generation* episode) 96

Heiman, Mark 184

Herbert, Frank 20, 22

Hercules: The Legendary Journeys (TV series) 184

Hicks, Catherine 132

The Hidden Fortress (film) 13, 20, 22

"Hidden Hunger" (*Battlestar Galactica* fan poetry) 179

High Noon (film) 2, 43

Hill, David 53

Hill, Judge Irving 33, 34

Hoffman, Morrie 127

Holcomb, Rod 41, 64, 94, 98

Holland, Erik 128

Holland, John 68, 94

Holliday, Fred 128, 138

Holman, Jena 53

Holt, Nick 111

Horsley, Michael 111

Houston, David 19

Howe, Cynthia 179

Howe, David 127

Hoyt, John 50, 105, 107, 112

Hughes, Barnard 59

Hunter (TV series) 124

Hyde-White, Wilfrid 54

"I Have Seen Earth" (unproduced *Battlestar Galactica* teleplay) 28

The Immortal (TV series) 134, 144
In Search of Ancient Gods (book) 16
"In the Hands of the Prophets" (*Deep Space Nine* episode) 154
The Incredible Hulk (TV series) 136, 181, 214
Independence Day (film) 6, 133, 189, 207
"Into the Great Wide Open" (*Battlestar Galactica* fan fiction) 179
The Invaders (TV series) 50, 72
Irene, Georgi 135
It Takes a Thief (TV series) 15
It's a Wonderful Life (film) 109
Izvestia (Soviet periodical) 37

J.A.G. (TV series) 42
James, Brion 128, 134
Jarrell, Amy 144
Javna, John 40, 120
Jaws (film) 179
Jaws II (film) 27
Jeager, Richard 214
Jefferson, Herb, Jr. 4, 17, 32, 34, 52, 85, 102, 119, 126, 147
Jeffreys, Ann 94
Jennings, Junero 81
Jensen, Maren 17, 34, 53, 62, 70, 85, 103, 117, 179, 215
John Carter of Mars (book) 20
Johns, David 53
Johnson, Brian 11, 22
Johnson, Chip 54
Johnson, George Clayton 41
Johnson, Janet Louise 62
Johnson, Joe 17, 173
Jones, Claude Earl 65
Jones, Clifton 49

Jones, James Earl 59
Jones, Mickey 128, 134
Jones, Sam J. 125
"Journey to Oasis" (*Buck Rogers* episode) 42, 123, 212
Journey to the Far Side of the Sun (film) 72
"Journey's End" (*Battlestar Galactica* Maximum Press Comic) 203
Joyce, Michael 53

Kadish, Ben 126
Karpisak, John 183
Kellerman, Sally 107
Kellin, Michael 135
Kelly, Dennis 53
Kenner 184, 187, 188
Khambatta, Persis 67
Kimble, Robert 53
King, Stephen 40, 89
King Kong (1976 film) 23, 176, 177
Kitman, Marvin 39
Klugman, Jack 14
Knight, Don 136
Knight Rider (TV series) 4, 14, 35, 50, 71, 110, 124, 143
"KOBOL" (*Battlestar Galactica* fan fiction) 178
Kolbe, Winrich 42, 105, 107
Kolchak: The Night Stalker (TV series) 1, 14, 143, 208
Koslo, Paul 130
Kreinberg, Steve 28
Kubrick, Stanley 86
Kurosawa, Akira 13, 20, 75, 78

Lagenbach, Frederick 53
Landau, Martin 107
Landers, Audrey 79
Lange, Jessica 35
Lantz, Phillipe 53
LaRocque, John P. 183

Larson, David 135
Larson, Eric 135
Larson, Glen A. 4, 6, 12–25, 28, 29, 31–33, 34, 36, 41, 42, 44, 52, 54, 55, 61, 75, 77, 83, 89, 90, 106, 113, 119, 123, 125–182, 135, 138, 140, 141, 146, 147, 149, 150, 165, 179, 194, 195, 205, 207
Larson, Michelle 135
Laserblast (film) 146
Lasley, Richard 53
Lassie (TV series) 3
"The Last Outpost" (*Star Trek: The Next Generation* episode) 41, 59
The Last Starfighter (film) 72
"The Last Sunset" (*Space: 1999* episode) 152
Lateef, Ahmet 41, 101
Laverne & Shirley (TV series) 4, 14, 31
The Leech Woman (film) 143
"The Legacy" (*Planet of the Apes* episode) 67
LeGault, Lance 50, 68, 94, 105, 107
"Legend of the *Rising Star*" (*Battlestar Galactica* fan fiction) 179
Lenard, Mark 214
Lenz, Kay 34
Leonard, Tice 179
"Let That Be Your Last Battlefield" (*Star Trek* episode) 151
Levi, Alan J. 20, 41, 59, 71
Levine, Philip 144
Little House on the Prairie (TV series) 3
Live and Let Die (film) 64
"The Living Legend" (*Battlestar Galactica* episode) 29, 41, 45, 47, 48, 51, 58, 62, 74,

81–84, 86, 90, 94, 104, 107, 115, 123, 147, 158, 170, 178, 180, 184, 194
Lockhart, Anne 34, 53, 62, 83
Lockhart, June 83
Logan, Michael 207
Logan's Run (film) 9, 177, 199
Logan's Run (TV series) 2, 5, 9, 11, 12, 13, 144, 175, 214
"Lonely Among Us" (*Star Trek: The Next Generation* episode) 151
"The Long Patrol" (*Battlestar Galactica* episode) 2, 29, 41, 44, 46, 47, 50, 68–71, 75, 76, 100, 155, 169, 172
"The Long Sleep" (*U.F.O.* episode) 49
Longo, Ronald 53
"The Lore of Adama" (*Battlestar Galactica* poetry) 178
Los Angeles Philharmonic Orchestra 53, 196
Lost in Space (1998 film) 36
Lost in Space (TV series) 18, 22, 37, 55, 79, 83, 146
"Lost Planet of the Gods" (*Battlestar Galactica* episode) 19, 29, 35, 41, 42, 45, 61–64, 70, 74, 80, 83, 85, 87, 88, 115, 148, 153, 167, 168, 194, 200
"The Lost Warrior" (*Battlestar Galactica* episode) 25, 29, 41, 43, 45, 47, 65–68, 75, 76, 79, 109, 114, 115, 157, 168, 205, 213, 214, 216
Lowens, Curt 128
Lowry, Illyanna 53
Lubin, Sarah 179
Lucas, George 9, 11, 13, 20, 26, 33, 52

Lupo, Frank 78, 124, 126
Lynch, Richard 72, 128, 136, 138, 214

MacGyver (TV series) 146
Mackay, Jeff 85, 99
Mackenzie, Duncan 128
Macnee, Patrick 50, 52, 90, 91, 92, 103, 185
Magar, Guy 28
The Magnificent Seven (film) 2, 43, 75, 78
"The Magnificent Warriors" (*Battlestar Galactica* episode) 25, 29, 41, 43–46, 66, 75–78, 80, 121, 156, 157, 169, 205
Magnum, P.I. (TV series) 35, 42
Majors, Lee 9, 123
The Making of Star Trek (book) 95
Malden, Karl 178
Man, Adam 79
"The Man with Nine Lives" (*Battlestar Galactica* episode) 6, 26, 29, 43, 44, 50, 68, 94–98, 100, 103, 105, 107, 114, 154, 171
The Man with the Golden Gun (film) 72
Manetti, Larry 53
Mantooth, Randolph 50, 102 104
"Mark of Gideon" (*Star Trek* episode) 151
"Mark of the Saurian" (*Buck Rogers* episode) 124
Marriott, Angelo 53
Martell, Tasha 68, 71
Martin, Michele 178
Martin, Pamela Sue 14
Martin, Todd 128
Marvel Comics 9, 105, 179, 199–203
*M*A*S*H* (TV series) 11
Matheson, Murray 102
Mattel 4, 23, 26, 181, 185–188, 192

"A Matter of Perspective" (*Star Trek: The Next Generation* episode) 99
Matthews, David 54
Maverick (TV series) 43
Maximum Press 36, 92, 179, 203
McClory, Sean 68
McCloud (TV series) 4, 14
McCord, Kent 32, 122, 126, 130, 137, 138, 150
McCrum, Cory 53
McCullough, Robert 144
McDonnell, Terrence 84, 85, 98, 110
McFarlane, Todd 189
McGoohan, Patrick 1
McIlhoney, Lawrence 38, 120
McKenzie, Roger 200
McNeill, Robert Duncan 99
McQuarrie, Ralph 17, 53, 193
Mego 9, 10, 26, 184
Melville, Herman 165
Menzies, Heather 9
Mercer, Charles 196
Merton, Zienia 49
"The Metamorph" (*Space: 1999* episode) 46, 152
Metropolis (film) 13
MGM 9
Milford, Kim 146
Milland, Ray 5, 54, 55, 156
Miller, Alan 124, 136
Mills, Jed 140
Miracles of the Gods (book) 15
Miratti, Tony 140
"Miri" (*Star Trek* episode) 81
Les Misérables (novel) 136
Misfits of Science (TV series) 2
"Missing Link" (*Space: 1999* episode) 45
Mission Galactica: The Cylon Attack (*Battlestar Galactica* telefilm) 29;

see also "The Living Legend"

"Mission of the Darians" (*Space: 1999* episode) 45

Moby Dick (novel) 165

Moffatt, Donald 9

Monahan, Ray 53

Monogram 23, 26, 190, 191, 205

Monroe, Sharon 178

Moon Zero Two (film) 43, 72

Moore, Roger 92

Moreau, Harry 53

Morgan, Maxwell 53

Mork & Mindy (TV series) 31

Morse, Barry 49

Moses, David 128

The Most Dangerous Game (film) 134

"The Most Toys" (*Star Trek: The Next Generation* episode) 110

Moulds, John 53

Mulhare, Edward 50, 105, 107, 109, 125

Muller, Brigitte 79

Murder in Space (*Battlestar Galactica* telefilm) 29; *see also* "Murder on the *Rising Star*"; "The Young Lords"

"Murder on the *Rising Star*" (*Battlestar Galactica* episode) 20, 35, 41, 50, 94, 98–101, 160, 213, 216

Murder She Wrote (TV series) 100

Murdock, George 53, 64

Murvin, Robert 111

"The Mutiny" (unproduced *Battlestar Galactica* teleplay) 28

Mystery Science Theater 3000 (TV series) 101, 146

Mystery Science Theater 3000: The Movie (film) 146

Nash, N. Richard 166

Nation, Terry 1

Navarro, Anna 144

NBC 4, 10, 28, 31, 180

Nelson, Barry 75, 78, 80

Neufeld, Sigmund, Jr. 123, 140

"The Neutral Zone" (*Star Trek: The Next Generation* episode) 124, 143, 152

The Neverending Story (film) 34

New York Times 25, 37

Newsweek (periodical) 19, 24, 37

Neyland, James 195, 199

Nicholson, Jack 35

"The Night the Cylons Landed" (*Galactica: 1980* episode) 29, 119, 123, 126, 140–145

Norihiro, Masaki 53

The Nude Bomb (film) 30

Nyby, Christian, Jr. 41, 61, 68, 84

Oakes, Randi 54

O'Connell, David 53

O'Connell, Maureen 53

The Odyssey (book) 101, 169

Official Battlestar Galactica Blueprints 195, 202

Official Battlestar Galactica Scrapbook (book) 195, 196

Okrand, Marc 55

Olson, James 43, 72

"Olympiad" (*Buck Rogers* episode) 124, 150

Ortiz-Gil, Leon 53

O'Sullivan, William 53

Oswald, Gerd 41

Othello (play) 112

The Outer Limits (TV series) 1, 41, 42, 89, 107

Outland (film) 43, 214

Paine, Cathy 68, 71

Palance, Jack 64

Pappas, Chris 183

"The Paradise Syndrome" (*Star Trek* episode) 77

Parker, Bill 127

Parker, Lara 124, 140

Parker Brothers 192–194

Parkes, James R. 111

Parsons, Estelle 59

Parts: The Clonus Horror (film) 101

Pathways to the Gods (book) 16

"Patterns of Force" (*Star Trek* episode) 77

"The Pegasus Chronicles" (*Battlestar Galactica* fanzine) 178

Penner, John 53

Peppard, George 43, 78

Perry Mason (TV series) 99, 100

Persoff, Nehemiah 107, 108, 110

Pertwee, Jon 43

Petala, Alexander 140

Peters, Brock 99, 100, 101

Peterson, Mark 127

Peterson, Wolfgang 34, 149

Pfeiffer, Michelle 34

Phantom in Space (*Battlestar Galactica* telefilm) 29; *see also* "The Hand of God"; "The Lost Warrior"

Phillips, Stu 17, 127, 196, 197

Phinney, David 53

The Phoenix (TV series) 136, 144

"The Piece of the Action" (*Star Trek* episode) 77, 108

Piller, Michael 1

"Planet of the Amazon Women" (*Buck Rogers* episode) 212

Planet of the Apes (TV

series) 1, 9, 21, 87, 152, 184, 208

"Planet of the Slave Girls" (*Buck Rogers* episode) 64

Playton, Paul 53, 78

"Plot to Kill a City" (*Buck Rogers* episode) 124

Pohl, Frederick 40

Polito-Puma, Jennifer 127

The Postman Always Rings Twice (film) 35

Powell, Randy 214

Predator 2 (film) 125

The Prisoner (TV series) 1, 41, 89, 152

Prisoners of the Lost Universe (film) 34

Probert, Andrew 17, 173, 184

Profiler (TV series) 14

Pryor, George 53

Quade, John 124, 135

Quantum Leap (TV series) 42

"A Question of Priorities" (*U.F.O.* episode) 49

The Questor Tapes (TV pilot) 41, 58

Quincy (TV series) 14

Raiders of the Lost Ark (film) 14

The Rainmaker (play) 165

Ramsay, Logan 107

Rashomon (film) 13

Raymond, Alex 20

"The Red and the Black" (*The X-Files* episode) 64

Red Dwarf (TV series) 178

"Red Squadron" (*Battlestar Galactica* fan fiction) 179

Reed, Robert 128

Reeve, Christopher 64

Resnick, Michael 194, 195

"The Responsibility Seat" (*U.F.O.* episode) 49

"The Return of Starbuck" (*Galactica: 1980* episode) 67, 108, 122, 123, 128, 143, 145, 147–150, 213, 214, 216

"Return of the Archons" (*Star Trek* episode) 67, 108, 151

Return of the Man from U.N.C.L.E. (Telefilm) 42

"Reunion" (*Star Trek: The Next Generation* episode) 96

Reynolds, Sam 127

Rich, J.D. 178

Rich Man, Poor Man (TV miniseries) 18

Richard Hatch Enterprises 182

Richard Hatch Fan Club 182

Richard Hatch Web/Home Page 182

Richman, Mark 124, 140, 143

Rickman, Eldon 53

Ripple, Richard 53

Rist, Robert 122, 126, 133

Robman, David 53

Robocop (film) 72

Rocketship X-M (film) 83

Roddenberry, Gene 1, 11, 21, 22, 36, 58, 83, 97, 149, 194

Rogers, Tom 200

Romero, Ned 144

Rosario, Bert 138

"Rules of Engagement" (*Deep Space Nine* episode) 99, 213

Rush, Sarah 53

"Saga of a Star World" (*Battlestar Galactica* episode) 17, 19, 20, 23, 24, 29, 41, 42, 44, 54–61, 63, 64, 66, 105, 106, 115, 121, 123, 141, 154, 156, 160, 167, 168, 172, 184, 186, 196, 200, 201

Saga of the Battlestar Galactica (unused *Battlestar Galactica* title) 17

St. Elsewhere (TV series) 35, 143

Sardo, Louise 140

Satloff, Ron 146

"The Satyr" (*Buck Rogers* episode) 66, 67, 103, 212, 213

Schell, Catherine 43, 49, 62

Scheltz, Paul 178

Scholastic Book Services 196

Schulman, Charles 53

The Sci-Fi Channel 33, 35, 36, 116, 125, 180, 182

Sci Fi Vortex (TV series) 38

Scott, George C. 35

Sea Hunt (TV series) 83

"The Seance Spectre" (*Space: 1999* episode) 46

SeaQuest DSV (TV series) 2, 116

Seidel, Eddie, Jr. 30

Seinfield (TV series) 14, 179, 180

Serling, Rod 1

Server, Eric 75

The Seven Samurai (film) 13, 75

Seymour, Jane 19, 50, 54, 55, 62, 80, 83, 196

Shales, Tom 27, 38, 159, 184

She-Devil (film) 35

Shoop, Pamela Susan 124, 134

"Shuttle Diplomacy" (*Battlestar Galactica* Marvel comic) 202

Signs of the Gods (book) 16

Silent Running (film) 21, 33, 46, 75

Singer, Marc 67

"Sins of the Father" (*Star*

Trek: The Next Generation episode) 96
The Six Million Dollar Man (TV series) 9, 10, 135, 137, 199
Sloan, Michael 42, 53, 71
Smiley, Richard 53
Smith, Wayne 53
Something Is Out There (TV series) 41, 59, 144
Somewhere in Time (film) 64
Sommers, Brett 75
"Soul Hunter" (*Babylon 5* episode) 52
Soule, Olan 90
Soylent Green (film) 101
Space: Above and Beyond (TV series) 6, 52, 206, 207
Space Academy (TV series) 18
Space Casanova (*Battlestar Galactica* compilation film) 29; *see also* "Take the *Celestra*"
"The Space Croppers" (*Galactica: 1980* episode) 112, 119, 121–123, 126, 144–148
"The Space Croppers" (*Lost in Space* episode) 146
"Space Mimic" (*Battlestar Galactica* Marvel comic) 202
Space Mutiny (film) 146
Space: 1999 (TV series) 1, 4, 10, 11–13, 16, 22, 25, 27, 37, 41, 43, 45, 46, 50, 58, 61, 62, 97, 98, 107, 108, 117, 130, 136, 152, 160, 175, 178, 180, 185, 199, 208
Space Patrol (TV series) 22, 51
Space Prison (*Battlestar Galactica* compilation film) 29; *see also* "The Long Patrol"

"Space Vampire" (*Buck Rogers* episode) 52, 212
"Spaceball" (*Galactica: 1980* episode) 119, 122, 133, 138–142, 145, 147
Spang, Laurette 20, 31, 70, 112, 117, 166
Spawn (comic book) 189
Spelling, Aaron 17
Spielberg, Steven 2, 93, 194
Spiner, Brent 78
"Spock's Brain" (*Star Trek* episode) 124
Springfield, Rick 50, 54
SSSSSSS (film) 17
Stacey, Adam 183
Star Gate (film) 36
Star Gate SG-1 (TV series) 36
Star Trek (TV series) 1, 3, 6, 9, 10–13, 16, 18, 21, 24, 27, 36, 37, 41, 45, 46, 50, 59, 71, 73, 74, 77, 81, 83, 88, 89, 97, 98, 99, 104, 106, 108, 113, 115, 130, 137, 149, 151, 160, 161, 175, 176, 180, 199
Star Trek: Deep Space Nine (TV series) 1, 6, 11, 35, 42, 86, 95, 96, 99, 101, 107, 154, 184, 205, 206, 213, 214
Star Trek: Generations (film) 86
Star Trek: The Motion Picture (film) 6, 17, 67, 95, 189, 194
Star Trek: The Next Generation (TV series) 6, 13, 14, 28, 41, 42, 47, 50, 59, 64, 68, 72, 86, 95, 96, 97, 98, 99, 107, 110, 116, 117, 122, 124, 134, 143, 151–153, 171, 178, 206, 214
Star Trek: Voyager (TV series) 18, 35, 42, 70, 71, 87, 96, 97, 99, 107,

113, 117, 176, 205, 206, 213, 214
Star Trek II: The Wrath of Khan (film) 47
Star Trek IV: The Voyage Home (film) 6, 101, 131–133, 207
Star Trek V: The Final Frontier (film) 64, 149
Star Trek VI: The Undiscovered Country (film) 73, 86, 87, 101, 150
Star Wars (film) 2, 3, 5, 9, 11, 15, 16, 17, 20, 21–24, 33, 34, 37, 42, 44, 51, 58, 60, 61, 67, 73, 96, 117, 160, 161, 162, 173, 176, 177, 180, 184, 185, 199, 206
Star Wars — The Special Edition (1997) 36
Star World (unused title for *Battlestar Galactica*) 117
"Starbuck" (*Battlestar Galactica* Maximum Press comic) 203
Starlog (magazine) 15, 22, 24, 28, 33, 40, 63, 106, 133, 137
The Starlost (TV series) 2, 9
Starman (TV series) 144, 214
Starship Troopers (film) 36
Stauffer, Jack 53
Stevens, Andrew 125
Stevens, Leslie 1, 42, 53, 71
Stevenson, Parker 14
Stipes, David 53
Stitch, Patricia 94, 99
Stock, Alan 72
Stone, Sharon 34
Stratton, W.K. 99
Streamers (stage production) 18
"Streets and Stars" (*Battlestar Galactica* fanzine) 178
Streets of San Francisco (TV series) 17, 178
Streep, Meryl 35

Streisand, Barbra 23
Strong, Larry 53
Stuart, Norman 54, 90
Stuart, Patrick 122, 125, 126, 138
Stumpf, Randy 111
Sturua, Melor 38
"Sub Smash" (*U.F.O.* episode) 87, 214
"The Super Scouts" (*Galactica: 1980* episode) 119, 133, 135–139, 141, 142, 145, 214
Superman (radio show) 15
Supiran, Jerry 135
Surrender the Galactica (*Battlestar Galactica* novel) 194
"Survival" (*U.F.O.* episode) 148, 214
"Survive the Alliance" (*Battlestar Galactica* fan fiction) 178
Swan, Michael 135
Swarcz, Jeannot 64
Swartz, Tony 53
Swofford, Ken 50, 107
Sword of Justice (TV series) 14

T.J. Hooker (TV series) 41
"Take the *Celestra*" (*Battlestar Galactica* episode) 26, 29, 41, 49, 50, 110–114, 146, 158, 172, 184, 216
Tales of the Gold Monkey (TV series) 14
Taslitz, Eric 135
"A Taste of Armageddon" (*Star Trek* episode) 108, 151
Tektronix 18, 53, 77, 121
"Testament of Arkadia" (*Space: 1999* episode) 41, 50, 108, 162
"Testimony of a Traitor" (*Buck Rogers* episode) 99
"That Which Survives" (*Star Trek* episode) 124

The Thing from Another World (film) 46
Thinnes, Roy 72, 73
Thiokol 18, 54
The Thirteenth Tribe 177
This Is Spinal Tap (film) 92
This Island Earth (film) 22, 144, 146
"The Tholian Web" (*Star Trek* episode) 45, 104
Thurston, Robert 194
Time (magazine) 20, 40, 44, 184
The Time Machine (film) 77
"Time of the Hawk" (*Buck Rogers* episode) 43, 107, 212, 214
The Time Tunnel (TV series) 130
Timko, John 65
Titanic (film) 13
T.J. Hooker (TV series) 41
"The Tomb of the Cybermen" (*Doctor Who* serial) 77
Tomblin, David 41
The Tombs of Kobol (*Battlestar Galactica* novel) 194; *see also* "Lost Planet of the Gods"
Topper 108
The Towering Inferno (film) 51, 56, 88
"The Trap" (*Planet of the Apes* episode) 87
Trendmasters 36, 189, 190
Troll (film) 83
"The Trouble with Tribbles" (*Star Trek* episode) 37
Trumball, Douglas 33, 46, 76
Tuerpe, Paul 140
TV Guide (periodical) 24, 38, 176, 207
TV Zone (periodical) 33
20th Century–Fox 20, 21, 22, 23, 26

"Twiki Is Missing" (*Buck Rogers* episode) 124
The Twilight Zone (TV series) 1, 50
"Twisted" (*Star Trek: Voyager* episode) 86, 214
2001: A Space Odyssey (film) 22, 24, 86, 199

U.F.O. (TV series) 1, 22, 41, 48, 49, 86, 99, 148, 153, 213, 214
The UFO Incident (TV movie) 41, 59
"Unchained Woman" (*Buck Rogers* episode) 43, 76, 212
Univeral Hartland 24, 53, 127
Universal Studios 20, 21, 22, 23, 29, 30, 34, 35, 43, 54, 75, 77, 116, 143, 195

V (TV series) 50, 67, 101, 129, 144, 152
V— The Final Battle (miniseries) 101
Van Dyke, Barry 32, 112, 122, 125, 126, 130, 138, 150
Vanguard, Wendy 53
Vaughn, Robert 43, 78
"Vegas in Space" (*Buck Rogers* episode) 72, 112, 123, 124
"Vengeance on Varos" (*Doctor Who* serial) 70
Vertibird 194
Victor, Paula 90
A View to a Kill (film) 92
Vigil, Troy 184
Viskocil, Joe 12
Vivian, Tina 179
Von Däniken, Erich 5, 15, 16, 25, 65, 124, 131, 162, 180, 216
Voyage to the Bottom of the Sea (TV series) 2
Voyagers (TV series) 130

Wagon Train (TV series) 13, 37, 44, 84, 113, 128

Walker — Texas Ranger (TV series) 41, 100

"War Games" (*Space: 1999* episode) 162

"War of Eden" (*Battlestar Galactica* Maximum Press comic) 203

"War of the Gods" (*Battlestar Galactica* episode) 25, 41, 47–51, 89–94, 103–107, 110, 113, 115, 123, 136, 147, 149, 154, 157, 160, 167, 171, 180, 184, 216

War of the Worlds (film) 129

Washington Post (newspaper) 27

Waters, Harry 38

"Way of the Warrior" (*Deep Space Nine* episode) 96

Weddle, Vernon 128

Werewolf (TV series) 50, 124

West, Red 65

Wheaton, Wil 122, 182

"Where No Man Has Gone Before" (*Star Trek* pilot) 50, 113

White, Keith 53

Whitmore, James, Jr. 68

"Who Watches the Watchers" (*Star Trek: The Next Generation* episode) 153

"The Wildcats" (*V* episode) 67, 213

Williams, John 90

Willson, Karen E. 15, 133

Wilson, Robert 53

Winter, Gary B. 126

Wise, Robert 121

The Wizard of Oz (film) 104

Wolfman Jack 140, 143

Woods, Herbert 127

Wray, Fay 23

Wright, Bruce 54, 62, 90

WWOR 35

The X-Files (TV series) 1, 4, 14, 64, 181

York, Michael 9

"The Young Lords" (*Battlestar Galactica* episode) 29, 35, 44, 47, 50, 67, 78–81, 100, 109, 126, 148, 167, 169, 170, 172, 194

The Young Warriors (*Battlestar Galactica* novel) 194; *see also* "The Young Lords"

Zanetos, David 126

Zenda, John 128

Zimmerman, Howard 24, 25

Zraick, Robert 30